"When I saw some of the people included in *Script Partners*, I said, 'I've got to go out and buy this book.'"

> — **Carl Reiner**
> Writer, Director, Actor, Producer,
> and Father

"Why hasn't this book been written till now? A lively, knowledgeable, user-friendly guide to how not to be alone in what can seem the loneliest profession on the planet. Claudia Johnson & Matt Stevens know the collaborative process from the inside; and they have gathered insight, encouragement, wisdom, and wisecracks from some of the great writing teams of film and television."

> — **Janet Burroway**
> Novelist, Playwright, and Author
> of the Bestseller, *Writing Fiction*

"This is a charming book! A delight to read. A wonderful insight into how movies that you have loved were created. It is a step-by-step instruction book for becoming part of a collaboration. And it lets you know how much fun you could have. Made me want to find a partner and get to work."

> — **Joan Darling**
> Emmy and DGA Award-Winning
> Actress and Director

"A clever and well-crafted book. It will give you the best insight on writing with a partner you may ever read. Claudia Johnson & Matt Stevens' approach to writing with a partner is truly inspiring. They get to the bottom of the collaboration process with some of the best writing teams on the planet. You will refer to this book for years...."

> — **Mark Doyle**
> Writer and Managing Editor of *Film Festival
> Today Magazine*

"The joys, the tears, the pitfalls, and the triumphs of script partnering are all here for you to experience. This is a unique opportunity to learn from some of the very best in the business."

— **Sable Jak**
Scr(i)pt Magazine

"Successful writing teams share their 'secrets' of co-creating scripts. Be assured this is no cookbook approach to script writing. Instead this book describes the joys and agonies of the creative process and offers guidance for establishing a productive collaborative. It's 'required reading' for those engaged in or considering a writing partnership!"

— **Carol Nicolay, Ed.D**
TV and Film Program, University of
Washington Educational Outreach

"If you're considering the possibility of collaborating with another writer, SCRIPT PARTNERS just might be the answer to all your prayers. Johnson & Stevens have deftly combined entertaining anecdotes, incisive interviews, hard-core info, and sage advice into a no-holds-barred bible for writing with a partner."

— **Kathie Fong Yoneda**
Paramount Pictures Story Analyst/Development
Specialist, Author of *THE SCRIPT SELLING
GAME: A Hollywood Insider's Look at Getting
Your Book Sold and Produced*

MICHAEL WIESE PRODUCTIONS
www.mwp.com

Since 1981, Michael Wiese Productions has been dedicated to providing novice and seasoned filmmakers with vital information on all aspects of filmmaking and videomaking. We have published more than 60 books, used in over 500 film schools worldwide.

Our authors are successful industry professionals — they believe that the more knowledge and experience they share with others, the more high-quality films will be made. That's why they spend countless hours writing about the hard stuff: budgeting, financing, directing, marketing, and distribution. Many of our authors, including myself, are often invited to conduct filmmaking seminars around the world.

We truly hope that our publications, seminars, and consulting services will empower you to create enduring films that will last for generations to come.

We're here to help. Let us hear from you.

Sincerely,

Michael Wiese
Publisher, Filmmaker

SCRIPT
PARTNERS

What Makes Film and TV Writing Teams Work

CLAUDIA JOHNSON & MATT STEVENS

Published by Michael Wiese Productions
11288 Ventura Blvd., Suite 621
Studio City, CA 91604
tel. (818) 379-8799
fax (818) 986-3408
mw@mwp.com
www.mwp.com

Cover Design: Objects of Design
Book layout: Objects of Design
Editor: Brett Jay Markel

Printed by McNaughton & Gunn, Inc., Saline, Michigan
Manufactured in the United States of America

ISBN: 0-941188-75-2
Library of Congress Cataloging-in-Publication Data
Johnson, Claudia (Claudia Hunter)
      Script partners : what makes film and TV writing teams work
      by Claudia Johnson & Matt Stevens
       p. cm.
      Includes bibliographical references.
      ISBN 0-941188-75-2
      1. Motion picture authorship. 2. Television authorship.
      3. Authorship--Collaboration. I. Stevens, Matt, 1963- II. Title.
      PN1996 .J627 2002
      808.2'3--dc21

                                   2002013031
                                       CIP

Dedicated to the Memory of

Billy Wilder

One of the Greatest Script Partners of All Time

"I always collaborated with somebody, because if you think that I am speaking lousy English now, you should have heard it then."

— from *Conversations with Wilder*

Probably the most famous punchline of the countless ones that broadcast comedians have ever offered us owed its creation to two members of Jack Benny's writing staff, Milt Josefsberg and John Tackaberry.

Working together, Tackaberry came up with a straightline for a burglar pointing a gun at Benny and demanding, "Your money or your life."

Josefsberg, lying on the couch (it is mandatory in any collaboration that one of the partners lie on the couch), heard the line and said nothing.

Tackaberry waited an impatient moment or two, then said to Josefsberg, "Well, have you got a comeback?

Not having thought of anything suitable yet, Josefsberg replied, "I'm thinking, I'm thinking."

Unwittingly, the process of collaboration had been memorialized as a punchline.

— Larry Gelbart

TABLE OF CONTENTS

FOREWORD

Whenever I am asked what advice I might offer to young people who want to break into film, I always say that there are already far too many people in film and what we really need are more people in health care.

Nevertheless, each year there are those who, armed with a combination of courage, ignorance, and hope (which is a form of both ignorance *and* courage), reject medical school, trade their LSAT manuals in for a screenwriting program and a coffee pot, and confront the blank page.

"Here comes another one," giggle the Muses, as they watch the poor fellow pore through his dog-eared Syd Field or Robert McKee in hopes of writing the next *Casablanca* or *The Lady Eve*. "Six weeks max," they say, "before he starts talking to himself. Eight and they'll pick him up naked in a bus station outside Cleveland, muttering about character arcs, climaxes, and whammeys."

Yes, it's a terrible business, this intersection of art and commerce and science and opinion and intuition and rules and contempt for rules; a business in which, to quote the poet, the best lack all conviction, while the worst are full of passionate intensity. And yet, despite the crater-sized pitfalls, there is something undeniably exhilarating about writing for the movies.

I don't refer to the delicious possibility of bankrupting a global corporation or the ability to make hard-bitten men weep (the exhibitors) or even the chance to move an audience in one direction or another. For me, the mysterious appeal has always been that it all starts from some low-voltage electrical activity in the recesses of somebody's brain, something you dream up inside your head.

It's an enormously powerful feeling, not to be underestimated: the seductive, infantile omnipotence with which someone alone in a room, though he appears to be staring off into the middle distance, is in fact inventing people, starting a war, perhaps, or if it's been an especially rotten day, destroying an entire planet. In what other line of work can a person make a beautiful girl fall in love with, say, a giant ant? Or bring to the masses a detailed description of interplanetary travel, right down to the non-gravity suction-toilet?

As your psychoanalyst will confirm, this is not an insignificant capacity, this omnipotent control over an entire universe. It is, in fact, what separates us from the animals: The animal understands one act: survival. The human understands three, with a climax occurring somewhere around page 90.

When it all works, it can be satisfying, therapeutic, and financially rewarding. When it doesn't, and the infant who a moment ago controlled the world suddenly finds the world spinning out of control, it can be terrifying.

This is, perhaps, one of the reasons we collaborate. Larry Gelbart, in a slightly different context, described collaboration as "consorting with the enemy." In the current context, however, the description would be: "two people fighting the common enemy."

The enemy has many names. One is loneliness. In my romantic period, when I lived alone and worked at night, I believed the best work in any field was accomplished by people working alone at night: Mozart. Goya. Tolstoy. Jack the Ripper. Experience has made me wiser, and I can now admit that sometimes two people working alone can be better than one. Especially if it's the right two people.

There are as many reasons for writing teams as there are teams (actually twice as many reasons, if you think about it). Loneliness I have mentioned. The bringing to bear of different sensibilities and experiences to a subject is another. The sobering effect of someone who can expose your dementia to the light of reason so it will shrivel and evaporate like Dracula in the sun. The usefulness of conversation as a tool for exploring and developing ideas is yet another.

When I first started writing, alone in my room at night, I would type out imaginary exchanges with myself, having schizophrenically invented a doppelganger/collaborator with whom I could argue about ideas in dialogue form. One night, and I am not making this up, I typed out, "I'm hungry." On the next line I typed, "OK, how about Chinese?" On the next line I typed, "I'm sick of Chinese, how about a pizza?" On the next line I typed, "You are going crazy," at which point I went for a walk around the block.

Every writer harbors two personalities: the infant who generates the raw material and the editor who evaluates it. Both are crucial to the process and each is inescapably at war with the other. A balance must be struck, an internal negotiation which often has as much to do with blood sugar, hormone levels, and one's personal life as with wisdom, logic, and experience. If the infant gains too much control, you get a 300-page screenplay with too many speaking parts, giant ants, and no architecture. If the editor gets the upper hand, you wind up with twenty-five aborted starts and the conviction that you are in fact the fraud you always suspected, that all the good ideas have been taken, that you have less talent than that pigeon staring at you from the window sill, and that your mother was right.

So the presence of another person functions as a stabilizer, like the two-man launch rule for ICBMs. The chances that two people will lose their mind at exactly the same time are exponentially smaller.

In a world fueled mostly by animal ego and self-interest it's encouraging to know that two personalities can accommodate each other to achieve a result. The whole can be — and often is — greater than the sum of its parts. This speaks well not only of the medium, but gives one hope for the very future of the civilization. Read and enjoy.

MARSHALL BRICKMAN
Award-Winning Writer/Director

Cecilia (Mia Farrow): You do believe in God, don't you?

Tom (Jeff Daniels): Meaning?

Cecilia: The, the reason for everything, the, the world, the universe.

Tom: Oh, I think I know what you mean: the two men who wrote *The Purple Rose of Cairo*, Irving Sachs and R. H. Levine. They're writers who collaborate on films.

— The Purple Rose of Cairo

INTRODUCTION & ACKNOWLEDGMENTS

Once, co-teaching a screenwriting class, we heard a knock on the door. We opened it. Two frantic undergraduate students (is that redundant?) stood in the hall. "Tell us how to collaborate! We have to write a script together and we don't know how!"

"Hey," we said, "you're interrupting our class."

"It'll just take a minute!"

"You want us to tell you how to collaborate in sixty *seconds?*"

They nodded.

A ridiculous request. More ridiculous, we tried to answer. We tried to reduce all we'd learned as script partners to a sound bite, little more than a log line.

It would've been great just to hand them a book on the subject, but one hadn't been written. Of the more than two hundred books on the market about writing scripts, not one focused on collaboration (amazing when you consider that many of the most important and successful films of the past and the present have been written by screenwriting pairs, from Billy Wilder's legendary collaborations with Charles Brackett and I. A. L. Diamond to half of the 2001 Academy Award nominees for Best Screenplay).

After class (and two G&Ts), Matt suggested that Claudia make this her next project since she'd recently finished a book about writing short screenplays. When she mentioned this possibility to her husband, he suggested the two of us write it together.

A collaboration about collaboration. It had a nice ring. And Matt loved the idea.

So did our colleagues. One woman, a former assistant to Oliver Stone, told us she'd tried to co-write a screenplay, but the collaboration had fallen apart. "I wish I'd had a book to consult about how to do it," she said. "Or do it better."

Another colleague put it this way: "People are hungry to know how to write creatively with another person, how to bring out the best in each other, how to keep it fair, and make it successful."

We decided to do it, to co-write a book about co-writing scripts, to demystify the process, if that's possible. ("The thing about the creative process," says Marshall Brickman, "is that if you could really demystify it everybody would be doing it and who would fly the planes and run the government? I mean this.") We would write it for those who want to know how to work with a partner and for those who want to know how other script partners work. As William Goldman says in *Which Lie Did I Tell?*: "I think the one thing writers are all interested in is how others do it."

Life, of course, intervened — Matt got a better job and moved to L.A., Claudia continued teaching in Tallahassee, we wrote two screenplays... (Insert calendar pages falling and clock hands spinning.)

A few years later, out of the blue, a grad student, Amy Ellison, knocked on Claudia's office door and asked if she could be her research assistant. Claudia told her about our idea for this book. Not only did Amy augment our research (there was *still* no book on the subject), she called two friends from Yale, Andrew Reich & Ted Cohen, head writers of *Friends*, and told them about our project. Andrew Reich said, "This book needs to be written." They agreed to be interviewed. We're grateful to Amy, Andrew, and Ted for providing the jumpstart we needed.

Matt flew to Florida, and we retreated to a friend's beach cottage on St. George Island (thank you, Christie Koontz) and wrote a proposal. Our friend, Linda Seger, suggested we send it to Michael Wiese, president of Michael Wiese Productions, who — after conferring with his vice-president, Ken Lee, and editor, B. J. Markel, bought the book immediately. We thank Linda and everyone at MWP for their enthusiasm and guidance, and our literary agent, David Hale Smith, for hailing the book and negotiating a collaborative contract.

Linda also helped us build a list of potential interviewees, including Lee & Janet Scott Batchler, Harry & Renee Longstreet, and Carolyn Miller. We added some of our own: Claudia had met Nick Kazan years before when they had plays on the same bill at Actors Theater of Louisville, where she also met her lanky friend, Stuart Hample, who suggested we write his friend Marshall Brickman. Another friend, Goody Cable, had met Larry Gelbart in an Oregon Starbucks and still had his e-mail address. Claudia's daughter, Anne Loomis, put us in touch with a writer at *Newsweek* who put us in touch with the Farrelly brothers. As a film reviewer for E! Online, Matt worked with James Lewis at mPRm Public Relations, who helped us contact Matt Manfredi & Phil Hay and Olivier Ducastel & Jacques Martineau (thank you, Dan Leonard, for translating their French into English). Matt's friend, Brett Hedlund, put us in touch with Jim Taylor through Taylor's assistant, Kaile Shilling. Matt Danelo at Bumble Ward & Associates facilitated our interview with Brad Anderson.

We requested interviews via phone, e-mail, and fax. The response was overwhelming. Again and again, writers echoed Andrew Reich — "This book needs to be written" — and agreed to talk to us about their own idiosyncratic collaborative process.

The list continued to grow even during our interviews in L.A. Scott Alexander & Larry Karaszewski suggested we talk to Robert Ramsey & Matthew Stone and Ed Solomon and gave us their contact information. And Peter Tolan put us in touch with Harold Ramis. When we told Aaron Ruben we'd love to interview Hal Kanter, Ruben asked his wife, Maureen, to bring him the phone. She did — a flimsy, cordless contraption Ruben hated. "Don't we have a *real* phone?" Maureen laughed and dialed Kanter's number. "Hal!" Ruben said. "I'm talking to you on a toy phone!"

Kanter countered, "That's why you sound so young!"

Hal Kanter, in turn, put us in touch with Fay Kanin.

We scheduled interviews on our way to interviews. Stuck on the 405 Freeway (that *is* redundant), Claudia called the Farrelly brothers' assistant to arrange an interview with them. "Bad news," he said. "They can't do it. They'd love to, but they can't. They're looping *Shallow Hal.*" Assuring him that she understood, Claudia thanked him and turned off her phone.

"You called him 'darling,'" Matt said.

Claudia laughed, "No, I didn't."

"*Dahling.* Like you're an old-time agent."

"I did not!"

"You did." Matt laughed. "*Dahling!*"

Writers met us in coffee shops, restaurants, their offices, homes. We drove all over L.A. in Matt's old dusty dented black Mazda pick-up (he'd ordered a new car, but it hadn't been delivered), usually parking the truck out of sight, but when we interviewed Peter Tolan at his home in Pasadena, he buzzed us in the front gate. As we approached Tolan's large, stately house ("the shack," Tolan jokingly calls it), Matt realized there was no way he could hide the hunk of junk he was driving, but he tried — roaring past the front door and tucking the truck between two of Tolan's luxury cars.

In the end, we interviewed twenty script partners or teams: Scott Alexander & Larry Karaszewski, Brad Anderson, Lee & Janet Scott Batchler, Marshall Brickman, Olivier Ducastel & Jacques Martineau, Larry Gelbart, Fay Kanin, Hal Kanter, Nicholas Kazan, Harry & Renee Longstreet, Matt Manfredi & Phil Hay, Carolyn Miller, Harold Ramis, Robert Ramsey & Matthew Stone, Andrew Reich & Ted Cohen, Aaron Ruben, Ed Solomon, David Sonnenschein, Jim Taylor, and Peter Tolan. It's a rich sample — TV, film, mainstream, indie, domestic, foreign, friends, lovers, spouses, serial collaborators, career collaborators, and relative newcomers.

Their collaborative credits are listed in our Filmography (see page 281). Quotations from writers not listed there are from other sources, cited in the Bibliography (see page 291).

We also interviewed entertainment attorneys Brooke A. Wharton and Eric Weissmann, who kindly took the time to give us the skinny about the business side of collaborative writing, as did agents Alan Gasmer, Dave Brown, and Jennifer Good. Thanks, too, to their assistants, especially Allen Goss, and to Matt's friend, Graeme Stone, for putting us in touch with Good and Brown.

And we're grateful to Lise Anderson at the Writers Guild of America, west, for granting permission to reprint the "Writer's Collaboration Agreement" (see page 256), and to Grace Reiner for illuminating the agreement's usefulness and importance.

Additional thanks to: Anne Loomis, for our wonderful Web site; Aaron and Maureen Ruben, for the martinis and dinner and pep talks and brunch; Marti Hagen and Elizabeth Wilson of Word Wizards for their help with the transcriptions; Pacific Theatres for giving Matt their old, clunky transcription machine; Matt's Dinner Club for their encouragement as he worked on the book; Mark Litton for loaning us his copy of *Session 9*; Frank and Mary Ann and the rest of Matt's family for emotional support, and the Bank of Frank and Mystery Gifts, Inc., for financial support; Pat and Mark Sellergren for the R&R in St. Croix; Claudia's "coven" — Janet Burroway, Elizabeth Stuckey-French, and Pamela Ball — for their help with Chapter Two and the title; Dr. Alan Kagan, for keeping Claudia happy, sane, and productive; Claudia's son, Ross Loomis, for the laughs and for guiding us to current research about laughter, and her husband, Ormond Loomis, for his invaluable technical assistance throughout the project, and for suggesting that we co-write the book in the first place.

Above all, we're grateful to the writers we interviewed for their generosity of time and spirit and their candor about the collaborative process. Their experience, insight, advice, and humor are the very heart of this book.

"Yes, I'm saying it out loud. In print," Dennis Palumbo says in *Writing from the Inside Out.* "Writers are the smartest people in the room. Any room. Anywhere in town."

If we ever doubted that, we don't now.

"She got gaps. I got gaps. Together we fill the gaps."

— Rocky Balboa (Sylvester Stallone), *Rocky*

CHAPTER 1

WHY COLLABORATE?

What do feature films like *Annie Hall, The People vs. Larry Flynt, Batman Forever, Shrek, Election, Good Will Hunting, America's Sweethearts, There's Something About Mary,* and *O Brother, Where Art Thou?* have in common besides their success?

They were co-written by collaborative screenwriting teams: Marshall Brickman & Woody Allen, Scott Alexander & Larry Karaszewski, Lee & Janet Scott Batchler, Terry Rossio & Ted Elliott, Jim Taylor & Alexander Payne, Matt Damon & Ben Affleck, Peter Tolan & Billy Crystal, Peter & Bobby Farrelly, and Joel & Ethan Coen.

Many episodes of successful TV series are also co-written by teams like Andrew Reich & Ted Cohen, executive producers and head writers of *Friends*.

Each year the list of script partners and their successes grows longer. Why? Because as we and the writing teams interviewed here have discovered, collaborative scriptwriting is one of the most productive and successful ways to write.

And the rewards often transcend success, as we and so many others have found.

"We both know on some level we could do this by ourselves," Andrew Reich tells us over an El Pollo Loco lunch at their Warner Bros. office. "We both could, but we're better together and prefer it that way."

1

Harold Ramis has co-written scripts with different partners, from Douglas Kenney & Chris Miller (*Animal House*) to Peter Tolan (*Analyze This*). "It just adds so much to the work," he says during a break from editing *Analyze That*. "Peter, for instance, will add just tremendously funny things and great scenes, great dialogue. And there's this synergistic benefit — it makes my work better, and together we're better than probably either of us alone. I can enjoy writing alone, but I think I've never been as good as with other people. If I were limited by my own ability, my own imagination, I would be probably less than half as successful as I am," he confesses, laughing.

Husband and wife Andrew Schneider & Diane Frolov (*Northern Exposure; Dangerous Minds; The Chris Isaak Show*) both had successful solo careers, but after more than a decade of collaboration, they wouldn't consider returning to writing alone. "Now it would be almost inconceivable for me to be a solo writer," Schneider tells *Written By*. "It seems like such a lonely, hopeless position to be in."

Matt Manfredi & Phil Hay (*crazy/beautiful*) agree. "I can't think of a screenplay that I would want to write by myself, that I don't think Matt would be able to contribute to," Hay says in a loud, crowded deli in West Hollywood. "I feel he would always be helpful, so it never occurs to me to write a screenplay alone. It would be very lonely and upsetting."

We've written screenplays alone, and we've written screenplays together, and we're not going back. But for our money — and experience — Jim Taylor, who also wrote *Citizen Ruth* and *About Schmidt* with Alexander Payne, says it best. "Writing with Alexander at my side is much more pleasurable than working on my own," he tells us. Or, as he tells *Scenario*, "Just the writing process itself, of writing on my own, is very unpleasant and unproductive, and it's just no fun."

Fun, in fact, is the reason Harold Ramis started writing with others.

"Here's the secret: When I was in college, there were things I was interested in academically, but nothing was as much fun as sitting around a room with really funny guys and laughing all the time. I couldn't think of anything better to do. It started in a fraternity house, then moved off campus, and it occurred to me that people actually make a living doing this, but I didn't know it was possible until the end of college. My very good friend in college was a guy named Michael Shamberg, who is Danny DeVito's partner in a company called Jersey Films. And Michael and I literally shook hands and said, 'Let's never take jobs we have to dress up for, and let's only do what we enjoy.' Then again, this was the late 60s; we were prepared to be hippies and live communally. But young people still do that now, have always done it. You know you're gonna struggle anyway; you might as well enjoy it."

IT'S A COLD WORLD OUT THERE

The misery curve for screenwriters is legendary. It's a daunting task to write a screenplay and even more daunting to write a good one. Conventional wisdom says it takes five to ten years to learn the *craft* of screenwriting, and five to ten screenplays before you finally sell one. There are exceptions, of course, keeping hope alive that perhaps, just perhaps, writing screenplays is easy.

It isn't.

And getting a screenplay produced is even harder. Screenplays are like sperm: There's a one-in-a-million chance they'll get made.

3

Jim Cash & Jack Epps Jr. wrote six screenplays before *Top Gun* was produced.

"The business is very difficult," Epps tells William Froug in *The New Screenwriter Looks at the New Screenwriter*. "It's a hard-hitting business. Let's face it, it's the major leagues. Very competitive; there's a lot of pounding going on. You get it from the directors, you get it from the studios."

Nicole Yorkin & Dawn Prestwich (*Judging Amy; The Education of Max Bickford*) spent their first four years writing scripts that didn't sell. The Farrelly brothers spent nine years hawking their screenplays around Hollywood before they made their first film. So screenwriters must find effective ways to keep discouragement from overcoming determination.

Over coffee at Starbucks in Pacific Palisades, Lee & Janet Scott Batchler tell us that writing together helps them stay motivated.

JANET: Sometimes we both get down at the same time. It just works that way. Sometimes we sort of pull each other through.

LEE: The best baseball player in the world has a batting slump.

JANET: And the best baseball players in the world are batting somewhere in the .300s. Nobody hits a thousand. We just have to keep reminding each other of that. We sort of have to goose each other to get going sometimes.

It may be a cold world out there for screenwriters, but one of the best ways to stay warm is collaboration.

"You've always got one person in town who's looking out for your best interests," says Robert Ramsey, who writes with Matthew Stone

(*Destiny Turns on the Radio; Life; Big Trouble*) in an office overlooking Griffith Observatory and the famous Hollywood sign.

Yes, you have to find the right writing partner, and once you start selling your screenplays, you'll make half the money, but most writing teams believe that's a small price to pay. Bottom line: From better brainstorming to better mental health to better screenplays, the advantages of sharing the writing outweigh the disadvantages of sharing the bottom line.

TWO IMAGINATIONS ARE BETTER THAN ONE

In *Which Lie Did I Tell?* William Goldman grouses about the way the Farrelly brothers and the Coen brothers collaborate on their screenplays. They write too quickly. They break the rules. They write without knowing — or outlining — their story. They *deliberately* get themselves into a corner with their stories, then take a few days or a week or even a month off until they find a way out. Goldman insists there's madness in their method, but he grudgingly admits that for them it *works*.

"Okay," Goldman says, "my theory as to why it works for them is simplicity itself: numbers. Not because they are brother writing teams, although that doesn't hurt. They certainly know each other so well, and can deal with each other's idiosyncrasies. But it's because there are two of them. I can't do it that way. If I get into a dark place, I can't say to my writing partner, 'Here, fix the fucker.' There's only me, trapped helpless in my pit, no way out."

If you've written alone, you know what Goldman is talking about. That trapped, helpless feeling. Your story gets stuck in the corner. You think, *No way out.*

What do the Farrelly brothers do when this happens?

"We just drive," Peter Farrelly tells Goldman. "You know, it frees everything up. We just get in the car and drive."

Madness!

Or is it? The truth is, we're big fans of driving. There's something about motion that's magic. But hurtling down highways sometimes isn't enough. Once, on a road trip from Tallahassee to Memphis, we tried to develop an idea for a screenplay, but the story kept getting stuck. One dark corner after another. That trapped, helpless feeling began to set in. Finally one of us had the wisdom to say, "What about that *other* idea we had?" We set the first idea aside and started brainstorming the second. Bingo! We were off. The idea spun into story like silk off a spool. By the time we got to Memphis, a ten-hour trip (the way that we drive), we'd written an entire scene-by-scene for a screenplay.

We learned a couple of things on that trip: Some stories deserve to stay in the corner (R.I.P.). And though Peter Farrelly is right when he says driving frees everything up, Goldman's right, too: We got out of the "dark place" because there were two of us in the car. When one couldn't see that we needed to change ideas and direction, the other one did. Then we started brainstorming. And found a way out.

BETTER BRAINSTORMING

There are some terrific techniques (clustering, for example) for exploring ideas alone on paper, but brainstorming (Goldman likes to call it "spitballing") by definition requires more than one person. According to *Conceptual Blockbusting*, it was invented as a group problem-solving technique and given its name by Alex Osborn, a leader in advertising, who outlined four rules for successful brainstorming sessions:

1) No evaluation (internal or external criticism) of any kind is permitted.

2) All participants should be encouraged to think of the wildest ideas possible (because, as Osborn believed, "it's easier to tame down than think up").

3) Quantity of ideas should be encouraged (quantity helps control our internal evaluation, and quantity, he also believed, leads to quality).

4) Participants should build upon or modify the ideas of others (because, in Osborn's words, "combinations or modifications of previously suggested ideas often lead to new ideas that are superior to those that sparked them").

We were amazed and impressed (with ourselves) when we recently read these rules, because over the years we've developed a similar set of unwritten rules for brainstorming our screenplays.

Before we make an outrageous suggestion, we say, "I'm just playing." That's code for, "Brace yourself, this could be bullshit," but it buys us a license to offer the dumbest ideas without getting dumped on (Rule 1).

Okay, in our more insecure moments, if we think the idea is *really* outrageous, we'll say, "You're gonna hate this" or "Get out your barf bag," but we throw the idea into the mix anyway so we can explore it. Because, like Alex Osborn, we've learned that the more outrageous the idea the better (Rule 2).

A wild idea can always be tamed (unless, of course, it turns out to be brilliant), but it can also release a whole herd of ideas (Rule 3).

And when we play off each other's ideas, we almost always come up with something better (Rule 4).

It's the "synergistic benefit" Ramis refers to. "Another analogy I've used is like getting an assist in basketball. One person puts the ball up near the hoop, and the other person slams it in. Or makes a great pass that results in a shot."

He, too, often offers an apologia before he makes a suggestion. "I preface my ideas with saying, 'This really is bad' or 'You're gonna hate this' or 'How lame is this?' or 'Is this too stupid?' You know, particularly in comedy. Comedy depends so totally on the approval you get from the audience, and your collaborators are your first audience, so you're just desperate to please them." He laughs.

Ramsey & Stone have a similar tactic:

MATTHEW: We say, "This is probably a really terrible idea."

ROBERT: "This is probably the worst idea I've ever had."

MATTHEW: Happens all the time. Like fifty times a day.

ROBERT: It's the lunatic ideas that you feel safe sharing with your partner. If you're afraid he's gonna think this is stupid, then you're never gonna say it. Maybe he'll think it's great. You've just got to put it out there. The more risk, the more reward.

It's no accident that this method works. As *Conceptual Blockbusting* says, a study group at Harvard listed the following behavioral reasons why brainstorming this way is such a success:

1. Less inhibition and defeatism.

2. Contagion of enthusiasm.

3. Development of competitive spirit; everyone wants to top the other's idea.

Less inhibition means more freedom and willingness to take risks — one of the great benefits of collaborative writing. As psychologist and creativity researcher Howard Gruber observes in *Creative Collaboration*, "What a collaboration does for you is, by spreading the risk a little bit, it encourages you to take more chances." We're all told to be bold (there's magic in it), but it's easier when we write with others. It takes a great deal of trust — in yourself, your partner, and the creative process — but the rewards are profound. A greater willingness to take chances expands and enriches the creative field for you. Increases your options. Opens your mind — and your screenplay.

"It carves out a lot of territory for you to operate in," says Harold Ramis.

The boldness comes in part from another benefit of collaboration: instant feedback. When you write alone, if you're anything like us, you're your own worst critic. You start to question your work and your judgment. You have no idea how your words come across. A co-writer can see the potential in an idea you might otherwise shoot down. This feedback energizes and encourages experimentation. Discourages defeatism. You spend less time at the pity party Goldman so aptly describes — *there's only me, trapped helpless in my pit, no way out* — and more time creating your screenplay.

A contagion of enthusiasm (derived from the Latin *en theos*, "with God," in case you doubted it was divine) means more excitement about the screenplay you're writing. And, as you bounce ideas back and forth ("creative ping-pong," we call it), the excitement increases. As Epps says in *Written By*, "We sort of feed each other." It's working — no, *playing* — together that makes breakthroughs happen.

Finally, better brainstorming develops a competitive spirit. As we'll explore in Chapter Eight, a *healthy* competitive spirit inspires you and your partner to try and top each other and ultimately to offer your best.

Still, the sweetest moments for us will always be solving creative problems together. That's the real joy and reward of collaboration. We laugh, crow, high-five. We've even been known to jump up and do a victory dance — trusting we won't make fun of each other's moves.

THE THIRD VOICE

"Collaboration is a merger of the aesthetic of two different people," says Nicholas Kazan, who wrote *Matilda* with his wife, Robin Swicord. "It's distinct from the individual aesthetic. And I think what happens in a good collaboration is that you form this other psychic or psychological identity."

That's one of the more marvelous and mysterious benefits of the collaborative writing process. Somehow, through the merging of the aesthetic, experience, and talent of two writers, a "third voice" emerges.

"Jim likes to say, and it's true," Jack Epps tells Froug, "there's three egos involved here: there's Cash's ego, Epps' ego, and then there's the ego of Cash & Epps. And that's the one."

Cash adds, "We're writing our best when the third personality takes over."

Prestwich says the same thing about working with Yorkin. "We're actually very different voices as writers," she tells *Written By*. "When we come together to write, we create a third writer. Basically that third writer writes the script. It's this third writer who has so much more experience and knowledge than we have individually."

Scott Alexander & Larry Karaszewski (*Ed Wood; The People vs. Larry Flynt; Man on the Moon*) have only written screenplays collaboratively. "So it's hard to say what that individual voice would be anymore," Karaszewski says. "There's definitely a third voice."

"Sort of a mixture of real and ridiculous, funny and poignant, and absurdism," Alexander explains. "So we do tend to shove our scripts into that voice. Unless we're doing a two-week polish, in which case we're idiots for hire."

We create a third voice, too, when we write scripts together, and we've learned to welcome that third writer into the room.

So has Ed Solomon, who collaborated with Chris Matheson on *Bill & Ted's Excellent Adventure, Bill & Ted's Bogus Journey,* and *Automatons.* "Try to be in love with that third entity," he advises. "It's neither you nor them, neither your idea nor that person's idea, but it's that third thing which is a product of the two of you. Try to always keep your eye on that. Nurture *that*."

11

The whole *is* greater than the sum of the parts. And the partners.

COMPLEMENTARY STRENGTHS

Talk to any screenwriting team and they can tell you, chapter and verse, what they have in common. We met as colleagues at the Florida State University Film School, we're both from the South, we adore comedy, and we have the same sensibilities about what makes a good story. As we'll examine in Chapter Two, similar sensibilities are crucial for you and your partner, but your *differences* — the creative yin-yang — are just as important. It is this combination, this complementarity, that gives each collaboration its unique richness and range of experience, knowledge, and talent to tap.

In *Written By*, Jack Herrguth describes how he and Seanne Kemp Kovach (*Sister, Sister*) complement one another. "The fact that I'm a man and she's a woman, I'm white and she's African American brings different points of view to our partnership that enriches it." And Billy Van Zandt, who writes and executive-produces with Jane Milmore (*Newhart; Martin; Bless This House*), tells *Creative Screenwriting*, "I think the male/female dynamic, as far as a team is concerned, is important. Because I clearly don't know what it's like to be a woman."

Like Herrguth & Kovach and Van Zandt & Milmore, we're different genders. But male/female is only the beginning of our differences: urban/rural, single/married, no children/children, pessimist/optimist, good dancer/bad dancer, pop culture/literature, actor/playwright, neurotic/Zen (Matt's suggestion).

We complement each other, too, with individual strengths as screenwriters: visual/verbal, character detail/character arc, scene/structure, dialogue/description, shtick/depth, first draft/

revision. This doesn't mean we don't share the work, but we often defer to each other's expertise. It's a nice safety net. When we hit a snag, we can turn to the expert and say, as Goldman so delicately put it, "Fix the fucker."

"I think the key to collaboration is knowing what your strengths are and knowing what your partner's strengths are," Epps says. "And not trying to compete with each other."

"Usually, Jack works ahead of me, planning scenes," Cash adds. "His story instincts are exceptional, and I give him all the room he needs to develop the main body of the work. He'll pitch several scenes to me at a time, and we'll talk about each one of them for a few minutes, turning them inside-out a couple of times, reshaping something, adding something else. His job during this is to make sure the story stays on track. My job is to make the scene interesting. He's looking at the whole sky; I'm looking at the incoming bogey."

A nice metaphor since they wrote *Top Gun*.

Lowell Ganz & Babaloo Mandel (*Splash; Parenthood; City Slickers*) are also well aware of their complementary strengths, as they tell *Written By*:

LOWELL: I know a lot about sports.

BABALOO: And I know nothing. I bring ignorance!

LOWELL: I tend to think every day is our last day in show business... or on earth. I've always said about myself, that I'm the first man in the lifeboat. I'm the guy who gets in the dress, pushing women and children out of the way.

13

BABALOO: He would, and he would travel with that dress… and he'd have a little stuffed baby….

LOWELL: Seriously, to answer it… He has a great sense of tracking the audience — to take himself out of the movie and put himself in the theater…. Babaloo is also, aside from everything else, as good a joke writer as I ever met in my life. And I have an ability — I have a willingness — to construct scenarios and toss them into the air… to just say, "All right! How about this for a construction on this act?" When we get stuck… to just sort of get to it quickly and go through various solutions.

Like traveling with a dress and a little stuffed baby.

BETTER MENTAL HEALTH

In *Traveling Mercies*, Anne Lamott describes a moment in the Idaho mountains when she needed to talk to a normal person about a parenting decision she had to make. "Needless to say, there was no one around remotely fitting the description of a normal person: I was at a *writing* conference."

Okay, we all know "normal writers" is an oxymoron, so writing and mental health may seem like an odd combination. But remember, we're talking about *collaborative* writing, and better mental health, we believe, is one of its greatest rewards.

Take anxiety. Please. Anxiety is so rampant in writers (especially women, but men suffer, too — just ask Matt) that a recent conference sponsored by the Institute for Psychoanalytic Training and Research was devoted to finding ways to assuage it. One of the strategies that the conference predicted would be most successful was an effective creativity support group.

Writing with a partner is having your own creativity support group. As Aaron Ruben (*The Comic; Caesar's Hour*) tells us while munching a cigar on the patio of his Beverly Hills home, "It takes the terror out of being in the room with that sheet of paper and typewriter and not one word is there."

That terror is all too common. "Every time, my first day of writing I think, *I can't do this*," Andrew Reich confides. "I'm a fake. I'm gonna get found out this time that I really suck. One of the things I've learned in collaboration is to trust Ted when he says, 'This is good enough.' I trust that."

Anxiety may attach to any creative project, but writing with a partner, we've found, is the best antidote. When we work together, we keep each other from sliding into self-doubt, the slough of despond. Again, we've developed a code, an emotional shorthand: When one of us starts looping about some gloomy thought, the other makes the sound of a hollow pipe organ — *boop boop, boop boop* — and that gets us laughing and working again (well, it works for us).

In fact, for us, laughter is the heart of the art of maintaining mental health when we work together. Even when we aren't together, if we're having a terrible day, we'll call each other and say, "Make me laugh!" Because, like brainstorming, laughter is hard to do on your own. It's a social act that connects us to others. And satisfying the human need for connection is one of the reasons laughter increases mental — and physical — health.

Neuroscience is beginning to understand other reasons. Laughter is one of the few times we use our whole brain. Peter Derks, professor of psychology at the College of William and Mary, says when we get a punch line, both sides of the brain are engaged (collaborating!), "the left hemisphere working on the joke's verbal

15

content while the analytic right hemisphere attempts to figure out the incongruity that lies at the heart of much humor."

"After you laugh, you go into a relaxed state," explains John Morreall, president of Humor Works Seminars in Tampa, Florida. "Your blood pressure and heart rate drop below normal, so you feel profoundly relaxed. Laughter also indirectly stimulates endorphins, the brain's natural painkillers." More to the point for screenwriters, laughter makes us more creative. "Humor loosens up the mental gears. It encourages out-of-the-ordinary ways of looking at things."

WD40 for the creative wheels.

But what happens when those wheels screech to a halt? Writer's block.

"I turn to my partner and scream 'Help!'" says Paul Guay, who wrote *Liar Liar* and *Heartbreakers* with Stephen Mazur.

"You just call up the other person or go talk to the other person, and you deal with the problem," Nick Kazan says at his Santa Monica bungalow, "and the problem usually goes away. Something that would keep you stuck and perhaps deeply depressed for a week or two is going to evaporate in a matter of minutes. So it's a great solace."

Without Ted Elliott, Terry Rossio claims to have "a permanent case of writer's block," as he says on their Web site, *Wordplayer.com*. His recommendation? "Get a writing partner, so there's somebody other than yourself you don't want to let down."

And a partner can offer insights, ideas, or inspiration and get your creative wheels turning again, as Scott Alexander & Larry Karaszewski have found.

LARRY: On the days when I just am brain dead —

SCOTT: That was yesterday.

LARRY: Exactly. 2001 was actually a brain dead time for me. Your partner can spark you and push you forward. And then when he's not feeling up to it, I can say, "All right, we gotta get to work." There are very few times when we both shut down completely. It's happened.

SCOTT: I think it happens all the time. The thing with writer's block with teams is that it's more embarrassing because it's two people staring at the wall for hours and not a sound being spoken. You can cut the tension with a knife after a certain point. It's more humiliating because if a guy's alone and staring at a computer and doesn't know what to do, he'll just go off and make a sandwich or turn on the TV.

LARRY: It's hard to masturbate when Scott's around. (Laughter.)

Ron Osborn, who collaborates with Jeff Reno (*Radioland Murders; Meet Joe Black*), tells the Writers Guild, "When we both hit a roadblock... you know it's major. Painful, in fact. I know of no shortcuts we use. I tell Jeff a close family member of mine's died, flee the office, and seek the comfort of strangers. He's usually solved it when I return."

Hey, whatever works. Script partners also recommend taking breaks, exploring alternative story setups and directions, and trusting the process and the other person. If all else fails, they remind each other that they've got deadlines to make and bills to pay. As many teams tell us, that's the quickest cure for block.

17

All these advantages — the creative support, the trust, the complementary strengths, the improved mental health, and the inspiration — increase morale. "You have another person who is pushing you forward if you're feeling like you don't know if you can do it," Frolov says about working with Schneider. "We trade off in the role of being encouraging. We take turns saying, 'Yes! We can do this!'"

"What ends up happening is one person bolsters the other," Matthew Stone says. "Nobody's a bigger fan of each other than we are. We think we're fucking great." They laugh. "But I think that's an important thing."

It is. As we said earlier, there's a one-in-a-million chance a screenplay will get made. But they do get made. If you hang in there. If you keep writing and honing your craft, even when you feel like the world's biggest loser.

Most writing teams, like Cash & Epps, have had to deal with long stretches of failure. The *real* F word. "It was very difficult because Jim's and my history was that we had written six unproduced screenplays," Epps admits.

Their partnership kept them going, Cash says. "We had some times when we were not successful, so we got together and said, 'Look, we want to make this work. We want to make this happen.'"

Prestwich & Yorkin, too, credit their collaboration for their success. "Through all the ups and downs and setbacks and such, we've always had each other to depend on for a reality check," Yorkin says. "'Is this as insane as I think it is?' And since we can do that with each other, we are able to present a strong united front to the world we deal with every day."

18

Prestwich adds, "I think it gives us a lot of confidence."

This inner and outer strength is especially important when you sell your script and you have to deal with the insanity of studio notes, the bane of every scriptwriter's existence. Because they're a team, Ramsey & Stone believe they're better able to protect and preserve their screenplays from the opinions of studio executives who too often know more about business than writing.

"I'm always looking for a peaceful solution to a situation," Ramsey says, "and Matt is really good at defending our borders. He is quicker to anger, I would say, actually. I think both functions are really necessary in dealing with all these know-nothing cocksuckers." They laugh. "But I have total respect, 'cause they're very intelligent people."

BETTER MOTIVATION AND WORK HABITS

But all the confidence in the world is no substitute for actually doing the writing. Developing productive work habits. And having a partner helps here, too. A writing workout partner.

"You have to show up because the other guy's showing up," Ramsey says. "Matt's going to the office, I gotta get there. Otherwise, I would probably be the least productive person on earth."

Jim Taylor agrees. "Having an appointed time to show up for work and someone whom you are accountable to on a daily basis makes each workday more productive," he says. "When one of us gets tired or discouraged, the other one can take over and keep things going. Plus, Alexander is a great cook."

For Scott Alexander & Larry Karaszewski, their productivity doubles, too, when it comes to taking phone calls, an essential part of the business. "This is a great trick that teams can do," Alexander says. "Oftentimes someone will call us up, and we're talking to some person, and the second line will ring. One of the two of us will discreetly leave the call, and the caller has no idea they've lost one of us. So this is a good trick that collaborators can do. Invaluable."

Partners also bring different work habits to the collaboration, and these habits often improve over time. When we started writing our first screenplay, we tried to write once a week (Claudia's idea), but this wasn't frequent enough to create a productive momentum. Things picked up when we started to write every day (Matt's better idea).

Brian Helgeland & Curtis Hanson remain virtual opposites when it comes to work habits — Helgeland needs to know he has two months to write without interruption; Hanson works "in whatever way works" — but working together on *L.A. Confidential* pulled them through the tough patches, they tell *Written By*. As Helgeland so beautifully puts it, "When there was no wind, we rowed."

MAKES YOU A BETTER WRITER (AND MAYBE A BETTER PERSON)

No internal or external criticism may be allowed in brainstorming (Rule 1), but at other times in the creative process, your writing partner can be an invaluable critic — your first audience. His or her response produces a better script than you could have come up with alone.

"It's almost like the script gets a second draft in the first draft process," Prestwich says.

"I think we get a better-edited first draft than we could writing separately," Matt Manfredi says, "just because it's got to get by two people."

"Two very cranky people," Phil Hay adds, laughing.

But perhaps more important, most teams tell us that working together has made them better people. Less ego-involved and controlling. More open and trusting. The long-term effect of writing with someone else, we and others have found, is far more profound than expected. It's humanizing. We've learned to accept and welcome our differences and most of our idiosyncrasies.

"I think it makes us very tolerant people," Prestwich says. "It makes us understand the human condition a little bit better because we have such an intimate view of it."

And since the best scripts are about the human condition, what better way to learn to write better scripts?

As we said, the rewards of collaboration often transcend success. Many script partners found success on their own, but it wasn't until they wrote with each other that they found real fulfillment.

"What we do together has been not just professionally but personally very nourishing," Lowell Ganz says, "to have done it with, and to still be doing it, together."

SCRIPT PARTNER POINTS

✪ Writing with a partner helps you stay motivated, focused, and productive in the face of countless rejections (and it's cheaper than antidepressants).

✪ It's a dog-eat-dog business — and vice versa — but there's always one person in town looking out for your interests.

✪ Two imaginations really are better than one — better brainstorming and creative breakthroughs.

✪ Yin, meet Yang. Complementing (and complimenting) each other can lead to stronger scripts.

✪ A writing workout partner encourages — and enforces — better work habits.

✪ A partner helps you work through writer's block, if only because it's embarrassing when both of you are staring at a blank page.

✪ Collaboration not only improves mental health, it makes you a better writer — and a better person.

"Actually, none of us on this planet ever really choose each other. It's all quantum physics and molecular attraction. There are laws we don't understand that bring us together and break us apart."

— Annie Savoy (Susan Sarandon), *Bull Durham*

CHAPTER 2

THE RIGHT WRITING PARTNER

Matt Manfredi mops up the iced tea he's accidentally spilled all over our table — and his lap. The waitress at Canter's Deli in West Hollywood returns to our booth with a stack of napkins and a fresh glass of tea. "Try to keep this one on the table," she wisecracks over the racket of clattering dishes.

We crack up.

Manfredi is a good sport, but still red-faced from his *faux pas*, he lets Phil Hay answer our question about finding the right writing partner.

"It's such a big deal to throw your lot in with somebody to do this," Hay sighs. "And it's so hard to break up collaborations. I guess the advice that I would give to people who are considering collaboration is — it's really great if you find the right person."

Okay. But how do you do that?

It's a question many writers have asked us since we started our collaboration, and a question we've asked many collaborative writers. But it's a little like asking how you find a friend or a lover or any significant other. Collaboration is an intimate creative relationship, and whether you're looking for a partner to co-write a particular project or someone to share a writing career, finding the right person is a mysterious process governed by "laws we don't understand," as savvy Savoy says in *Bull Durham*.

23

We certainly don't understand the laws that brought us together as collaborators. We consider it a Christmas miracle that it ever happened at all. In fact, we *hated* each other when we met on the faculty of the Film School at Florida State in 1992.

MATT: To be honest, Claudia scared the shit out of me. I thought of her as a white tornado. Maybe you remember the TV commercial for Ajax, where you open the cap, and — look out! — this "white tornado" sweeps through the room cleaning everything in sight. I thought the label was appropriate, not because Claudia ever cleaned anything, but because she could burst into a room and boy, look out! Well, over lunch one day, I made the mistake of telling her and other faculty members about a freelance writing job I'd accepted for a documentary about nuclear waste. The real kicker was the producer wanted it to be a *comedy*. Huh? About leaky nuclear waste containers and the need for reform in the Department of Energy? (Insert laugh track here.) Ironically, the D.O.E. was funding this little project (to the tune of $1.2 million). Hearing this, Claudia took the high moral ground (read: high horse) and accused me of making a pact with the Devil. *Ouch.*

CLAUDIA: But many months and drafts later, you discovered I was right.

MATT: Yeah. Bigger *ouch*. Stinging from Claudia's criticism, I refused to even share the sidewalk with her on the walk back to our offices. I crossed the street, hung back, and sulked to my office thinking, *I can't stand her!* But the big lesson learned was that nuclear waste, the U.S. government, and film producers are about as funny as —

CLAUDIA: Our faculty meetings.

MATT: Mind-numbing.

CLAUDIA: Soul-sucking.

24

MATT: But otherwise fun! (Laughter.)

Many of our professorial pow-wows turned into pseudo-development meetings for students' short screenplays. We began to notice we often offered similar notes and found ourselves on the same side of creative arguments, er, discussions. It was there that we said to each other for the first of countless times to come, "Hey, get out of my head!"

We gradually let our guard down as we discovered our shared sensibilities, and eventually Matt felt comfortable enough to share a problem he was having with a script. A producer in L.A. had just optioned the project and was demanding changes in the third act before sending it out. Claudia gave Matt some helpful notes, and another piece of our improbable connection was in place. So maybe it was safe to try lunch again. CUT TO:

We became regulars at a local greasy spoon, Manny's, a Southern-gothic *Cheers*, where the waitresses knew our names and our standing orders. Over heaping portions of buffet-style fried chicken, mashed potatoes, cornbread, and cobbler (and Matt wondered why he gained so much weight!), we started swapping story ideas.

CLAUDIA: I wanted to write a screenplay inspired by my experience as an expert witness for the defense in a criminal obscenity trial in Tallahassee — a local mom-and-pop video store had been busted for renting homosexual porn — so over a series of lunches, we discussed and developed a fictional framework for the script.

MATT: We probably yapped louder than we should have — not because other idea-hungry writers might be eavesdropping, but because talk of gay porn doesn't sit so well in a small Southern dive. More than a few diners shifted to distant tables, believe me.

CLAUDIA: But we discovered how much we liked the process of working together — and each other. And we both loved the story.

MATT: So at some point in some lunch (ironic, huh?), Claudia asked me to officially co-write the courtroom drama. We figured each of us could bring a certain perspective to the material. (No, I've never done gay porn. Did you *look* at my photo?)

CLAUDIA: I had the First Amendment and courtroom experience, but Matt was a more experienced screenwriter and a real taskmaster about our work habits. I call it his "steely fiber."

MATT: The White Tornado meets the Steely-Fibered Taskmaster. Sounds like the title match at the WWF Smackdown or a disastrous combo for collaborators. Thankfully — and surprisingly — it wasn't.

COLLABORATION HAPPENS

"I don't know that anyone ever goes shopping for a collaborator," says Fay Kanin (*My Pal Gus; The Opposite Sex; Teacher's Pet*) at her Santa Monica beach house. "Maybe they do, but not in my experience. Generally it happens. It comes out of friendship, or someone puts you together with someone and it works."

The collaboration of Marshall Brickman & Woody Allen began when someone put them together — and it worked. "We both had the same managers, Rollins & Joffe, who had developed Nichols & May into, well, Nichols & May," Brickman tells us. As Allen's career took off and he started using more material for his TV appearances, the managers suggested that their two comic clients give co-writing a whirl.

"So we started. Very formal, guarded. All business," Brickman says. "At first it was writing material for his act, then we tried a movie, a few TV specials. Woody had already done a few movies, collaborating on the scripts with his old friend Mickey Rose. I'm not sure what happened — this might have been around the time Mickey moved to California (maybe a change was in order). So we tried a screenplay, which nobody loved, which is in a drawer somewhere — don't ask me about it because I'll never tell — and then we wrote *Sleeper*."

And the rest is film history: *Annie Hall, Manhattan,* and *Manhattan Murder Mystery*.

But most of the writing teams that we've interviewed were not put together. They evolved out of close personal relationships. Friends and lovers and family.

FRIENDS **AND FRIENDS**

"We were friends, and we started writing together," Andrew Reich says of his collaboration with Ted Cohen on *Friends*. "We knew each other so well. And that's crucial."

They became best friends and roommates at Yale, but they didn't start writing collaboratively until they were living on opposite sides of the country. After graduation, Reich went to L.A. and became a book agent, while Cohen went to Harvard and became a law student. Neither was happy with what he was doing. Reich eventually left the agent business ("I quit/was fired," he laughs), and in 1993, Cohen took a break from his studies.

"Ted said, 'Hey, I'm gonna come out there for a vacation. Why don't we write a script?'" Reich suggested they take a whack at a spec for *The Simpsons*. "It was just like, 'Sure, what the hell.' Not really expecting anything to come of it, but, 'Yeah, why not?' We just wanted something to show to our friends that would make them laugh and make us laugh, and it was really for fun. It was so lovely."

Reich & Cohen never considered a career as co-writers until the first draft was finished. And no one was more surprised than they were that it didn't suck. "We thought, 'This is actually pretty good,'" Reich says. "'Wow, this is pretty funny. This could maybe get us an agent, and we could maybe try doing this for a living.'"

An accidental collaboration.

"You have to stumble into it," says Scott Alexander, " just like you have to stumble into your own style."

He and Larry Karaszewski met in the meal-card line the first day of their freshmen year at the University of Southern California. Like Reich & Cohen, the two film majors became roommates and friends long before they became collaborators. Four years later, on a cross-country road trip during summer vacation, they were inspired to write their first script. And just where did the future Ed Wood/Larry Flynt/Andy Kaufman biopic writers get this inspiration? Where else? Ann Landers!

"She was running a series of columns about a kid who was vandalizing a high school gymnasium," Alexander explains. "He'd fallen through the roof while committing the crime and had gotten paralyzed when he hit the ground. And his parents had sued the school district and won; they won a couple million dollars. So I mentioned this to Larry, and we started laughing about this tragic

28

story, saying, 'That would be a funny movie if it weren't some poor kid, but some really slick thief, like a Morris Day kind of a guy.'"

Morris Day? Obviously, this was the '80s. Like, totally.

The idea stuck with them. When they returned to USC, they started writing together two to three hours every night. Their goal of finishing a feature-length screenplay was unusual among their fellow film students.

"We weren't encouraged to write full screenplays," says Karaszewski. "You were supposed to write the first forty pages, or come up with just an idea."

"So we had no ulterior motive in deciding to write the script," adds Alexander. "It wasn't like we thought we'd write it, sell it for a lot of money, and break in. It was like, 'Hey, we don't know anybody who's written a whole script. I wonder if we could.' We figured it was something none of our friends had done. 'If we can get to page 120, wouldn't that be cool?' That was really it — it was just a goofy lark."

That goofy lark — a crime caper called *Homewreckers* — sold to Twentieth Century-Fox for $300,000, one week after they graduated.

All good collaborations don't evolve from good friendships (God knows, ours didn't!), but they endure because good friendships evolve from the collaborations.

"These teams that have lasted, they have to also be great friendships," Harold Ramis tells us. "You've really got to want to spend a lot of time with someone, because obviously you're not working eight hours. You're processing everything that happens in your life, in the news, in the world; it all gets in there somehow. That's

29

a big part of collaboration: what you talk about away from the work. At Second City, Joe Flaherty, Brian Murray, and I used to start our day by having breakfast and reading the newspaper together — 'Did you see this? Did you see that?' Even when we moved from Second City to National Lampoon — that was me, John Belushi, Bill Murray, Brian Murray, Joe Flaherty, Gilda Radner — we'd call each other when we were watching TV and say, 'You watching that? Check this out.' Because everything becomes potential material, either the actual content or your response to what you're seeing. That's how you forge a shared point of view, by processing lots of other stuff and by sharing your past with everyone. One of the first things we did on *Animal House*, one thing we did constantly, was recite a complete oral history of our educational experience — all the people we remembered from college, all the teachers, every amazing event, every apocryphal event, everything that our cousins, brothers, uncles ever told us about college. We didn't know if it would be relevant or not to what we were writing, but it is this information-sharing that provides the background for what you write."

LOVE AND MARRIAGE

"*C'est notre rencontre qui nous a décidé à travailler ainsi et pas le désir de faire des films qui nous a fait nous rencontrer,*" Olivier Ducastel & Jacques Martineau say in their e-mail from Paris. Since *nous ne parlons pas le français*, a friend translates for us: "It wasn't our desire to make films that brought us together, but rather it was our meeting one another that led us to make films together."

An aspiring director, Olivier studied film as an undergraduate and wrote a feature, but he couldn't raise the funds to produce it. Meanwhile, Jacques — who teaches literature *à l'Université* — wrote his first feature for some friends in the film industry, but he didn't want to direct it. When he and Olivier met in 1995, it was *l'amour* at first sight. "It was for us, first and foremost, a relationship as lovers."

Olivier read Jacque's script, *Jeanne et le Garçon Formidable* (*Jeanne and the Perfect Guy*), and offered to direct the film with him. "We did it, it worked well, and we've worked together ever since." It certainly worked well for their film, *Drôle de Félix* (*Adventures of Felix*), which became a U.S. art-house hit and one of the most successful French imports of 2001.

Fay Kanin and her late husband, Michael — one of the longest and most successful collaborations in Hollywood — did not choose each other as writing partners, they chose each other as spouses. And they both fell in love with a *New Yorker* story called "Sunday Punch" about a boarding house for fighters. Convinced it would make a good film, they bought the rights to the story and decided to adapt it during their honeymoon in Malibu.

"We rented a house right on the beach — I guess that's when we first fell in love with the beach — and we wrote the screenplay on spec. Then we sold the script. That said to us, 'Listen, you can do this.' We had each written separately. Michael had written a couple of the B pictures at RKO, and I was a reader, but I had written some short stories with another reader. I had not written a screenplay yet that I'd sold, so we said, 'This is it. We could do this together. We've got a career here.'"

Harry & Renee Longstreet (*Fame; Alien Nation: The Udara Legacy*) also discovered a career together, one that evolved from their marriage — and the ghosts of marriages past. A few months after their wedding, Renee was struggling to write a screenplay while working five — yes, five — jobs. She couldn't stand the thought of financial dependence. "I'd had difficulties with my ex-husband stopping paying," she tells us over coffee at their dining room table. "Then he'd pay sporadically, then he'd get behind. It was just a nightmare, and I would never again be dependent upon a man to support me and my kids. Ever."

But Harry thought she should devote herself to her craft, and he offered to pay her to write. Renee refused. "I said, 'I'm not ever going to let you support me. What do you think, I'm going to let you be my *patron*?' He goes, 'No, just let me be your husband.'"

She accepted his proposal and threw herself into her scripts. She also let Harry read pages as she wrote them.

RENEE: He would come home at night from work, and he'd read what I'd written. And he'd start to say, "Well, what about if you do this? Or what about if you do that?"

HARRY: I started to noodle with it.

RENEE: And then he said, "Could I do that scene with the drama teacher?" So he took that and he wrote that scene. And then he tried to write another scene. And then another.

Their career collaboration was under way.

You and your writing partner don't have to be married (God knows, we aren't!), but it's important to think of your partnership as a marriage of sorts — not to be taken lightly.

"It's really a marriage," insists Hal Kanter (*Move Over, Darling; All in the Family*) over breakfast at Sportsmen's Lodge in Studio City, "and you'd better make sure you've got the right woman or the right man, depending on whether you're a woman or a man — but not necessarily today!" He laughs.

Larry Gelbart (*Caesar's Hour; M*A*S*H*) waves the marriage metaphor away. "I will avoid the marriage analogy because it's tougher than marriage," he tells us at his home in Beverly Hills.

Why? we ask.

"Because there's no sex!" he laughs. "There's no way to kiss and make up." (Unless you and your partner are married or otherwise romantically involved.) Still, Gelbart agrees in spirit with Kanter. "You really have to love the other guy/girl. You really have to."

O BROTHER (OR SISTER), WHERE ART THOU?

And then there's brotherly/sisterly love. That's not to say other familial combinations aren't possible — the father-son team of Sherwood & Lloyd Schwartz (*The Brady Girls Get Married; A Very Brady Christmas*) springs to mind — but the sibling collaboration is far more prevalent. Obviously, you can't go shopping for a sibling, but if you are biologically blessed, perhaps you will join the growing number of Hollywood heavy-hitters who have kept it all in the family: Jerry & David Zucker (*Airplane; Naked Gun*), Joel & Ethan Coen (*Blood Simple; Fargo*), Larry & Andy Wachowski (*Bound; The Matrix*), Peter & Bobby Farrelly (*Dumb and Dumber; Me, Myself & Irene*), Albert & Allen Hughes (*Menace II Society; Dead Presidents*), Shawn & Marlon Wayans (*Scary Movie; Scary Movie 2*), Jim & John Thomas (*Mission to Mars; Behind Enemy Lines*), Peter & David Griffiths (*Collateral Damage; The Hunted*), Chris & Paul Weitz (*Antz; About a Boy*), Jill & Karen Sprecher (*Clockwatchers; Thirteen Conversations About One Thing*), Nora & Delia Ephron (*Michael; You've Got Mail*).

Ironically, no one in the Farrelly family thought the future *Dumb and Dumber* guys would amount to anything. "Peter and Bobby were a couple of screw-offs. A+ screw-offs," their father, Bob Farrelly, tells *Newsweek*. "But the family is so close. Mariann and I both tried hard, and I think the word is *love*. L-O-V-E."

Raised in Rhode Island, the young jokesters may have been l-o-v-e-d by their family, but they didn't find the school system so affectionate. "Due to the fact that we were horrible students, we ended up going to a lot of different high schools," Peter admits. "My parents were afraid for us. 'What the hell's gonna happen to you?!'"

Despite the family's fears, the siblings ended up pursuing higher education: creative writing for Peter, geological engineering for Bobby. Initially, Peter co-wrote screenplays with fellow grad student Bennett Yellin, and for about two years Peter asked his younger brother for feedback on their work, since he trusted Bobby's story skills and comedic instincts. "Finally after a couple of years of this, I felt like we were taking advantage of him," Peter says on *Randomhouse.com*, "because he was doing a lot of the work but he wasn't getting any credit, so we ended up writing a screenplay with him, and it was our best one. He just wrote with us from then on, and after a couple of years Bennett quit."

After selling two *Seinfeld* scripts and several screenplays, the brothers got their big break with *Dumb and Dumber* (co-written with Yellin).

You've Got Female: Nora & Delia Ephron were raised in a very writerly environment, along with siblings Hallie and Amy. "If one of us said something at dinner, Father would yell, 'Write it down!'" Delia recalls on *Bookmagazine.com*. Their parents, Henry & Phoebe

Ephron, were a successful screenwriting team in Hollywood during the 1940s and '50s, with such credits as *Desk Set* and *Carousel*.

Collaboration begat collaboration, though Delia and Nora had established solo careers before they ever started writing together. An essayist, novelist, and screenwriter (*When Harry Met Sally; Sleepless in Seattle*), Nora first joined forces with Delia, a novelist and journalist in her own right, on the screenplay for *This Is My Life*, Nora's directorial debut in 1992. Since then, the sisters have conquered the male-dominated planet Hollywood with hits like *Michael* and *You've Got Mail*.

Living together in New York after college, Joel & Ethan Coen began picking up jobs from producers who needed low-budget scripts written and rewritten. That experience led to writing the script for their genre-bending indie, *Blood Simple*, in 1984.

Even at an early age, the Brothers Coen experimented with the film form, shooting Super-8 remakes of feature films. But, as they say in *My First Movie*, that didn't reflect a strong desire to become collaborative writers/filmmakers.

ETHAN: It was another way of goofing off. I don't know when it got sort of serious for me. Certainly later than Joel, since he went to film school, and I didn't. For me it was more an opportunity that presented itself through Joel's work than any long-harbored ambition I'd had.

JOEL: But these things are sometimes just pursuing what might be a casual interest in the path of least resistance. Even the decision to go to film school. Something that strikes you at that moment as being a bit more interesting than something else. It's not as if you really know what you're going to do with it. Or if you're going to do anything with it.

ETHAN: Yeah. There are other people you read about like Scorsese for whom it seemed like a religion from an early age. It certainly wasn't that with either of us.

DESPERATELY SEEKING SOMEONE

But what if you don't have a partner-worthy friend/lover/ spouse/sibling? If you can't find a collaborator among the people you know, get to know more people, obviously.

If you're in college, wake up and smell the collaborations! Ramsey & Stone took film classes together at Northwestern, Reich & Cohen did improv together at Yale, and Manfredi & Hay did improv together at Brown. Follow their successful example. Enroll in film or screenwriting classes. Or join a drama or comedy group.

If you're not in college, *nil desperandum*. Take classes anyway. Attend writers' conferences. Start a writers' support group. Join writers' organizations. Socialize.

"I used to think that it would be great if, instead of the kind of seminars the Writers Guild gives, that they gave tennis lessons because so much was happening on tennis courts," Carolyn Miller (*Here's Boomer; Mystery at Fire Island*) says over iced tea (*sans* spills) in her living room. "Maybe now it's the golf course."

Whatever venue you choose — class, court, or course — as the group of writers you know expands, so do your chances of finding a script partner. But if you *still* can't find a collaborator among contacts and colleagues, consider this option:

36

*Writer/director seeks scriptwriting partner.
Goal: funny movies that are completely original
and totally unlike Hollywood's endless parade of
remakes. Ideally your forte is solid character
development. Please contact me. Are we a
match?*

— Ad posted on the Internet

Hey, if you can find Mr./Ms. Right with an ad, why not the right writing partner? Whether you're seeking a career collaborator or a co-writer for one particular script, you can post notices — as many do — in any number of places on the Internet like *www.screenwritersutopia.com*, *www.hcdonline.com*, *www.scriptfly.com*, and *dir.groups.yahoo.com/dir/Entertainment_Arts/Movies/Filmmaking/ Screenwriting*. You can also place ads in publications such as *Variety*, *The Hollywood Reporter*, *Backstage*, *Los Angeles Times*, *Screenwriter Magazine*, and *Hollywood Scriptwriter* (and their online versions as well).

Tony Urban & Michael Addis, who co-wrote the comedy *Poor White Trash*, met on the Net. A struggling screenwriter in Pennsylvania, Urban started e-mailing story pitches to industry people, including L.A.-based writer/director Michael Addis. "Absolutely everyone turned me down, including Mike," Urban says on *Wired.com*. "Except Mike was more polite than everyone else, and asked me what else I was working on." So Urban pitched another idea: a true story about a waitress mom who resorts to crime to send her son to college.

Addis was hooked, and the two writers "went AOL," trading ideas back and forth via e-mail until they had a detailed outline. "I started feeling like a real Web junkie/shut-in," Addis says of the online partnership. "But the process was working."

Whether you look for the perfect partner among perfect strangers or people you know, it's best to look for someone with the following qualities that we — and the writers we've talked to — consider crucial to a good partnership.

SIMILAR SENSIBILITIES

"There are a lot of things to ask yourself when you are getting into a collaboration," says Carolyn Miller. "Certainly, do you care about the same things? Are you going to want to write about the same kinds of story?"

The collaboration of Ted Elliott & Terry Rossio began when they realized they did. Though they differed in many ways ("let's not bring up politics, hmm?" Elliott says), they both loved films and books, and they aspired to be screenwriters, something Elliott strongly recommends in a partner. "Try to avoid getting a partner who wants to be, say, a convicted murderer, or worse, a performance artist," he says on their Web site. But it was their shared sense of story, their common goal of creating unforgettable films, that made — and continues to make — their collaboration work, with such credits as *The Mask of Zorro, The Road to El Dorado,* and *Shrek.*

Goal: *funny movies… Are we a match?*

In the midst of our mind-numbing faculty meetings, sitting on opposite sides of the room because we couldn't stand each other ("White Tornado!" "Sell Out!"), we discovered that we had similar sensibilities about what makes a good story. And we had the same sense of humor. We cracked up at each other's jokes.

Let's face it: It's hard to have contempt for someone who laughs at your jokes. Humor studies show that this is one of the most powerful ways to reverse a bad first impression (which is why Matt laughs a lot on first dates). Such is the power of humor in creating human connection. And good collaborations. In fact, the same sense of humor between you and your partner may predict, as nothing else can, a closeness and compatibility in your writing life.

One thing that made Robert Ramsey & Matthew Stone gravitate toward each other was their respect for each other's "whimsical perspective."

ROBERT: The guy cracks me up. That's always been really helpful. In writing comedy. (They crack up.)

MATTHEW: If Rob says something, and I laugh, it's funny.

ROBERT: That's a good sign.

MATTHEW: That's a good sign. It goes in, and of course, it's manipulated till it's not funny anymore. (Laughter.)

Their sensibilities, from humor to work habits are so fused that Ramsey calls it "the Vulcan Mind Meld." ("We're a little on the anal side, too," Ramsey confides. "Matt's mother once said we're like *The Odd Couple*, only we're both Felix.")

If you're looking for a partner to co-write comedy, "Say something that you think is comedy or you know to be funny or try out your favorite joke," Larry Gelbart suggests, "and if the other person doesn't laugh, *run do not walk* to the next candidate!"

There is the rare exception, of course, like Peter Tolan's "unlikely collaboration" with Denis Leary on the darkly comic detective series,

The Job. Tolan wasn't very familiar with Leary's work, but from what he did know, he thought the partnership was doomed. "Our senses of humor and everything are completely different," Tolan tells us at his Pasadena home, where part of *Gods and Monsters* was filmed. "He has a really dark outlook on things, and I'm a little more versed in having that same outlook but making it palatable for a mass audience. He roughs up my smoother edges, and I smooth down his rougher edges, so the collaboration really works well. Definitely a surprise to me."

So it's possible that another shared sensibility like a dark outlook can compensate for dissimilar senses of humor, even when you're writing comedy. But we've found that the same sense of humor is invaluable when we're writing together, even if we're writing drama.

Our screenplay, *Obscenity*, is extremely heavy in places, especially when the main character's brother, Sam, dies in a gaybashing. We dreaded writing that scene. We dodged it for weeks. And we were *totally* depressed the day we knew we had to write the damn thing. Fortunately, something struck us as funny — probably the long, mournful looks on our faces — and we started howling with laughter, the comic relief we needed so badly to get through the scene.

Other sensibilities we share helped us with *Obscenity*, too: our taste in films in general and courtroom dramas in particular. We both love *To Kill a Mockingbird*, so when we were struggling to write the scene in our script where the jury announces the verdict, we said, "Let's see how Horton Foote did it." We looked at his screenplay, and inspired by his style, we wrote an *homage*.

"The same rule applies to a pair of writers who want to do drama, action, whatever, except without the laughs," Gelbart says. "What do you like? Who do you like? Which movies? Which this? Which that?"

Or what — or whom — do you *dislike*?

"It's probably more important that the two people share the same dislikes than the same likes," Marshall Brickman says, an opinion that clearly informs some of his and Allen's greatest comedic moments (the professor pontificating about Marshall McLuhan in *Annie Hall* leaps to mind). "That is, it's better if you hate the same things, rather than like the same things. It narrows things down a little."

Our shared dislike — okay, *hatred* — of hypocrisy fueled the writing of *Obscenity*. In the actual court case that inspired our screenplay, the State Attorney busted the mom-and-pop video store in the name of morality, but he was really in bed with a major "family values" video chain that bankrolled his campaign so he could put their competition out of business. That kind of thing just pisses us *off*.

Still, for all the likes and dislikes you and your partner may share, it's good to have "a dissimilar taste," Gelbart says. "You can be black and white. You can be yin and yang. It's okay if the other person's take is interesting and it opens you up a little, and presumably the reverse is happening. But it helps if you occasionally say the same thing at the same time."

The Vulcan Mind Meld. Or, as we like to say, "Get out of my head."

COMPLEMENTARY STRENGTHS

"I think collaborations are much more successful when people have different strengths," say Peter Tolan. "That way, nobody has everything. Nobody brings everything to the table. The best collaborations are when you shore each other's weaknesses up."

It's important to keep this in mind as you search for a partner.

"You're looking for someone hopefully with complementary strengths," Janet Batchler says, "but that means that you have to have an understanding of your own strengths."

Or to quote the Oracle at Delphi, "Know thyself."

"It takes remarkable self-awareness to get into a collaboration," Tolan says. "I think you have to be remarkably self-aware to say, 'I can do that and that; I just can't do *that.*'" And in a successful collaboration, partners play to their strengths. "They understand how it works, and they're able to feed it and keep it running."

Fay Kanin credits her success writing with Michael to their complementary strengths. "Michael was an artist, and you can see he was very good," she says, pointing to his paintings and sculptures around the living room. "So his strengths in terms of movies were the visual. And I was a people person. I really liked the characters and the dialogue and all of that. Not that he couldn't write dialogue, but I loved it; he did it."

When we ask about complementary strengths, Larry Gelbart nods. He and his co-writers on the classic 1950s TV variety show *Caesar's Hour* had similar sensibilities — "Sid knew that if you threw enough Jews up in the air, they'd all come down funny" — but there were important differences, too.

"Mel Brooks didn't write jokes," Gelbart says. "Mel didn't and doesn't. His specialty is genius. He majored in genius."

We agree (and ask if he knows how we can get tickets to *The Producers*...).

"What Mel does is come up with whole pieces of business — a whole song, a whole dance. Not a concept but an execution of a concept. The concept is his mind, and anything can roll from there. I'm sure he can think of a funny line and a funny word and a funny name, but his specialty is just being the only Mel Brooks in the room. I do lines and I do characters and I can do plot and I'm *good* at it. But it's more convention. He is not conventional. Doc — Neil Simon — is the same way."

Marshall Brickman describes his and Woody Allen's complementary strengths in similar terms. "I tend to be somewhat more bound by logic than Woody Allen, and I say that as a criticism of me rather than of him. His approach to a problem or material in general is more intuitive than mine. I like to kind of back into things logically; he seems to have a genius for making some kind of intuitive leap which defies logic but solves the problem."

It's important to know your weaknesses, too. As our favorite meat-punching, egg-gulping, flying-high-now boxer, Rocky Balboa, mumbles, "I got gaps." How else will you know what strengths you need from a partner?

Peter Tolan confesses that his gap is coming up with ideas — somewhat of a surprise from "the funniest man in Hollywood," as Billy

43

Crystal has called him. But Tolan insists it's true. "If I could have a guy come in who was my collaborator, who just sat here and said, 'I have an idea for a screenplay,' I would love that guy. I'd collaborate with that guy because I am not fertile when it comes to ideas. I'm not spinning eight different plates in the air of fantastic screenplay ideas that I have. But if you come to me with a great idea, I'll say, 'Oh, I know what to do with that.' That's my strength."

Nick Kazan was well aware of his own limitations when he asked a friend, Margo Katz, to collaborate on a screenplay adaptation of the book, *In Memory's Kitchen*. Based on a cookbook compiled by Jewish women in a Czechoslovakian settlement camp during World War II, the book tells their story: They knew they were going to die and the recipes passed down through oral tradition would die with them, so they wrote the recipes down and smuggled them out of the camp.

"Not being Jewish and not being a woman, I didn't think I would be the ideal person to do all of this," Kazan says. "So I collaborated with Margo." Working from an outline they created together, Katz did the first draft, which Kazan rewrote. He then gave it back to her for comments. "It would be inappropriate for me to do the first draft, then for her to come behind and correct it," Kazan says, "because I just have more experience than she does. So, yes, I wanted her perspective and her input."

Like Kazan, you need to be clear about what perspective and input — or other strengths — you're looking for in a prospective partner. You also need to be clear about each partner's role. Katz and Kazan were not equally experienced writers, so Kazan's experience guided the project. And equality wasn't the point.

It never is, according to Marshall Brickman. "A successful collaboration can never be equal, or democratic. As we know, art is not a democracy but an autocracy."

He freely acknowledges that Woody Allen was the dominant creative force for obvious reasons: He was the star of the film; the character he was playing was more or less pre-formed from his stand-up act and other public appearances; he was not perceived by the audience to be an actor like Brando or Olivier, who would create a work of art in the creation of a role.

"The important thing was to get Woody Allen's sensibility onscreen, in a coherent and satisfying way that had some dramatic logic," Brickman says. "Oh, yes, and to be entertaining and if possible enlightening and observant about that slim slice of life from which we took our material, which was the slice of life we happened to be living, or living in — New York, Manhattan."

They had a clear sense of purpose. Most successful partnerships do.

"You have to have the same goal," Andrew Reich says. "If one person is just looking at this as a way to quickly cash in on something, and the other person just really wants to do good work, that's never going to work out. You have to have the same sort of focus on an end result."

How that result comes about, how the collaborative process leads to a finished script, can be as mysterious as finding the right writing partner.

"As in the marriage bedroom, you never really know what's going on unless you're there in the room," Brickman says.

Sometimes you're there in the room, but you'd *still* be hard-pressed to say how it happened.

"The biggest mystery of all," Phil Hay says, "is how it gets done."

PLAYS WELL WITH OTHERS

Since collaborative writing is such a close-knit creative relationship, you have a greater chance of working successfully together if you've worked out the bugs of *being* together. How you behave in good times — and bad. During arguments, for example (a subject we'll explore more fully in Chapter Eight).

Disagreement is an important part of the creative process, so crucial to any collaboration that Andrew Reich recommends looking for "someone you've had arguments with or you know you can settle things with without throwing tantrums. If you're casual friends, how are you going to deal with each other in an argument?"

This may sound like a minor thing to consider when choosing a partner, but it's intricate interpersonal stuff that comes from knowing the person. Your relationship. And yourself.

Peter Tolan can't argue. He can't even say, "No, that's not good." And he considers this his greatest weakness as a collaborator. "In a successful collaboration, you've *got* to be able to argue," he says. "I mean, you've really got to be able to say, 'I don't like this and here's why. Here's why this doesn't work.' And you've got to hope, too, that the other person is open to hearing that." He doesn't mind when people argue with him (he can take it, but he can't dish it out); in fact, he admires writing partners like Harold Ramis who argue with grace and wit. "We've had a very playful collaboration," Tolan says.

One such creative disagreement occurred while writing the remake of *Bedazzled* (an average schmo, played by Brendan Fraser, swaps his soul for a series of wishes granted by the Devil, Elizabeth Hurley). "I wanted to do a 'call-back joke,' where the Brendan Fraser character goes to the Devil's club for the first time, and there are all these people dancing. And there's a guy just standing there with a really big rooster. Fraser asks, 'What's that?' and the guy says, 'Guess.' And that's the whole joke. It's obvious he's asked for a very large cock. So then in the original draft, he gives this final wish away to somebody that he's met. I wanted the audience — at the end of the movie — to see that person with a very big rooster."

After all, Tolan reasoned, given the opportunity, every guy in the world would ask for a very large, er, rooster. The first time he pitched the joke, Ramis laughed — because Ramis thought he was kidding. Then Tolan pitched it again. "I said, 'Hey, what *about* that idea?' Harold looked at me like *we're not doing that*. So, it was, you know, playful. It was funny. But he definitely had a list of what he thought would work. That wasn't on it."

So what *should* be on a list of things to consider when choosing a partner is how well you both deal with disagreements and other sticky situations. That knowledge, of course, can only come from knowing each other and how you relate under pressure. Success in show business may rely on who you know, but creating a successful collaboration relies on *what* you know about who you know — and write with.

A WRITER YOU RESPECT (AND VICE VERSA)

Aretha was right. Respect matters most.

We ought to know. We went from zero to sixty on the issue, from contempt to respect. And only when we hit respect, only then, could we write together.

"That's the most important thing about a writing partner," Ted Elliott says. "Find a writer you respect, whose abilities you envy — and hope he or she feels the same about you. You should both feel like you're getting the better part of the deal."

"What I advise people to do is identify the most talented people around you and stick with them," Harold Ramis says. "It's one of the most obvious things about my own career path. I started *Animal House* kind of on my own. I wrote a treatment for a college film which I called "Freshman Year," and I was writing it for the *National Lampoon*. I had my own very independent point of view, and it wasn't quite a *Lampoon* point of view. They wanted me to keep writing it, but I suggested — which they loved, they jumped at — that I work with someone from the *Lampoon*. I got to pick my own collaborator initially, so I chose Doug Kenney, and what a fortuitous thing for me. But if you're an acting student or in a film school, you're probably going to gravitate naturally to the most talented people around. And if you can hook up with them, great."

We've emphasized the importance of knowing yourself and your prospective partners, but it's equally important to know their work. If you don't, read something they've written. If your prospective partners are strangers, request a writing sample and offer one of yours. If you don't have respect for their writing (or vice versa), run don't walk to the next candidate.

"I still have trouble to this day, in this non-collaborative period of my life, having any real respect for someone whose work I don't respect," Gelbart says. "It's not that I don't have respect for them. I drift away. I don't care about a relationship. And you have to have a relationship. You just really have to."

No respect, no relationship. But if you *do* respect the work, even before you have a relationship, there's a good chance a good one will develop.

Marshall Brickman didn't know Woody Allen that well before their managers put them together, but he already had great respect for his work. The future partners met while Brickman was a member of a folk music group called the Tarriers. "I played a lot of folk instruments — banjo, guitar, etc.," Brickman says. "That's me on the *Deliverance* album — you know, 'Dueling Banjos' — but another story...." In 1963, the Tarriers headlined at the legendary Bitter End Cafe in New York City, and Woody Allen was the opening act. "Woody went on for his twenty minutes to usually a confused reaction from the audience. They weren't sure what to make of him."

But Brickman stood in the wings and marveled at Allen. "It was like discovering a great novelist or poet you never knew existed," he says. "Even at that early date his stuff was wildly brilliant, though as yet unfocused. He experimented with a variety of material in addition to the personal/psychoanalytic/relationship stuff." Brickman, of course, was no slouch himself. He, too, was damn funny, which was why Rollins & Joffe thought Brickman & Allen would make a good team.

There is, however, such a thing as too much respect (see also: awe). "I can't envision any situation from here on out where I would team up with someone," Gelbart says, "or go to work somewhere

where I would be one of a group. By this time, there's too much respect paid and too much deference, so people are likely to say, 'It's wonderful!' when I know it isn't. That's the flip side of respect. Too much of it. Well, it only takes what, fifty years?"

So when it comes to respect, equality does matter. Mutual respect is the key.

"Don't think of the other person as the one who types," Gelbart says. "Don't think of the other person as the one who fills in what I don't have. Just think of yourselves as *one* and give them the same respect you give yourself. And you can be that honest about their shortcomings, too, since any writer jumps at the chance to downgrade himself or herself."

JUST DUET

In the end, collaboration — like love, friendship, or film — is experiential. No one, not even close friends or spouses or family members, can possibly know if writing together will work until they try it.

"I remember going for a walk at Zuma and talking about our *Simpsons* idea," Andrew Reich says. "All of a sudden, Ted said something, and I said, 'Then we could do *this*.' And he said, 'We could do this and *this*.' Funny ideas started flowing, and it just felt like *wow*, this is really a good idea! And *boy* is this more fun than I've been having sitting by myself trying to write. With Ted, there was that moment of *wow*, this is so much better. It just clicked."

So choose the most promising partner and see if it clicks when you work together. See if you say, "*Wow.*" That's the real acid test. The journey of a collaboration begins with one script.

SCRIPT PARTNER POINTS

☪ Know Thyself. Thy strengths and thy weaknesses. How else will you know what you need from a partner?

☪ Know Thy Partner. Look among those you know well: a friend, spouse/lover, or family member. If none is partner-worthy, get to know more people or post notices online or in print.

☪ Know Their Work. If you must look for the perfect partner among perfect strangers, look for someone whose work you respect (and vice versa). Exchange writing samples, preferably in the genre you plan to write.

☪ Make sure you share similar likes and dislikes. As Ted Elliott says, it's probably best to avoid politics. It's probably also wise to avoid religion (unless thou art co-writing the next *Omega Code* sequel).

☪ As Larry Gelbart says, if you're planning to write a comedy, say something funny. If your prospective partner doesn't laugh, run don't walk to the next candidate.

☪ Make sure you find someone you can argue and settle things with — without tantrums, resentment, or bloodshed.

☪ Make sure you share the same goals for your project.

☪ Just duet. The journey of a collaboration really *does* begin with one script.

"Some choices must be made that are difficult. Nonetheless, we must make them....The fate of the entire space-time continuum may rest on your shoulders!"

— Professor Emmet Brown (Christopher Lloyd),
Back to the Future (screenplay, fourth draft)

CHAPTER 3

THE SPACE-TIME CONUNDRUM

Once you've found the right writing partner, you have a new problem to solve: the space-time conundrum. Where and when will you work? It's a tricky enough problem for *solo* writers, but the difficulty is doubled for writing teams. You have to consider two sets of creative habits. Two circadian rhythms. And two lives packed with family commitments, relationship issues, social obligations — and that pesky problem of making a living.

For us, where and when we write together has evolved over the years — a process itself. From 1995 to 1997, we lived in Tallahassee and switched writing days at Claudia's house/Matt's apartment. In 1997 Matt moved to L.A., but we still work at each other's place; we just travel farther to do it. As a result, we do more writing apart and rely more on technology to keep us connected.

The evolution of your space and schedule may not be as extreme. Again, you can only discover by doing, but it doesn't hurt to give it some thought before you begin.

Why?

Because the place and the time that you choose can influence how well you write.

Unless, of course, you're Larry Gelbart.

"I am really the best or the worst to talk to because after all of these years I can work anywhere, anytime," he says. "I worked with

53

Bob Hope for four years — in planes, in jeeps, in limos, in tents, on trains, on planes. With a pencil, with a pen, with a typewriter, with all three at once. Now I switch from Beverly Hills to Palm Desert. Every week I spend four days down there, three days up here, but it's just a different computer monitor to look at rather than a different place. I'm just so *trained.*" He laughs. "Paper-trained, it used to be. Now it's monitor-trained."

Lesser mortals, however, may profit from finding a specific workplace and time.

THE RIGHT PLACE

A writer's first concern, Tennessee Williams once said, must be "to discover that magic place of all places where the work goes better than it has gone before, the way that a gasoline motor picks up when you switch it from regular to high octane. For one of the mysterious things about writing is the extreme susceptibility it shows to the influence of place."

Unfortunately, what worked for Tennessee Williams didn't work for Hal Kanter when they rewrote Kanter's adaptation of Williams' play, *The Rose Tattoo.* "I had to go to his apartment every morning, a small crowded apartment that reeked of cat urine," Kanter explains. "I got to the point where I couldn't take it any more. Just the aroma in that place was enough to kill me! So I would work at home, and he would work at his apartment. Then we would meet and exchange pages and go over the pages again. And we got a script out, a final script I was proud of, but to my disgust, he insisted on getting sole screenplay credit. That's why I wound up with an 'Adapted by' credit. I should have taken it to the Guild; I would have won. But he was a fierce little fighter to protect his own turf."

Just as you need to click with your partner, you both need to click with the place where you work. On the macro level, this means finding the geographical setting where you both write best. It doesn't mean that you have to pick up and move, though you might decide that you want to. Wherever you live, you have all kinds of choices. Fay & Michael Kanin fell in love with the beach, so they moved there to live and to write.

For us, living on opposite ends of the country can be a huge frustration at times, but it doubles the possibilities for geographic locations. Like the Kanins, we love to write at the beach. It's the magic place Tennessee Williams is talking about "where the work goes better than it has gone before." And fortunately, a wonderful friend loans us her cottage on St. George Island off the Florida Gulf Coast where there are no distractions except the cry of the odd bitchy seagull and the siren call of Bombay Sapphire gin (not that we aren't pretty skilled at distracting ourselves, but we'll talk about that when we talk about the Right Schedule later in this chapter). So when we're under the gun to finish a project or facing that difficult prospect of starting a new one, Matt flies to Florida, and we head for the Gulf. That's where this book began.

We also love to write in the country. If the beach cottage is booked, we'll drive to Claudia's farm, a cracker house with big wraparound porches overlooking a ten-acre meadow surrounded by pines. Absolute privacy. Quiet. Nothing but wildlife: white-tailed deer bounding across the meadow, sand-hill cranes warbling off in the distance, and two wild-eyed screenwriters duking it out over dialogue.

For others, an escape from the big city creates its own pitfalls. When Peter Tolan & Harold Ramis were struggling to write a new sequence for the remake of *Bedazzled*, Ramis suggested they meet in Cape Cod. He'd secured a room in the old public library where they could work.

"We set up the computer and sat down and looked at each other," Tolan recalls. "In five minutes, Harold said, 'You wanna eat something? You hungry?' And I said, 'Yeah, I could eat.' So we walked down a ways to the general store, got sandwiches, sat in rocking chairs in the front, and talked about everything except the movie. We went back, sat there for five minutes, looked at each other, and he said, 'You ever see the old part of the island?' I said, 'No, I haven't.' So we got in the car, drove there, walked around the dock for a while, looked around. 'Wanna see where I'm staying? Wanna see the house?' 'Sure, let's go!' Back over to the house, walked around for a while... "

We're certainly no strangers to work avoidance, but we're less likely to succumb when we flee those distractions that undermine our creative process: phone, friends, family, neighbors, and their Satanic leaf blowers. Then again, you and your partner might love the sound of leaf blowers. The shriek of small internal-combustion engines (or electric ones) might be just what you need to jump-start your writing. Far be it from us to tell others their process. God knows, Gelbart isn't bothered by noise.

"I don't have to have silence," he says. "For the four years I worked on *M*A*S*H*, my office was right next door, right above the sound-editing department of Twentieth Century-Fox. All day long I heard screeching brakes and gunshots and so forth. But I just did it."

The point is to find a place that works for you and your work. Where you can focus, relax, and create. Download from the universe.

As Mihaly Csikszentmihalyi says in *Creativity*, "It is not what the environment is like that matters, but the extent to which you are in harmony with it."

On the micro level, once you've found the right geographical setting, what kind of space is most harmonious for you? A public place? Home? Office? Or you may find, over the long haul of writing a script, a combination works best.

WRITING IN RESTAURANTS

We started working together at Manny's, over sweet tea and collards and Southern-fried chicken. In spite of those people who got up and moved because we were discussing gay porn, we enjoyed developing the story for *Obscenity* there. Something about the energy of the place — the conversations all around us and the clatter of dishes — fueled the back-and-forth of brainstorming.

Brad Anderson tells us that he, too, seeks out public places when he starts a script with Lyn Vaus, who co-wrote *Next Stop Wonderland*, or Steve Gevedon, who co-wrote *Session 9*. "The process begins with endless brainstorming, throwing anything into the hopper, kind of like free association," Anderson says. "It usually occurs at the nearest bar."

Harry & Renee Longstreet have also found public places conducive to starting a script.

HARRY: In the old days we used to go to this one coffee shop. It was our lucky coffee shop.

RENEE: In the old days.

HARRY: And we were younger. We had a lot more brain cells because we were quick.

RENEE: We'd go in there at eight in the morning. We'd sit and have breakfast, and we'd do Scene One, Scene Two, Scene Three — *boom boom boom* — and by noon, we'd be done with the story.

Still others like Matt Manfredi & Phil Hay find public places conducive to starting their writing day (or postponing it). "We go nine-to-five pretty much," Manfredi says, "but sometimes the nine is at the bagel shop."

Andrew Reich & Ted Cohen start their writing day by talking long walks. "We walk," Cohen says. "We always walk at the beginning."

"Somehow there's less distraction," Reich adds. "And we both think better walking."

But they're leery of writing their scripts in restaurants. "We never take our computers to Starbucks or whatever and sit there and work," Cohen explains. "That's actually a thing that I have a superstition about. I don't like to move around too much writing-wise. I like to have one or two places where I can do it, so yeah, we work at Andrew's house or we'll work here [at Warner Bros.]."

Robert Ramsey & Matthew Stone don't write in restaurants because it's distracting. "I see people writing in coffee shops," Stone says, shaking his head. "We have enough distractions in this very spare office. We could sit here and talk about Osama bin Laden. We would never get any work done. We don't need any distractions."

But restaurants play an important part in their writing day. "We always go out for lunch," Ramsey says. "Think how much we could save if we just brought baloney sandwiches! But we always go to the same restaurant. We sit there and read the paper all through lunch. And we know that the people who see us every day never talking to each other are thinking, *They don't talk!* We've been sitting there talking to each other all day. We don't need to talk at lunch."

For them, this silence — like negative space in a painting — is crucial to the creating they do. And it's crucial that the place be the same. In fact, they're in a mild crisis the day we interview them because their favorite restaurant has gone out of business.

ROBERT: They just closed it. We've been thrown into chaos. It's a problem. We may have to move our office now.

MATTHEW: It was a health food restaurant called Evergreen.

ROBERT: For like $5.75, you had this sprouty — You got almonds and cauliflower. It was so unglamorous. It was healthy. It was so wonderfully not Hollywood.

You may find that public places are perfect for breaks or breaking out stories or other brainstorming when you're starting a script or your writing day. Walking on the beach and talking over lunch in Southern-fried restaurants have been a big help to us, but like Ramsey & Stone and Reich & Cohen, when it comes to the actual writing, we avoid public places. Drafting the script, we've discovered, demands a more private space.

Olivier Ducastel & Jacques Martineau say the same thing; they just say it in French. "*Pour les discussions, nous l'avons dit plus haut, tous les lieux sont bons, même les plus bizarres...* " they tell us: "All places — even the most bizarre ones — are good for our discussions. As far as writing goes, we have to confess that Jacques only writes in his bed with his laptop on his knees. For him, any other space is uncomfortable and lacks the power to inspire him."

Ultimately, that's what the right place — public or private — should do: offer comfort and inspiration.

YOUR PLACE OR MINE?

Like Dorothy Gayle, some writers believe there's no place like home. Fay Kanin prefers writing at home. Larry Gelbart does, too (three days a week), as do Ducastel & Martineau, Peter Tolan, the Longstreets, the Batchlers, Manfredi & Hay, Reich & Cohen, Carolyn Miller, and many others. It's familiar. Private. Cheaper than renting an office. A shorter commute — for one of you, anyway, unless you live together. And it offers the comforts of, well, *home.*

Marshall Brickman describes such comforts writing *Sleeper* with Woody Allen. "We would meet at his house and talk, and his housekeeper would occasionally bring out a tuna fish sandwich and a brownie, and then we'd go for a walk and talk. It was like anything but work."

We don't have a housekeeper to bring us brownies, but working at home does let us stock the fridge with the food and drink that we require to write: iced tea, fresh fruit, albacore tuna. The same thing, every day. Like Ramsey & Stone, we find familiarity breeds comfort and creativity.

If you and your partner prefer working at home and you don't live together, you'll have to decide whose house you'll work in, or you can trade back and forth. Manfredi & Hay choose to work at Phil's house, "which used to be both of ours before Matt got married," Hay says. The space is familiar to them, and there are fewer distractions. Other people, even — especially! — people you love, can be a major distraction.

Like Henry Morgan's wife when he and Aaron Ruben were working on a half-hour sketch-comedy show. They wrote in Morgan's New York hotel room — with his wife nearby on the couch. "She's sitting there swinging her leg, and whatever we came up with, she made a comment on," Ruben remembers. "Now that's strictly forbidden, or as Germans say, *streng verboten*. You don't do that. You leave writers alone. You don't even sit in the room with them, even if you're ready to laugh. You let them do their work. But there she is, swinging her leg and saying, 'That's not very funny.'"

By the end of the writing session, Ruben was fed up, but he agreed to work with Morgan again the next evening — on one condition. "I said, 'No wives, huh?' And Henry had a look like, *How am I gonna tell her?* Well, he did tell her. That's the cardinal rule of collaboration — no third person in the room. No. No way. No non-combatants."

When we were both living in Tallahassee, taking turns writing at each other's place, we tried to work when Matt's roommate or Claudia's family weren't home. Eventually, Matt got his own apartment, and we worked there frequently — at the dining room table in the main room, which was larger and lighter than the room he'd turned into an office. But most writers we've met prefer writing in a space set aside for an office. Some married teams, like the Batchlers and Longstreets, maintain separate offices.

"We used to write in the same room, but when we had more room, we got them separated," Harry Longstreet says.

"When we had a big six-bedroom house," Renee adds, "we had two offices where we wrote next to each other." But when we interview them, their offices are at opposite ends of their home — Renee's with a view of the mountains surrounding the San Fernando Valley, and Harry's more tucked away, lined with posters of the projects they've written. (They've since moved to Washington state.)

The Batchlers have two offices, too. "Lee's is downstairs," Janet says, "a cozy cave with a wall of curved windows that somehow remind one of the bridge of the Starship Enterprise. I have a huge office/library/family room upstairs where I write and also where our assistant works, but not while I'm writing."

Ducastel & Martineau tell us, "We do have an office, but it isn't used for writing. Well, it's rarely used for writing." Bed, as they've said, is where Jacques likes to write.

So *where* you work in the house can affect how you write. Again, find the space that's best for you both. Over time we've found it's the porch. At the farm, we write at a small round table overlooking the meadow. In Tallahassee, we write at a small round table overlooking a pond. At St. George Island, we write at a big picnic table overlooking the Gulf. The sound of the waves helps us think and create.

Water works wonders for writing, we've found. We're not sure why. A friend saw a piece in *The London Times* that said negative ions in running water stimulate creativity. Whatever the reason, the power of water is well documented: Einstein's greatest ideas reportedly occurred in the shower, and Greek mathematician Archimedes' principle of displacement occurred to him in the bathtub ("Eureka!").

But the shower and tub may be too intimate — and too cramped — for most writing teams.

"We've taken showers together," Scott Alexander says, deadpan. "It gets things going. Even if you don't write a scene that day, your back is clean. He's got a loofah. It's fantastic."

Larry Karaszewski gapes at his partner. "I don't know *what* you're talking about!"

OFFICE SPACE

For Alexander & Karaszewski, there's no place like an office *outside* the home.

"It does amaze me how many professional writers still work at home," says Alexander. "It's a funny profession where you can be at the top of your game but, 'Hey, I got a little computer in the back of my bedroom I work at.'"

He and Karaszewski now write together in their airy Beverly Hills office. But it was a journey to find the right space. A space odyssey. Until they made their first sale, they wrote together in the apartment they shared.

SCOTT: We were still living together when we sold a script.

LARRY: Yeah, we were still roommates. So after we got that big check, we instantly got our own apartments. And that's when we sort of made it become more of a job-like thing.

SCOTT: Larry bought Jane Mansfield's old house. (Laughter.)

For a while, when they weren't working in a studio office, they went back and forth between Jane Mansfield's old house and

Alexander's new apartment, but this soon interfered with their work and their lives.

SCOTT: Actually, around *Ed Wood*, we started having kids, and then it became, *Oh, God*. You can't be trying to work when some kid is running around with a rattle and trying to get your attention. So then we had to have an office to go to. If the studio makes us a deal that's remotely central to our two houses, we'll take it. Or now we're here in a rented space.

LARRY: We like having a neutral space. It works better because if you have a bad day at work, it doesn't affect your house. You don't have that big blowout and fight over some scene, and then he gets to leave and drive home, and you're stuck there. You're just in the funk.

You may also prefer the neutral space of an office. Both of your homes (assuming you're not living together) may be too distracting. Going back and forth might be too much trouble. It may be psychologically important to you, as it is for Alexander & Karaszewski, to keep home and work in separate spheres.

Or having an office outside the home may enhance your sense of professionalism, as it has for Ramsey & Stone. Their move to an office was important and symbolic.

MATTHEW: It took it away from being like something you did in your house. When we first started, we lived together and we wrote at home.

ROBERT: About three feet from Matt's bed. (Laughter.)

MATTHEW: When we sold a project to Universal, they gave us an office. And that changed our lives. We got up in the morning. I would drive to Rob's house, go over the hill —

64

ROBERT: We'd actually bathe and go to work.

MATTHEW: Yeah, we'd bathe. We looked like normal people, except for the job.

ROBERT: That's when we started to feel legitimate.

MATTHEW: It's a long road, a feature-length script. It's a long road. So even if you're working for somebody, you're not gonna be talking to them for a few months at a time. It's a completely structureless environment you work in. So we do anything we can to create the illusion that it's a job.

Now they make the daily trek to their office on Wilshire Blvd. This routine not only makes their work feel more "job-like," it increases their discipline. "Matt and I require dogged, habitual predictability in our work habits," Ramsey says. "There are days when we don't get much of anything done, but we still come into the office and sit here till we do it."

An office, of course, is no guarantee you'll *be* disciplined. When Alexander & Karaszewski got their first studio office at Twentieth Century-Fox, discipline went straight out the window.

SCOTT: We were just so excited to be on the lot. We were inviting friends over every day and taking them to the commissary and saying, "Look, there's Mel Brooks."

LARRY: We were having five o'clock Bloody Marys.

SCOTT: Four o'clock.

LARRY: Four o'clock Bloody Marys.

SCOTT: It wasn't dark yet. (Laughter.) We were making Bloody

Marys for all the other writers on the lot every day. We were just two giddy kids. And it took us many years to figure out that you have to be professional, you have to sort of clock in, you have to keep your employers happy, and you have to make everyone involved in the movie think that you're making the movie that they want to make individually. Even though none of them are.

THE RIGHT STUFF

Once you've found the right place to work, fill it — to the extent that you want it filled — with objects that have significance for you (and carefully arrange them, if you're a fan of *feng shui*). Alexander & Karaszewski line the walls of their office with posters of movies they've written. So do Harry Longstreet and Ramsey & Stone. Lowell Ganz & Babaloo Mandel decorate their walls with pictures of their children and cardboard cutouts from *Splash, Parenthood*, and other hits that they've written.

Ramsey & Stone also keep a small statue of Buddha on their computer, though for the life of them they can't say why.

MATTHEW: I'm not a Buddhist. He's not a Buddhist. Somehow or other we ended up with this Buddha, and he always stays on top of our computer. We could write with him not there. (They laugh.) You bought him from somewhere, right?

ROBERT: I got him somewhere.

MATTHEW: I don't know why we do it. We put him on our computer, and he's just always pretty much been there.

Wherever we're writing, we put a small statue of Pinocchio on the computer. When we're writing well and we feel triumphant, we make a silver-cup trophy for him out of a chewing gum wrapper.

When we're writing poorly and we think we suck, we knock him off the computer. Yeah, yeah, we know, that's Disney character abuse, but we don't feel so bad about it since we saw *Shrek.*

We also like to fill our space with music.

CLAUDIA: We've started our writing sessions with Vivaldi's "Four Seasons" for so long now, it's become an almost Pavlovian signal that it's time to work.

MATT: Except we usually lose Claudia during the *adagio* movement of "Winter." She stares into the distance and says upbeat things like, "I want that played at my funeral." (More about handling neurotic partners later in the book — just kidding.)

Speaking of funerals, while scripting Sam's service and wake in *Obscenity*, we underscored our writing sessions with a particular piece — the sorrowful *"Nunc Dimittis"* from Rachmoninoff's "Vespers" — to put us in the right frame of mind. In fact, we became so attached to the music that we specified the song in the scene description, something we rarely do. It's not unlike those filmmakers who decide that temp track music used during editing ultimately proves to be the best score for the finished film.

Stephen Mazur tells the Writers Guild that he and partner Paul Guay play music during their writing sessions "to drown out the horrifying silence."

The aural equivalent of the blank page.

"Used to think I could write only to the sounds of silence," Guay says. "Now I listen to all my CDs and albums (in separate rotations, in alphabetical order by artist, of course, limit one artist per day; if you're gonna be anal, do it right). This means a lot of Beatles, Simon and Garfunkel, Rolling Stones, Elton John, and 'Seasons in the Sun.'"

Manfredi & Hay have also found that music can help.

PHIL: We've had a lot of luck with Kruder & Dorfmeister, these two Viennese DJ re-mixer guys. And their music. I mean, ten hours just go by. It's very trancy. Occasionally — I think it's really geeky, and Matt doesn't condone it, I don't think. I will occasionally make a tape of music that I think is somehow appropriate or just in the vein or tone of what we're doing. I listen to it on my own time, or I try to impose it on Matt.

MATT: He hasn't done that. He hasn't done that.

PHIL: Yeah, I have.

MATT: This is obviously — This is gonna come up later. (They laugh.)

How you fill your space may seem unimportant or self-indulgent, but Csikszentmihalyi assures us, "The kind of objects you fill your space with also either help or hinder the allocation of creative energies. Cherished objects remind us of our goals, make us feel more confident, and focus our attention. Trophies, diplomas, favorite books, and family pictures on the office desk are all reminders of who you are, what you have accomplished.... Pictures and maps of places you would like to visit and books about things you might like to learn more about are signposts of what you might do in the future."

Though you might feel a bit sheepish unpacking all this stuff at Starbucks.

THE RIGHT SCHEDULE

Like Butch Cassidy (or Maria von Trapp), writers are hard to pin down. We like it that way. We love our freedom. That's one reason we chose this profession. But Larry Karaszewski is right: "You sort of have to clock in." Whether you're writing on assignment or spec, you'll need to keep a regular schedule if you're going to deliver the script.

"This whole thing is about delivery," Gelbart says. "We're really gifted UPS men. FedExers, you know, because it's gotta be there. It's gotta be there. So you don't have a lot of time. But it's enough time for us."

You will have to decide — or discover by doing — what writing schedule works best for you. Yes, it's doubly difficult because you both have busy lives, but that is precisely why you must do it.

"You wind up having to put together some kind of time structure," Karaszewski insists, "which is one of the things that makes writing with a team different than writing by yourself. Because writing by yourself you can let the Muse follow you wherever it goes. You're awake at 3:00 a.m., you got a good idea, you can get up in your underwear and start writing. When you have a partner, you can't do that."

You will need to consider your commitments and circadian rhythms, then carve a "time structure" out of the chaos. And, hey, once that's done, the rest is simple.

"You just show up and do the work," says Marshall Brickman.

THE COMMITMENTS

In the beginning, however, it wasn't easy for Brickman & Allen to show up and write. Brickman had quit the folk-music business ("I got frightened of the idea of reaching thirty and still having to carry guitars and banjo cases around," he says) and landed a job on *The Tonight Show* with Johnny Carson. Brickman rapidly became the head writer. Woody Allen, meanwhile, was starring in *Play it Again, Sam* on Broadway. Despite their hectic schedules, the two found a way to write together.

"Woody was on stage from 8:30 till about 10:15, 10:30 if the laughs were good," Brickman says. "So we used to meet between 10:30 and 1:00 a.m. and work on stuff. Very odd. Crazy, even. The kind of thing you can only do when you're young."

When we started writing together, we had to create a schedule around our full-time teaching and Claudia's family — no small feat since we both taught during the day, and Claudia felt strongly about being with her family at night. Fortunately, we were able to schedule our classes at similar times. This allowed us to write every day when we both had time off.

Even writing teams that don't have to accommodate outside work often have to accommodate family. The Batchlers have worked out an elaborate schedule to write and take care of their two young children.

"Our deal is, Jan gets them up," Lee says. "I get their sunscreen on, and she gets them to school. After dinner I get their baths, get them ready for bed. So after 8:30, 9:00 p.m., I have to take an hour to get into another world. Then at 10:00, I'm ready to get to work."

"He usually works till about midnight or 1:00 now," Janet adds. "I would rather stay up late, but it's easier for me to get up in the mornings, so I take that shift. Staying up till 2:00 a.m. is no longer an option."

Having children has also changed the writing schedules of Alexander & Karaszewski.

"We generally work an eight-hour day, though the eight hours slide around a bit," says Alexander. "If we're involved on a production job where there's a movie getting made in the imminent future, then we'll work ten-hour days or twelve-hour days or Saturdays and Sundays. But other than that, we work a forty-hour week. And now we've both got kids. In the old days, we'd be in the office probably till about 8:00 every night, and now we wanna be home to see our kids before they go to bed."

So do Ramsey & Stone, and they've created a schedule that honors that delicate balance between work and home.

MATTHEW: We show up sometime between 9:00 and 9:30 a.m., and we usually, on an average day, leave around 3:30, 4:00 p.m. It's good. We both have families.

ROBERT: It's a great lifestyle.

MATTHEW: When we're really kicking butt and we're close to finishing something, we work seven days a week. We work Saturdays and Sundays; we pull a morning shift. Sometimes we'll even come in for a night shift a couple times a week, like 7:00 to 10:00 p.m. If you can just get that leg up on that scene for the next day, you can maybe figure out a problem.

ROBERT: So we do burn the midnight oil every once in a while, but overall our schedule is pretty enviable.

Happy problems like production demands or those periods when you're "really kicking butt" need honoring, too.

Ducastel & Martineau, in fact, let the writing process itself dictate their schedule. "As far as how long we work, there really is no limit, unless fatigue sets in," they say. "Really, it depends on where we are in the writing process. Generally speaking, we stop when we're tired, but if we still have more ideas for the rest of it, it makes it easier to pick up where we left off the next day."

The important thing is to create a schedule that allows you to create and, when other commitments conflict, to remain flexible and find a way to keep writing. Like Manfredi & Hay. For most of 2001, the *crazy/beautiful* writers were crazy with work: production on their indie feature, *Bug*, and a slew of projects including a science-fiction film for Paramount. As a result, they returned to the writing schedule they'd kept when they had regular jobs — after editing *Bug* all day, they wrote nights and weekends, whenever they could find free time.

"Usually we don't like to do that," Hay says. "It's more productive to just try to limit ourselves to working five-day weeks. And we've figured out that a good day is four or five productive hours out of that day."

Though he and Manfredi have also discovered, as we have, that writing together allows them to work longer than they could solo. "Collaborating extends the work day," Hay says, "because we can find anything — many things — to talk about other than writing."

So can we.

There's always something going on in our lives or the world that's far more interesting than the script that we're writing. Distracting as this can be, we've learned to let ourselves talk before we start work. It's important connection time that greases the creative wheels by getting a dialogue going. It's not a bad warm-up for writing dialogue, either. And as Harold Ramis says, it's the way partners forge a shared point of view.

But we've also learned to contain it, especially when we're drafting a script. We give ourselves half an hour or so to shoot the breeze, then we start writing. If extraneous matters come up, we say, "Sidebar," and turn over the egg timer we bought for this purpose. When the three minutes run out, we get back to work.

THE RHYTHM METHOD

But there's no gadget we can buy that can change our circadian rhythms. Claudia's a morning person; Matt thinks mornings are *heinous*. Matt's a night owl; Claudia's a drooling zombie by 10:00 p.m.

You can move to find the right place to work. You can change jobs to create the right schedule. But you can't alter your biological destiny. If you try, it will only create bad feelings between you.

"My ex-husband had some issues," Carolyn Miller puts it politely, "because I was more of a late riser than he was." She couldn't help it, and he wouldn't respect it. This impasse became such a sore point in their collaboration, a career counselor had to help them work out a solution. "We found a compromise. We determined to start at a certain time, and we worked between 'x' hour and 'y' hour.

And we'd have a long lunch break, just to recharge. Generally we would not work after dinner, so that I could find my own pace, and he'd find his. It worked out, and it reduced a lot of stress. We wouldn't be arguing about, 'Oh, gosh, you'd better get up,' and, 'Come on, you've gotta work.'"

If you and your partner are lucky enough to have the same circadian rhythms, count your blessings and create a schedule that capitalizes on that, if you can. Reich & Cohen are both morning people, so they do their best writing then.

ANDREW: We have four really productive hours from 9:30 a.m. to 1:30 p.m.

TED: Usually after lunch we never get anything done. (Laughter.) After lunch we come back and it's like, *Oh, my God*. We've usually left the hard stuff, so we know we'll attack it fresh in the morning.

ANDREW: And we never work at night. If the script is here, and we're here, then we might work at night. But I can't write once it's dark out and I'm home. It's so depressing to me, I just can't do it.

If you also have the same circadian rhythms, but commitments prevent you from writing when you prefer, create the best compromise that you can.

And do the same if you have different circadian rhythms. We would prefer writing at opposite ends of the day, but we compromise by writing together during the six hours that seem the least heinous to both of us: 10:00 a.m. until 4:00 p.m. Sometimes we'll work later or a little earlier if we're really cooking or we have a tight deadline, but never late at night or first thing in the morning.

Like so much else in a good collaboration, the key is mutual respect.

CLAUDIA: We're real respectful — well, I'm more respectful. (Laughter.) It can be especially tricky during those weeks when Matt and I live and work together under the same roof. But there are advantages, too. I love the early morning hours to myself. Often I'll look over our script and have some ideas by the time Matt makes his appearance.

MATT: And I do a lot of mop-up at night, long after Claudia's comatose. Sometimes I'll leave her Post-it notes on the screenplay. Something like, *We have a problem on page 35. Fix it!*

It's the best of both circadian rhythms.

THE LONG-DISTANCE COLLABORATION

Absence makes the heart grow fonder, or so they say, but what does it do to the collective brain? In 1997 when Matt headed west, young man, we were about to find out. Would divided we fall into apathy about our creative relationship? We weren't sure how — or even if — we would maintain our collaboration. After all, with *Obscenity*, we'd written every darn word together, in the same room, huddled over the same computer. How would the process work 3,000 miles apart?

We decided to give the long-distance collaboration a shot with our family comedy, *Behind the Eight Ball*, which we'd started outlining on that road trip to Memphis a couple of months earlier. Before Matt left for L.A. with his entire life packed in a U-Haul, we hammered out a detailed scene-by-scene outline for the script, as well as bits of dialogue, jokes, sight gags. We also developed a loose plan of collaborative attack: Matt would write the first draft when he got to L.A., then Claudia would fly out and join him for the rewrite.

MATT: With our scene-by-scene, I had a solid road map. I knew where I was going and wanted to immerse myself in the first draft. As a result, I didn't want us to talk frequently via phone or e-mail about the dialogue or action I was putting into the scenes. I didn't like the idea of faxing pages or acts as I wrote them because I was afraid it would interfere with my momentum and tempt me into rewriting as I wrote. And Claudia was absolutely fine with this approach, which showed tremendous trust!

CLAUDIA: Yes, it did! Matt mailed me the first draft when he was finished, and I read it on the plane to L.A. When I arrived, I had extensive notes for the rewrite — a good thing since we only had ten days to do it. When I left, I was still shouting script notes to Matt as I walked down the jetway.

But we came up with a script that we liked, so we applied the same MO to our next comedy, *Psycho Bitch*. Again, it worked well — we outlined the script in three weeks at Claudia's farm, Matt wrote the first draft in L.A., and Claudia flew west for the rewrite. In both cases, however, we realized that there's an unmistakable creative dynamic — okay, magic — that occurs when we're writing in the same room. We vowed that for all our long-distance collaborations — regardless of who writes the first draft — we would bookend our process by getting together for the brainstorming/outlining and again for the rewrite.

When Ed Solomon & Chris Matheson started collaborating, they both lived in L.A. and wrote every word together. They decided to turn their series of comedy sketches about two high school kids, Bill and Ted, into a screenplay. "We spent three days outlining and four days pounding out a first draft in long hand," Solomon says. "Then I typed half, and Chris typed half."

Their script for *Bill & Ted's Excellent Adventure* was optioned for $5,000 and sold for $15,000. But after the surprising popularity of that film and its follow-up, *Bill & Ted's Bogus Journey*, the team split, with Matheson moving to Portland, Oregon.

"That was tough, like any break-up," Solomon says. "But looking back on it, it allowed both of us to pursue our own individual voices." (Solomon, for example, wrote *Men in Black*.) "And in many ways it made our return to collaborating even more rich."

That return happened several years later, when Solomon called Matheson in Portland and proposed creating a series of three to four-minute cartoons for the Internet called *Automatons*, based on an idea they'd conceived while working on *Bill & Ted*. Matheson agreed, and they began co-writing again — mostly by phone.

"We'd talk four or five days a week, for one to three hours," Solomon says. "I'd type, but we'd create every word together. Then I'd send Chris a disk. We'd each make notes on hard copies of the scripts. We just kept writing, and after about twenty-five pages, we said 'Screw the Internet.'" They decided to turn *Automatons* into a feature.

In addition to their lengthy phone conversations, they also met up in Las Vegas to draft the script. Why the gambling capital? "It was just a fun place," Solomon says. "We'd go for two to three days, maybe write for four hours a day. But Chris and I also write when he comes to L.A."

Tony Urban & Michael Addis did not say, "Screw the Internet." They co-wrote *Poor White Trash* entirely by e-mail. "Michael and I created a very in-depth outline/treatment, breaking down every single scene," Urban says in *Screenwriting on the Internet.* "Then we split the script in half. He took the first part, I took the second, and we wrote it in a few days. The next few months were spent polishing." They hadn't even met until Urban drove to the film set in Illinois, and they were "off to do rewrites."

Jim Cash & Jack Epps Jr. live half a country apart — Cash in L.A. and Epps in East Lansing, Michigan — but they *like* the distance. "One of the good things about our relationship is the fact that we're 2,000 miles apart," Epps tells *Written By.* "Jim goes off and has his life, and I have mine."

Their long-distance collaboration is done by phone, fax, and e-mail. "We have a program that allows us to have the same page on the screen at the same time — simultaneously across the country," Epps adds. "So I can make a change here, and Jim sees it in three seconds. Or he makes a change, and I see it in three seconds. We have the speaker phone on while we're working, so, in essence, we're there together." They admit their phone bills are high.

So are ours.

We communicate mostly by e-mail, sometimes a dozen e-mails a day, but there are times when we just need to talk — or hear the other one's voice. The phone is a poor substitute for being together, but it's better than nothing.

We've also bought the same screenwriting software, so we can e-mail our scripts to each other, a faster and cheaper method than snail mail, and we don't have to give up great chunks of our life to the glacial progress of post office lines.

If your collaboration is long-distance, we strongly recommend that you use the same software (we didn't as we wrote this book, and it drove us *crazy*). Or like Cash & Epps, you may want to invest in screenwriting software that lets you connect your computers and write together via the Internet in real time. *Final Draft* has a feature called *CollaboWriter*, and *Movie Magic Screenwriter* has *iPartner*. With either of these programs, you can read each other's work as you type, one of you having control of the script at a given time, so you can't type simultaneously and jumble the letters.

For more information and the latest upgrades, check out *www.finaldraft.com* or *www.screenplay.com/products/ mmscreenwriter*. Another excellent resource is The Writers Store in Los Angeles (1-800-272-8927 or *www.writersstore.com*).

Whether you're working at home, office, public place, or cyberspace, at the end of the day — and your script — *how* you work is not as important as how well how you work works for you.

And how well you work together, even if you're working apart.

SCRIPT PARTNER POINTS

☯ Explore different places to see where you both work best: Home? Office? Coffee shop? Chinese restaurant? Or a pu pu platter of all of the above?

☯ Consider your commitments and circadian rhythms, then carve a work schedule out of the chaos. Writing regularly — instead of waiting for the Muse to speak to you both at the same time (fat chance) — will create a sense of responsibility to each other and to your script.

☯ Fill your work space with music, items of significance, *objets d'art*, etc., that will focus your creative energies and put you in the right frame of mind for a particular project.

☯ If working long distance, figure out the most creatively-efficient and cost-efficient ways of co-writing: phone, fax, e-mail, and/or snail mail. You may also want to schedule times to get together in person during certain parts of the process.

☯ For heaven's sake, make sure both of you have the same scriptwriting software and/or word-processing software, especially if you plan on e-mailing files and drafts to each other. Trust us, this saves time and keeps you from wanting to shoot your computer — or Bill Gates.

"You must choose. But choose wisely. For as the True Grail will bring you life —
the False Grail will take it from you."

> — Grail Knight (Robert Eddison),
> *Indiana Jones and the Last Crusade*

CHAPTER 4

THE RIGHT SCRIPT: CHOOSING A PROJECT

You've found the right workplace and schedule — be they ever
so humble or complicated. Now you have a much more important
decision: Which script idea will you choose to write? You may be a
new team or a team that's established or, like Ed Solomon & Chris
Matheson, you may be back together after a break. You may be
writing spec scripts or the opposite of specs: assignment. Whatever
your situation, you have to go through this process.

"Every once in a while we stop and say, 'What do we want to do
next?'" Matt Manfredi says. "Do we want to write something for
ourselves to direct or a spec script or a pitch?"

You don't want to choose poorly. You want to pick the *right*
project. This, of course, means different things to different writers. It
depends on who you are, what you want to write, and where you are
in your life and career — and sometimes history.

THE RIGHT PROJECT

We wrote our first script, *Obscenity*, because the story and
issues compelled us to write it. Small and character-driven and
decidedly "left of center," as Robert Ramsey & Matthew Stone like to
say, it isn't exactly a studio piece. A recent finalist for Sundance, it will
be an indie for sure.

81

Long before their studio blockbuster, *Batman Forever*, Lee & Janet Batchler also wrote their first screenplay on spec. In fact, they did it just for practice — a good idea if you're beginners.

JANET: The first thing we did, just to see if we could do it, was to adapt a book which we didn't have the rights to, which was very stupid.

LEE: But we also realized that this was practice, that we weren't going to try to go out and sell it. But something that we always come back to is: If the story is no good, it doesn't matter how finely you polish it. So we looked around for a good solid story.

JANET: And we just said, "Let's try and see what it's like to put something into screenplay form, and to figure out what you leave out and what you put in."

Several years and screenplays later, the Batchlers found themselves barely surviving as writers in Hollywood. They hadn't sold what they wanted to sell and felt capable of doing far more than the world knew they could.

"We were our own best-kept secret," Lee explains. "We felt we were ready for a better agent. We wanted to play in the big leagues. And no one is going to invite you in until you show what you can do." They knew the right project for them had to be a script so compelling that it would take their writing and career to new levels. "We had to write a truly great script," he says. "A weekend read."

"A script so good that they had to read it, so good they didn't have a choice," Janet adds. "We knew we needed the idea that was good enough, the story that was good enough before we could write that script."

They were right. And after several months of searching, they landed on the right idea, based on real-life events: French magician

Jean Robert-Houdin is sent to Algeria in 1855 to prevent a bloody civil war led by a self-proclaimed sorcerer.

The Batchlers spent a year and a half writing the script — nine drafts! — but when it was finished in 1993, *Smoke and Mirrors* went out on Tuesday and, after a fierce bidding war, sold on Friday.

It was also a bumpy ride to success for Andrew Reich & Ted Cohen. Like the Batchlers, they wrote their first script just to see if they could do it — and for fun. A few years and cancelled shows later, they weren't where they wanted to be as writers, either.

"We had worked on *Minor Adjustments* and *Mr. Rhodes*, shows that didn't go a full season and weren't that good," Reich says. "Our career was not on a huge upward path."

Then the right project for them came along.

Warner Bros. invited Reich & Cohen, then freelancers, to write one episode of *Friends*, with the understanding that the studio might offer them staff positions if they liked the script.

"We had three days to write a show that was really our shot at a career," Reich says.

"There was so much pressure," adds Cohen.

A couple of days later, Reich showed a draft of their script to his ex-wife who "just kind of like, um, didn't love it," he says. "She was kind of critical of it. I was already kind of panicky, and it made me lose faith in it, and it was right before we were going to have our last day to go over it, and we were basically out of time. I remember being like, 'I just don't think this is that good.' I'm sure I was freaking out, and I was making Ted freak out, and I remember him going, 'You know what? It's good. It's good. We don't have any more time anyway, and seriously, it's good.' And we handed it in, and we got hired. And *that* I remember was a good lesson to trust the other

83

person. I know to trust Ted more than my ex-wife."

They laugh.

Writing the script was as far from fun as they've been as co-writers, but gutting it out got them on the show. The real lesson: If you've got a shot, take it.

Convinced their career *was* shot, Scott Alexander & Larry Karaszewski wrote *Ed Wood* on spec. After their early success with *Homewreckers*, they sold their pitch for *Problem Child* to Universal Studios, only to be replaced by a committee of no fewer than nine writers. The finished film was far from their original vision.

LARRY: We wrote it as sort of a black comedy for grown-ups.

SCOTT: We were picturing *War of the Roses*.

LARRY: Yeah, and it got dumbed down to a very silly kiddie movie. But it wound up being a big hit. And we wound up being corralled into doing the sequel. But weirdly enough, we had to write a sequel to the movie that was made as opposed to a sequel to the movie that we wrote, so it was a very awkward experience for us. And both movies were despised critically, so we actually had problems getting jobs after that. We were very disappointed by the whole working-for-Hollywood thing. We said, "If we can't get a job, we might as well just write the thing that we've always wanted to write." Back in college, we had talked about making a movie about Ed Wood, but we figured, "Who would make this kind of movie?" But fuck it — we didn't care at that point, so we went off and did it.

SCOTT: That was Larry swearing in your book. It wasn't me.

If freedom's just another word for nothing else to lose, the reverse, apparently, is also true. Or to quote *Risky Business*, "Sometimes you just have to say, 'What the fuck.'" So the right project for you might be doing just that and writing the thing you've always wanted to write. Something you give a fuck about.

After not writing together for seven years, John Rice & Joe Batteer were searching for an idea "that had some teeth," an idea that would be worth the months of hard work ahead. The one they chose — brought to them by producers Tracie Graham and Alison Rosenzweig — became *Windtalkers*, about the contributions of Navajo "Code Talkers" during World War II.

"We loved the idea of doing a war film," Rice & Batteer say in *scr(i)pt Magazine*, "loved the idea that we'd never heard of the code, loved infusing a war movie with a Native American timbre."

Passion for a project may be the best reason for writing a script, but sometimes the right project can't be your passion. Consider the case of Fay & Michael Kanin. During their long, prolific career as collaborators, their passion was writing on spec.

"We were offered studio deals at MGM because we did a couple of films there and at RKO, but no, we wanted to be our own boss," Fay Kanin says. "We liked that. And we wanted to write originals."

They enjoyed great success generating and writing their own ideas — until the McCarthy Era. Because they were liberals (*gasp!*), and Fay had taken classes at the Acting Studio ("taught by many Communist actors, terrific actors"), Hollywood slapped them on the Grey List. It wasn't as bad as the Black List, but it kept them from selling their work.

"We were *not* Communists, but you were red-baited even if you were not," she remembers.

Then the director Charles Vidor offered them an assignment: to write *Rhapsody*. The Kanins knew the studio execs would object, and they did, suggesting the director use a contract writer for the picture instead. But Vidor insisted.

"He said, 'Listen, don't give me all that. If you don't let me hire the Kanins, I am going to the press, and I'm gonna bust this wide open. I'm gonna give a press conference and say why.' He knew that he was safe because we were not Communists, so they couldn't use that defense. But you know so many people's lives were destroyed. Oh, boy, we watched a lot of our friends — "

She looks away.

"We watched marriages break up and, oh, it was a terrible time. A terrible time."

Fortunately, times have improved, though ageism has created its own Grey List in Hollywood now. But even in the face of prejudice against your age, gender, race, or sexual or political preference, you have a greater shot at success if you find the right script idea.

WHAT HAVE YOU GOT?

You may already have an idea. Or your partner may have one. This is often the case with collaborative pairs.

"A lot of times when we're finishing up a project, we'll start saying, 'What should we do next?' So an idea will just sort of come," says Larry Karaszewski.

"Usually one of us has an idea," Phil Hay says. "Matt and I are just sitting around, and someone says, 'I have an idea for a movie.'"

But some gifted writers like Peter Tolan just aren't gifted at coming up with ideas, so their partner has to be the idea person. That tends to be the case with Olivier Ducastel & Jacques Martineau.

"Olivier brings ideas and always brings the desire to make a new film," they tell us. "Jacques is a bit lazy if you don't push him to work and to write. So Olivier always gives the starting impetus. He often gives a starting sketch, even if it's very vague. For example, with *Drôle de Félix* (*Adventures of Felix*), Olivier talked about wanting to film French landscapes and wanted to tell the story of a boy who would go in search of his father in Marseille."

Whatever the case in your collaboration, if one of you has an idea, run it past your partner. Give a starting sketch. For some teams, this part of the process is very informal. Others, like Manfredi & Hay, turn it into a mini-pitch.

"We'll kind of present it," Hay says. "Usually when you get to the stage where you present it to each other, it's a pretty good idea, because I have a million bad ideas all the time, and I'll realize in five minutes they're not good, and I don't bother Matt with them. But sometimes I think this is an idea that just might work."

Our style's a bit different. We bother each other a lot with ideas we're pretty sure might be bad. Then again, how can we know until our partner has heard them? With this buckshot approach, many ideas get shot down. Yes, this can be painful. So we've made up a routine to keep ourselves laughing. We pretend we're skeet shooting, tossing ideas up in the air like clay targets. If one has potential, we explore it. But if one sucks, we shout, "Pull!"

The Gong Show for screenwriting.

This keeps us loose, less ego-involved, more creative. The point is to toss your idea out there, whatever your style. Kick it around with your partner. Brainstorm a bit. And yes, give each other the freedom to suck.

"We spend a couple of days throwing things around," Karaszewski says. "You don't really try to put any kind of constraints on it. You're just randomly throwing out ideas. And usually when it's good, it comes pretty quickly. Because all of a sudden you'll throw out an idea, and it'll lead to another idea, and it will just naturally sort of write itself in a weird sense."

Manfredi & Hay draw on their improvisation background at Brown when they brainstorm ideas. "Ideally, what happens is the old improv thing," Hay explains. "'Yes and... ' is the rule. You always say, 'Yes and... ', then 'and something.' So I'll say, 'I think we should do an action movie, and I've come up with a high concept, and here it is.' And Matt will say, 'Yeah, and I think here's who the main character should be.' Or combining two genres we want to do. 'We're gonna do a science fiction movie. What if we made it a love story?'"

By exploring your idea's possibilities and the genre — or genres — that might serve it best, you're testing to make sure it's a movie.

"That's the first question we ask," Hay says. "Is this a viable movie?"

Answering this question can take time. So can coming up with the appropriate genre(s). It took us weeks to decide on the right genre for *Obscenity*. It was clearly a courtroom drama, but would it be more of a character piece? Or a high-stakes thriller? Horton Foote-ish? Or John Grisham-esque?

Brad Anderson and his writing partners also take time to explore the best genre for their ideas. "We riff off of what kind of movie we want to make, what genre, and how we must studiously avoid the clichés and hackneyed characters most often associated with that genre."

It's a fruitful part of the process, helping you find a fresh take on the universe you've chosen. "Pick a genre and take it to the moon," recommends Quentin Tarantino, who did exactly that with the gangster genre when he and Roger Avery wrote *Pulp Fiction*.

So did Manfredi & Hay when they wrote *crazy/beautiful* and turned the teen movie into a moving adult drama. And Alexander Payne & Jim Taylor re-invented the high school movie when they adapted *Election*. "I wasn't going to make a high school movie," Payne tells *Scenario*. "It was an adult movie set in a high school."

And as Larry Wachowski says in *Scenario's* interview with him and his brother Andy, they wanted to write "a well-contained, suspense/film-noir kind of movie, where you can use a lot of humor and can get away with a lot of sexiness and stylishness." Their script for *Bound*, turned into a taut thriller with Jennifer Tilly and Gina Gershon, was classic film noir — but with a feminist-lesbian twist.

"The core idea of the screenplay is based on the character of Violet," Larry says. "The idea of a woman you see on the street and make a host of assumptions about that were all dead wrong. We wanted to play with what you see on the surface and the truth that lies beneath. We tried to do that with all the characters."

"We also thought — and our wives felt the same — that it would be great to do a movie where the women were the heroes and got away," Andy adds, "which almost never happens in this type of film."

Once you've explored your idea and its genre(s), and you're sure it's a viable movie, make sure you're the right people to write it. The best idea can be the worst script to write if you don't find a way to make it your own. In some way, on some level, you both need to find a connection to the material.

Manfredi & Hay ask themselves, "Why is it interesting to work on? Why do we need to do this?" Hay says, "For example, in doing *crazy/beautiful*, it was like, 'Why would we be good at writing a teen movie? We *wouldn't* be good writing a teen movie, so we want to write a drama about teenagers that isn't a teen movie. We want to write a love story that is a serious adult drama, but the characters are teenagers.' That was what got us excited. There's always something that happens when we start to come up with these ideas where it seems different, and it seems like the reason to make the movie — something that fits into a commercial category of some kind but has something else, some other spark to it. Sometimes it takes a while to find that."

And sometimes it takes a while to find your connection to an idea. After co-writing *Analyze This* with Peter Tolan, Billy Crystal approached him with a new concept: a publicist has to get two stars/lovers back together to promote their latest movie.

"To be honest, I really didn't want to do *America's Sweethearts*," Tolan confesses. "I had just done, like, six years of *The Larry Sanders Show* and didn't want to do any more stuff about the business, inside the business."

But he'd enjoyed working with Crystal on *Analyze This*, so he finally caved — on one condition. "I said I'll do it if it's kind of an acerbic, biting, edgy, dark, mean-spirited movie. As long as people are behaving badly, that's my kind of — that's when I see the humor of things — when people misbehave."

In other words, he found a way to connect to Billy Crystal's idea and make it his own. That's what you have to do. In this business, however, there's no guarantee it will *stay* your own, that it won't become the Project From Hell. After all, the common metaphor for what happens to a script is "child molesting."

Tolan wrote a draft that he liked, but the studio at the time, Castle Rock, said they saw the project as more of a romantic comedy. "Which was like a knife in my heart," Tolan says. "I really don't do a lot of those. I'm not a real romantic." Though he doubted Castle Rock really wanted to make the movie, he wrote a more romantic second draft — "a fool's errand," he calls it. Sure enough, the studio passed. Tolan felt some relief, but a few weeks later, Crystal called him with the news that he'd sold the project to Joe Roth (who ended up directing the film). Tolan was less than thrilled. "I'm like, *Oh, God, I have to work on this again!* And I said, 'Does he have notes?'"

Two weeks later, Crystal phoned again. The news this time? Julia Roberts was attached to the project. "I'm like, *Oh, no,* because now it's not just a movie, it's a *Julia Roberts* movie, and that required a great deal of work."

Tolan stayed on the project through all the script incarnations. "It's like a curse!" he laughs. "Torture, really torture. And rather than go into all of the awful details, I worked through the actual production of the movie, which was very difficult from a writing standpoint."

In the end, Tolan lost his sense of connection, but you still need to find it before you begin. This is essential. You both need to care. If you don't, you'll get partway through the script and realize you don't give a damn. This is not a good feeling. It's akin to Wile E. Coyote running off a cliff and looking down and realizing he's gonna crash. Chances are your project will, too.

"That seems to me the only thing that can truly destroy a script," Phil Hay says, "which is why I feel the most important question we ask ourselves is, 'Why is this interesting? Why is this different? Why do I care?' Because it seems like the only real threat to having a script self-destruct is if you get halfway through it, and you just don't care. And nobody cares."

Harold Ramis finds it difficult to care about an idea until he finds its deeper emotional level. "I'm contracted to develop a film based on an existing script. It's really basically about male bonding, and Peter [Tolan] and I have started talking generally about friendship, not thinking about how anything might specifically apply to the screenplay. I want to know what he thinks and feels about his

91

experience. How did he form the most interesting friendships in his life? What either facilitates or prevents him from making friendships now? Which is sort of what this movie's about — how difficult it is to make adult friends, how easy it was in college, and how hard it is now as an adult. So it's not just 'What's funny about this?' It's 'What do you really feel about it?' Because the comedy I aspire to write is always based on some real emotional, philosophical, or moral content. So you've got to get at that somehow."

We co-wrote several screenplays — and this book — because we both cared about the ideas. Still, there are times — and this can get sticky — when one of us cares about an idea and does not want to scrap it, but the other one doesn't care and does not want to write it.

CLAUDIA: I have an idea I love for a script about football, but when I mention it, Matt makes loud gagging sounds.

MATT: My subtle indication of disinterest.

CLAUDIA: I've tried pointing out that there are characters in the story who also hate football, and that's how he could connect! But he doesn't buy it, so if I want to write it, I'll have to do it by myself — a miserable prospect.

If your script idea isn't right for you both, don't force it; write it solo someday. If it is right for you both, go for it. As long as you both connect.

But will an audience?

Before you and your partner lock your idea, it's wise to check it against the "Screenplay Paradox," as Claudia calls it in *Crafting Short Screenplays That Connect*:

We go to *The Full Monty* to see a story about unemployed steelworkers who save relationships, self-respect, with a strip-show, but we also go because, on some level, we want to see our own life.

But we don't want to see our own life up there on the screen because we've seen it already, and that would be boring. We want to see our own life — and we don't.

This seemingly contradictory statement is nonetheless true....So the screenwriter's job — our great sleight of hand — is to create a story that satisfies both...

The burning question is *how?*...

I've never poured steel in my life. I've never been unemployed (knock on wood), and I've never danced on stage in a night club. I can't even understand some of the things the characters in *Full Monty* are *saying*... but I connected like crazy. So did millions of others... Because under the surface particulars of the story, beneath its unique universe in Sheffield, England, lie the deeper, universal patterns of striving, failing, and striving again as well as connecting, disconnecting, and reconnecting...

And these patterns — recreated in unique ways — are the source of a story's shared emotions.

Is your idea at once unique and universal? If not, toss it and yell, "Pull!" And keep exploring. If it is unique and universal, you're in luck.

If your idea passes one last screen test: *Make sure your script idea hasn't recently sold or isn't currently in development.* Screenwriters' worst nightmare is working months or even years on a script idea, only to discover that a similar idea has just reaped six figures and/or a three-picture deal for somebody else.

Okay, so there's no way to know what's in another writer's head or hard drive. Ideas pop up simultaneously. Blame it on *zeitgeist* or the "creative smog" hanging over L.A. But to make sure you haven't already been scooped, do a little market research. Keep up with films in development/production and recent script/pitch sales by checking out trade publications like *Variety, The Hollywood Reporter, Creative Screenwriting, scr(i)pt, Fade In, Written By*. You can also surf showbiz Web sites (some free, some fee-based): *www.screenwritersutopia.com, www.moviebytes.com, www.script-sales.com, www.hollywoodlit-sales.com, www.upcomingmovies.com,* and *www.4filmmakers.com*, to name a few.

One cautionary note: Though invaluable, this research isn't infallible. Consider such dueling projects as *Deep Impact* vs. *Armageddon, Antz* vs. *A Bug's Life, Volcano* vs. *Dante's Peak, Robin Hood* vs. *Robin Hood: Prince of Thieves, Mission to Mars* vs. *Red Planet, The People vs. Larry Flynt* (just kidding), and multiple Alexander the Great biopics.

We've learned this research lesson the hard way. We were shopping a treatment for a comedy called *Romeo and Julia* (a time-traveling tomboy helps a lovesick William Shakespeare overcome writer's block) when — you guessed it — *Shakespeare in Love* hit the theaters. And Matt's comedy, *A Really Rotten Christmas*, ended up on the proverbial shelf shortly after it sold because the producers' angle on the rewrite was too close to *Jingle All The Way*.

When Nick Kazan & Robin Swicord developed the idea for *Loco for Lotto* (a Hispanic housekeeper wins the lottery), they knew someone could beat them to the high-concept punch, so instead of burning valuable time writing *Lotto* on spec, Kazan called a friend at Sony and pitched the idea. "We said, 'We would like to sell it now, even though we think that we can write a really funny movie, and maybe we'd do better selling it independently. We'd like the deal announced, so that nobody else decides to write this movie.'" The friend loved the story and helped set up a deal.

Ultimately, your best defense is to "write something unique," as Scott Alexander tells *Hollywoodlitsales.com*. "Hollywood is littered with first-time writers who cashed in on the hot trend of that week. You know, *Die Hard* in a blank, and sold a big spec and then they got fired one minute after the deal closed, and they never worked again. The writers who keep a career are writers who break out from the pack and write stuff that no one else is writing."

WHAT HAS SOMEONE ELSE GOT?

If you write and sell a script based on your own idea — and see it made into a movie you like — congratulations, you've reached Script Nirvana. Some successful studio writers like Ramsey & Stone still long to do this (scratch a hired gun, find a frustrated spec writer), but they've hit dead ends when they try.

ROBERT: We can't walk into a studio and just sell them our ideas. We have not perfected that particular activity. And it's very frustrating.

MATTHEW: Our impulses are decidedly left of center. So what happens is we take these impulses, and once in a while we kind of float these balloons to people that have money to see if they're feeling a little left of center today. Honey, they're not. We've been shot down many times pitching our own ideas.

ROBERT: You're having a meeting with somebody, and you're sitting there drinking your carbonated beverage. And they always ask you what you want to do. It's in the rule book, that studio executive's rule book I haven't seen. I know it's in there — page 37, I bet. It says, "Ask the writer what they want to do." And they politely dismiss it and move on. "Oh, that's interesting, now let's talk about what we want." Everybody has their own agenda.

MATTHEW: They've got stacks of scripts that need to be written. They've got projects. Julia Roberts needs something developed for her. "There's this new comedian; you've never heard of him, but he's going to be big, and we're trying to develop something for him." Okay, so, who's generating these ideas? I don't know. They're coming out of the ether.

Since their own ideas aren't selling, Ramsey & Stone write other people's — like Eddie Murphy's concept for a prison comedy called *Life*. The impetus for that project came in January 1996, when producer Brian Grazer asked the writing team to meet with the comedy star.

MATTHEW: At first we said, "Are you insane?"

ROBERT: We went down in the elevator thinking that's the most ridiculous thing we ever heard. Us writing a prison comedy for Eddie Murphy? They must be high. (Laughter.) But then we got this call saying, "They're really serious. Do you want to do this?" We're like, "Uhhh... all right." And suddenly we're on a plane to New York to meet Eddie.

MATTHEW: And really, all Eddie Murphy had was, "I wanna do a movie about two guys who get stuck in prison. I don't know if they know each other."

Ramsey & Stone wrote an eighteen-page treatment for *Life*, then the full-length script, which made it to the big screen with Eddie Murphy and Martin Lawrence, directed by the late Ted Demme. Their adaptation of the Dave Barry novel, *Big Trouble*, became a vehicle for Tim Allen and Janeane Garofalo. Obviously, Ramsey & Stone have become extremely successful writing other people's ideas. But they've also learned the hard way, as we have, that you have to be picky about the assignments you choose.

Heaven knows we've signed on for some bombs — literally — like that nuclear project Matt suffered through. There are others he won't admit to and didn't put his name on. Claudia has also suffered, spending close to a year of her life as a dialoguist on the world's worst soap, *The Catlins*, Turner Broadcasting's attempt to make a low-budget, family-values *Dallas*. Unfortunately, the budget was so low it didn't allow for minor considerations like second takes and sound design and trained actors (T. J. Catlin was played by a college basketball referee). The show was so bad it developed a cult following, prompting the late Lewis Grizzard to bemoan that *The Catlins* were "spreading across America like an outbreak of mouth sores." Fortunately, after eight months, Claudia found out she'd been fired: When her story outline didn't arrive, she called the studio and discovered that the calling card they gave her was no longer valid. *The Catlins* was mercifully cancelled after two years.

Yes, for writers there's no such thing as bad experience, just good material. And yes, that's part of the process, but this is your career we're talking about. If you're careless about the projects you choose, you could lose years of your professional life.

"I mean it, time is very precious in this business," cautions Carolyn Miller. She's right. After all, time *is* money.

And, okay, if you've been writing on spec but not selling (see also: starving) it may sound crazy to turn down an assignment.

Maybe it is. Only you can make that decision. If the right project for you is putting food (other than Ramen noodles) on the table, take the assignment. Eating is a wonderful thing. But if you don't have to take it, and it's not the right project for you at this time, it may be smarter to pass. Write a project that meets your objectives. That's how you craft a career.

And, as Ramsey & Stone have learned, the more successful you get, the more important it is to be choosy. Stone says, "People will easily pigeonhole you. When the *Life* script was done, and the town knew the film was getting made, suddenly we got every script for Chris Tucker, Chris Rock. It was like, 'Here are a couple of white guys who can write a movie for black guys!' And we had to say no to everything because otherwise that would be it. That's what we would be doing."

"The way we have sculpted our career is by being very particular about what we say yes to," Ramsey says. "We get a lot of offers. We say yes to a few things, and we try to do them as well as we can."

With *Ed Wood*, Alexander & Karaszewski escaped being pigeonholed as writers of silly kiddie movies. But after T*he People vs. Larry Flynt* and *Man on the Moon*, they've found themselves flooded with biopic offers.

LARRY: It's weird to be in the position that we are because people will call us, and their idea of pitching us is just a person's name. "I've got a great idea for you — Abraham Lincoln!"

SCOTT: "Idi Amin!"

LARRY: "Idi Amin. What do you think? What do you think?" You know, sometimes it sounds good. Sometimes it's like, *Oh, my God, Idi Amin?*

SCOTT: "Charles Manson! How about it?"

LARRY: So sometimes you say yes or no based on that.

SCOTT: I don't know if Idi Amin has a good second act. It's a hell of a third act! And then he eats his enemy! (Laughter.)

The biopic scripts have become increasingly demanding: *Ed Wood* took six weeks, *Larry Flynt* took ten months, *Man on the Moon* took a year, *Marx Brothers* took three years (including obtaining rights). As a result, Alexander & Karaszewski have become more selective.

Following the bidding war over *Smoke and Mirrors*, the Batchlers also became very choosy. They turned down several projects at Warner Bros., simply because they didn't think they were the right writers for them. But when the offer came in for *Batman Forever*, they connected. They were intrigued by the idea of exploring the duality of the hero as well as the villains — "the psychological reality underneath it," Janet says. And their duality-driven pitch connected with director Joel Schumacher and producer Tim Burton, who offered them the job.

That's the secret to satisfaction and success when you take an assignment: making sure you're the right team for the project and making it yours. And making sure it will make a viable movie.

When first approached with the *Windtalkers* concept, Rice & Batteer loved the idea but weren't sure what to do with it. They had difficulty envisioning the film as something more than an interesting historical documentary. Then the producers' research revealed a darker, more dramatic dimension to the story: If a Code Talker fell into enemy hands, his bodyguard was instructed to "protect the Code at all costs."

This moral dilemma was rife with dramatic potential. "We had no doubts this was a movie," they say. "The bones of it, in fact, flashed between us in a flurry of creative spark that lasted only an hour but gave us a great amount of resolve... resolve we would find we desperately needed in the coming months."

A script, as we've said, can be a long haul. You need a great amount of resolve. And you need to believe the idea's worth writing.

"Whatever a writer is doing," Lee Batchler says, "they should really believe in it, not just be trying to make a buck."

The gloomy truth is, if you take an assignment you don't believe is worth writing, you still have to write it. Ramsey & Stone were delighted to make their first studio deal, *The Earl of Hackensack* (Rodney Dangerfield inherits a title in England), until they realized they didn't connect. They freaked, but at least they freaked together.

MATTHEW: It was collective terror. I suppose if there's comfort from running out of a burning building with somebody else, you have somebody's hand to hold. But that's about it.

ROBERT: We literally thought, "We can't do this." Jeffrey Price & Peter Seaman [*Who Framed Roger Rabbit; How the Grinch Stole Christmas*] once told us something. They said, "You'll see it. In every project there's always a moment when you ask your partner, 'Can I give the money back?'" But this was worse.

MATTHEW: It was a job. And we got into the Writers Guild with it. But it was really hard. It was really hard learning what studios expect of you. It was an education. That was our Hollywood education.

You can always shelve a spec script that doesn't pan out. But when you're under contract, you have to write the assignment — or give back the money. And as Garson Kanin told his sister-in-law when she wanted to do that, "My God, Fay, *never* give back the money!"

YOU GOT NOTHIN'

Okay, it happens. Don't feel bad. It happens to all partners eventually. It's never happened to you before, but now — no matter how hard you try — you just can't come up with an idea.

So relax. Take a shower. Go for a walk. Stroll and scroll through your Rolodex of ideas. Maybe you have a good one, but you've just forgotten.

"Occasionally," Phil Hay says, "we'll come up with an idea that seems pretty good or seems okay, and then we kind of forget about it for a while because we're doing something else. And then we come back to it. Like this comedy idea we might be pitching soon — a big, broad comedy. A year later, it just randomly recurred in a conversation."

An idea whose time has come. That's what you're looking for — an idea you filed away that clicks for you now.

In January of 1997, having lunch at our old haunt, Manny's, we were brainstorming script ideas for Matt's upcoming meeting with development people at Pixar Animation Studios.

MATT: I was going to be talking with them about possibly doing rewrite work on the *Toy Story 2* script, but I wanted to have a few high-concept ideas handy in case the opportunity came up to pitch.

CLAUDIA: And out of the blue I said, "What if a kid lets a Magic Eight Ball make all his decisions for one day?"

MATT: It was a great hook. Not for animation necessarily, but an

101

intriguing concept for a live-action family film. So we mentally filed it away.

Half a year later, driving ourselves crazy driving to Memphis because another idea just wouldn't gel, one of us said, "What about that Eight Ball idea?" In a flurry of creative spark, we outlined the whole story. A few months later, the script was in our agent's hands.

There are real advantages to retrieving an old concept. Like wine, script ideas often improve with time. When you're not working on the story, your unconscious is ("the elves," Claudia calls it). And it gives you insights about your idea when you least expect it.

"You get this idea, whether it's a character or whatever, and you don't do it right away. You sort of think about it," Fay Kanin says. "And every now and then I say, 'Gee, I thought of something for that.' And then we tuck it away. And then when we suddenly see an empty moment, an empty period, we say, 'Well, how about that idea?' By then, we have talked about it on and off, and we have a lot of stuff already there."

If no good old idea flashes to mind, pull out your notebooks and journals and files. You never know when a stockpiled idea might work. Steven Soderbergh made an entry in a 1986 notebook: "A film about deception and lost earrings." Three years later, he wrote and directed *sex, lies, and videotape*.

Bennett Yellin, who co-wrote *Dumb and Dumber* with the Farrelly brothers, tells *Newsweek* that Peter Farrelly always keeps a notebook of comic ideas. "If anybody says anything remotely funny, he immediately goes and writes it down. At the beginning of a script, he'd take out the notebooks and say, 'Here are ten jokes — now let's write the script around these.' Literally, this was the technique."

The Batchlers learned the value of keeping notebooks and files when they searched for an idea worthy of that "weekend read."

They'd already presented several ideas to their writers group, who liked one idea, but the group's moderator, Jack Gilbert — who spent ten years running Warner Bros.' writers workshops and is now a script consultant — challenged the Batchlers to keep digging. He told them to come back to the next meeting with at least three more ideas.

"We spent probably close to a month digging through files, every time we'd jotted down an idea for a story," Janet says. "And one of the ones that wasn't the top one on our list at that moment was the story of *Smoke and Mirrors*. We took that back a month later to the group, and everybody said, 'That's the one. That's the one we want to read.'"

If you don't keep ideas in a journal or notebook or file, start now. Jot down any ideas you see in newspapers, magazines, malls, or bus stations — anywhere you happen to find them. Anything goes, anything that remotely resembles a script idea. And the best ones often come out of the blue.

When Nick Kazan & Robin Swicord heard about a couple of housekeepers winning the lottery, *Loco for Lotto* was born. When they read Roald Dahl's book, *Matilda*, they said, "This would make a great movie." So they wrote an adaptation, which later became the 1996 Columbia/TriStar release starring Danny DeVito, Rhea Perlman, and Mara Wilson.

Literary works can be excellent source material for adaptation, as can older films: Nora & Delia Ephron's *You've Got Mail* (1998) was a remake of *The Shop Around the Corner* (1940). Stephen Mazur & Paul Guay's *Liar Liar* (1997) with Jim Carrey was an update of the Bob Hope film, *Nothing But the Truth* (1941), which was an update of *Nothing But the Truth* (1929), which was an update of *Nothing But the Truth* (1920)! Rights issues can be tricky, so you'll need to secure them before you begin — unless, like the Batchlers' first project, your adaptation is just for practice. (For a full discussion of acquiring rights, see Linda Seger's book, *The Art of Adaptation: Turning Fact and Fiction into Film.*)

But probably the best advice we've heard about generating ideas comes from Fay Kanin quoting Orson Welles (who would sell no wine, er, idea before its time), "He said, 'Stop looking at my movies and start looking at life.' A lot of your ideas come out of your life."

The Longstreets have found this to be true. They spent a long day at home with their friend, producer Joel Robeson, trying to come up with an idea for a prime-time drama. "So we're thinking," Renee says, "we're sitting there for the day, and in that day the calls come from the ex-husband, the ex-wife. One kid has to be picked up from school. The kids come home, the teenagers, the this, the that. At the end of the day, Joel says, 'I know the hour drama I want to do. It's this. Your life.'" So they went to CBS and pitched a dramedy, *We Interrupt This Life.*

An idea can even spring from an idle comment — as it did for us in 1999.

MATT: I had just flown to Tallahassee so we could salvage a script that we were trying to write. Claudia was teaching a screenwriting class that summer, and when I arrived, she had just held her first meeting. And she came home crabby.

CLAUDIA: I always cap this screenwriting class at eighteen — I'm a real bitch about it — but that evening I'd let twenty-one students enroll. I don't know what came over me. They all looked so cute. I just couldn't say no.

MATT: And I'm thinking, *What have you done with the real Claudia Johnson?*

CLAUDIA: And I said, "Well, the bitch within really failed me tonight!"

104

MATT: Later that evening, we drove to the farm to commune with nature and write. The country air must have worked magic because I woke up the next morning, and Claudia's comment was flashing neon in my head. I stumbled into the kitchen and said, "I've got it — a script called *Psycho Bitch*, about a woman who releases the bitch within."

CLAUDIA: "But she isn't within, she's her roommate — and wrecking her life."

MATT: Bingo. The idea clicked. We abandoned Operation Salvage and wrote *Psycho Bitch*.

So if you can't find a story out there somewhere, follow Orson Welles' advice and examine your own life. What fascinates you? Compels you?

Brad Anderson's interests — he calls them "obsessions" — have been the source of his ideas. "I have so far pretty much written about what I know or what I'm madly interested in," he says. "I impose my own interests and ideas into the form of a screenplay story. The collaborators I have worked with have endured my often strange fascinations."

Anderson became fascinated, for example, with a big, abandoned asylum in a suburb of Boston where he was living. "I got very intrigued with this place," he says, "its spooky presence, its history." He shared his growing interest with writing partner Steve Gevedon, and they began exploring how to turn this obsession into a horror film. "We decided to check out the asylum and one weekend snuck in and explored. The script for *Session 9* evolved directly out of our experiences — from being spooked by this place and the research that followed."

That research revealed a history of lobotomy operations which inspired several scenes, as did the discovery of unmarked graves of former patients. "We also found audiotapes of conversations between a patient and a doctor, and this became the basis for the session tapes," Anderson adds.

The decaying asylum provided the inspiration for the script and its tag line: "Fear is a place."

From *Session 9*:

Gordon looks out at something as they pass a line of trees.

THEIR P.O.V. — a colossal red brick Victorian Gothic building. Three stories high. Sharp gable slate roofs. Huge iron barred windows. Concrete cornices overgrown with ivy.

Straight out of Poe.

          PHIL (OS)
    Jesus Christ.

EXT. DANVERS MENTAL HOSPITAL — KIRKBRIDE BUILDING — DAY

The TOWN CAR and VAN are parked in front. Everywhere are dead trees, crumbling wooden benches, cracked concrete walkways that criss-cross the grounds —

We creep in towards the main door and a sign tracked there: No Trespassing. Town Of Danvers Public Works Dept.

>   GRIGGS (VO)
> 1871. That's when she went up
> gentlemen. We call her the Kirkbride
> Building after Dr. Thomas Kirkbride.
> He designed all these monsters back
> in the mid-1800s. Pretty simple layout
> really. Consider a giant flying bat —

INT. CONNECTING HALLWAY — SAME

Phil and Gordon, lugging his TOOL BAG, follow
BILL GRIGGS, Danvers Town Engineer, 50s, a jolly
man with a red birthmark on his cheek. He
chuckles as he raises his arms like wings.

>   GRIGGS
> — you got your main staff building
> in the middle — the bat body. And
> slanting off to each side, a crooked
> bat wing. One wing for female
> patients. The other for male. A
> bat!

He flaps his arms. They laugh as they pass a
MEDICAL CART laden with rusty trays. <u>The ceiling
overhead is caving in.</u>

>   PHIL
> More like a dead bat, eh
> Bill?

>   GRIGGS
> Never know it but this whole place's
> listed in the national historic
> register.

107

Finally, if you just can't get an idea — if the pitch within fails you — go back to Go and brainstorm again. Review the rules in Chapter One and go for it. Throw everything into the hopper, as Brad Anderson says. It can be a dazzling process, as Larry Gelbart so vividly captures when he describes brainstorming a sketch for *Caesar's Hour* with Mel Brooks, Mel Tolkin, Neil Simon, Sheldon Keller, Michael Stewart, Gary Belkin, and Sid Caesar himself. "The most vociferous, intimate, biggest group I ever worked with," Gelbart calls them.

"You're at the table and first you start with premises. 'Let's do a domestic sketch. Let's do Sid and his wife, Nanette, Carl and his wife' — I can't remember names — 'and Howie and his wife, Ellen Parker' — I do remember her name. 'Okay, they're what? They bought a car, she wrecked the car. We did that. Did this, did that. Okay, they're going to the theater. Oh, they're going to the theater — that's a good idea! Six people are going to the theater. The three guys work in town, the three ladies are out in the suburbs, and they have to have tuxedos. So, okay, we'll do a series of phone calls with people arranging with each other and then someone changing it and then having sort of a log jam. Let's try it, let's try it.' After pitching the premise, we'd sort of have a rough idea of where it was going, because it's always good to know where you're going."

Indeed. And the best creative compass (or Global Positioning System, for the high-tech) is choosing the right idea at the right time. Then all the scrolling through old ideas or digging for new ones will have been worth the effort, because you'll have a project that's worth the hard work ahead.

SCRIPT PARTNER POINTS

☞ When choosing the right script project, determine first what "right" means to you.

☞ If neither of you already has an idea, brainstorm. Give each other the freedom to really suck, to say something appallingly awful. This process may lead to a great idea.

☞ Explore — and transcend — the appropriate genre or genres for your idea.

☞ Whether the idea comes from you or somebody else (e.g., a producer, a studio), make sure you both connect to the script idea on some level. Make it your own. Otherwise, you're in for a long, painful process.

☞ Run your idea through the "Screenplay Paradox."

☞ Search the trades — in print and/or online — to make sure no one else has sold a similar idea.

☞ Keep notebooks/journals/files of ideas. Or kernels of ideas. Or germs of kernels of ideas. You never know what might sprout.

"Just because you are a character, doesn't mean you have character."

— Winston Wolf (Harvey Keitel), *Pulp Fiction*

CHAPTER 5

CO-CREATING CHARACTER

One day, Billy Crystal called Lowell Ganz & Babaloo Mandel and pitched an idea: three guys from New York go on a fantasy cattle drive.

"Right away, more than anything that's ever been pitched to us, we said, 'That's funny!'" Ganz tells *Written By*. "'If we can't make that funny, then we can't make anything funny.'"

But they didn't start with the jokes about saddle sores or stampedes and other set pieces we laughed at in *City Slickers*. They started, as they always do, with one simple question.

"The first thing we do is we sit down here and we say, 'Who are they?'" Ganz says. "They can't just be generic."

"'Who are they and why are they?'" Mandel adds. "'What's lacking in their lives that this is going to fulfill?'"

Every script is a journey for the main character — or characters — and the audience, too. A magic carpet that lifts them up and takes them for a ride and sets them back down. So Ganz & Mandel ask themselves, "Who are our eyes on this journey?"

It's an excellent question to ask as you embark on creating your own characters. Like Ganz & Mandel, you may create character first. You may start with story. Or you may create them simultaneously. The order doesn't matter; what matters is what works for you. And this may change from project to project.

111

From their first "flurry of creative spark," John Rice & Joe Batteer knew the climax of *Windtalkers* even before they knew their characters. So they decided to approach the material "from a character-first basis." Before outlining the scenes which built toward the inevitable climax, they explored the types of men who would be best "to walk us through the emotional minefield of the film," they say.

Whatever your process, when you create character, you'll be asking these kinds of questions: Who are they? Why are they? Who are our eyes on this journey? What type of men — or women — would be best to walk us through the emotional minefield of our film? And as you explore the possibilities, you'll be bringing your characters into existence.

"With *Session 9*, Steve and I would riff on the kind of characters we wanted," Brad Anderson tells us. "We might toss in character traits, habits, and attributes. We might talk about people we both know who resemble the character. Eventually, it would get to the point where we would be arguing back and forth like, 'This guy would *never* do that!' or 'She wouldn't say that and laugh, she'd say it and cry!' Then you know you're on the right track. The characters are becoming fleshed out."

Think about that. It's amazing enough when a solo writer creates character, but you're co-creating. The two of you are inventing the same character.

"You begin to think along the same lines," Anderson explains. He and writing partner Lyn Vaus certainly got on the same page when co-creating romantic lead Erin Castleton in *Next Stop Wonderland* (about a lonely RN who suffers a string of suitors when her mother places a personal ad without her permission). Anderson & Vaus decided that Erin would randomly choose words from a book to interpret. "Big words like 'faith,' 'determination,' etc., lend her guidance and give her strength."

Writing a crucial scene toward the end of the third act, they had to decide on the word Erin would randomly pick. "She is at a crossroads in the story, in dire need of guidance, so this particular word was extra important," Anderson says. "What could it be? Lyn and I both went home and slept on it, and when we met the next morning, we had both independently come up with the same word: 'linoleum.' It was weird to come up with the same word for one thing, but to both choose a word that was counterpoint to the notion of fate we'd established in the story and therefore funny — this was spooky."

Co-creating characters is a mysterious — and intimate — process. No wonder writers have likened it to having a baby. Okay, we know scripts aren't babies, but now and then we feel a real sense of wonder bordering on parental pride when we look at the characters we've co-created. We marvel: *We did this?* They may be based on people we've met. They may be inspired by characters or actors we admire. They may leap fully formed onto the page. But they all begin with one question, "Who are you?"

Coming up with the answer can be difficult, messy — birth imagery may apply — but it's a remarkable process. When you stop and appreciate that, it almost makes the labor worthwhile. And if the movie gets made, your characters just might support you in your old age.

TO BIO OR NOT TO BIO

Some collaborators start the process of creating character by writing a bio. A synopsis of character traits. Renee Longstreet calls it "character notes."

RENEE: When we do character, when I do it for me, I write a whole page — I can show you fifteen of them. I make a character, and I write everything I can think of: Does she like to play gin rummy? What does she like to eat?

HARRY: How does she dress? How does she talk?

RENEE: What's important to her? What is her background?

Renee shows us some of her character notes for the Lifetime movie, *Mothers and Daughters*:

ANDREA LINDEN — age 44

Community college art history instructor — Portland, OR.

Attractive naturally — not chic... dresses in comfortable clothes, Doesn't pay much attention to appearance, Doesn't exercise much, eats whatever she wants... one of those rare birds that other women envy.

Single mother... widowed at 25; Alex was only 5 years old... raised child on her own. As Regina [her mother] was disinterested/uninvolved... and very unconscious as women of her generation often were. Andrea went the other way somewhat controlling, over sheltering, high expectations.

Parenting and working on career — getting degrees, etc. kept her too busy to involve herself with dating, etc. Likes men, has friendships, but not a focus for her.

Collector — pack rat, but in a good way — has collected rock posters, T-shirts, fad items... hula hoops from the '50s... TV star "art" — (Farrah throw rugs etc.) pop culture items.

TIME LINE — Andrea — born 1955

> College — '73 — 18 years old — REED College on ROTC scholarship.
>
> Pregnant — '75 — they marry, she continues with school.
>
> Alex born 1976 — Andrea is 21 years old.
>
> Mickey in military dies from aneurysm 1979.
>
> Assorted jobs — keeps up her school, a class at a time — stays in Portland...

Committed mother but has other priorities as well.

All the things Regina didn't provide for her, she has provided for Alex and even some for herself — horseback riding lessons... Fills in the missing gaps.

Likes her students.

Misses her daughter — harbors some anger at both daughter, mother and sister.

Jazz buff — has learned to play keyboard as an adult.

And the notes continue for the other characters, too.

"No one ever has to see them," Renee says, "but I have to write them. So when I do the plot, I already know the person. I really do that. I really have to have my characters."

But bios aren't for all writing pairs. When we ask Scott Alexander & Larry Karaszewski if they create bios, Alexander laughs and says, "Nah, that's for serious writers."

We have to be honest: We hate bios. With all due respect to Renee and other fine writers who find bios fruitful, they've never worked for us. When we pile up albeit important detail, it feels, well, like a pile of detail. Inert. Boring. One man's bio is another man's boredom. Interestingly, even Renee's husband and collaborator, Harry, doesn't do bios. So sometimes even within the same team, partners have different approaches to character.

Though we agree we don't care for bios, our respective approaches — which we respect — are also different.

MATT: I think because of my acting background, I prefer a non-verbal method of creating character. I like to gather necessary information and then absorb it, so the way the character speaks and behaves feels organic.

CLAUDIA: I have to write everything down. Pen to paper. Copious notes on my clipboard — which I call "my laptop." It's probably the playwright in me.

We meet in the middle and brainstorm until we see the same characters, hear them, know their backstories, their emotional baggage, their deepest desires, their names.

WHAT'S IN A NAME?

Color us crazy, but for us a great deal. Before we started working together on *Obscenity*, Claudia had created names for the main characters, Sam and Sara, from the Buddhist concept, *samsara*: the vicious cycle of existence arising from ignorance and characterized by suffering. That's what the script is about, ignorance — in this case, homophobia — and the suffering it causes. Though an audience may never know where the names came from, this connected Sam and Sara — and us — to the story's deep subject.

But it took a long time to name our antagonist, the State Attorney. We went through the Tallahassee phonebook (it's bigger than you think) looking for names that fit his character: real charisma and country-boy charm. Finally, we came up with Wayne Mueller. It just *sounded* right (and the person he's loosely based on has the same initials). It made him real for us and helped us relate to a character we found hard to like.

CONNECTING TO CHARACTER

Contrary to conventional wisdom, good characters don't have to be sympathetic. Interesting, yes, but they don't have to be likeable for you — or an audience — to connect.

"Appeal comes from truthful and complex characters," Alexander Payne says in *Scenario*. "I hate when movie people say, 'Your lead character has to be sympathetic,' which for them means 'likeable.' I don't give a shit about 'liking' a lead character. I just want to be interested in him or her. You also have to make the distinction between liking a character as a person and liking the character as a character. I mean, I don't know whether I like Alex in *A Clockwork Orange* or Michael Corleone in *The Godfather* as people, but I adore them as characters. Besides, 'liking' is so subjective anyway. So many American movies of the '80s and early '90s bent over backwards to make their protagonists 'likable' in a completely fraudulent way, and I detested them."

In Payne & Taylor's indie success, *Citizen Ruth*, their title character evolved as they wrote many drafts of the script. A knocked-up, glue-sniffing drifter who plays both sides of the abortion debate, Ruth became less sympathetic, more self-serving, and more active. And as she became less likeable, the writers felt more connected.

"That sort of character, who's like a bull in everyone else's china shop, is really fun," Payne tells *Scenario*. "It's great to have this amoral presence among all these people who think of themselves as supremely moral."

Jim Taylor agrees. "A big issue for us was she was this person who does all these things that are on the surface reprehensible, even repulsive — "

"But she's still an innocent," Payne adds. "You root for her."

It's hard to imagine a character more reprehensible than Larry Flynt. At first, director Milos Forman would not read Alexander & Karaszewski's script, *The People vs. Larry Flynt*.

"My only association with the word 'Flynt' was exploitation," Forman tells *Written By*, "so I thought that some dirty company is asking me to do an exploitation film."

Alexander & Karaszewski were also disgusted with their main character. "We had never met Larry Flynt," adds Karaszewski. "We didn't even want to meet Larry Flynt."

Still, they found a way to connect without changing the truth. "The movie only would work if Larry Flynt were despicable in the film. And so whitewashing him was totally beside the point to us," Alexander explains. "The point of the movie was, 'He's disgusting, and yet he did something important.'"

From *The People vs. Larry Flynt*:

EXT. U.S. SUPREME COURT - DAY

Pandemonium on the Court's steps. JOURNALISTS mob the exiting participants, circling in groups around Larry, Keating, and Falwell.

> REPORTER #1
> Reverend, are you confident that you will win the case?

> REV. FALWELL
> Absolutely! There's no way the Supreme Court will side with a sleaze merchant like Larry Flynt.

> REPORTER #2
> Mr. Keating, why are you here today?

> CHARLES KEATING
> To show my support for those who believe that pornography should be outlawed. This smut is the most dangerous menace to our country today! All decent citizens demand ACTION! They want pornography where it belongs — IN JAIL!

Larry has the biggest crowd.

> REPORTER #3
> Larry, why'd you bother appealing?
> Why didn't you just pay the fine?

> LARRY
> Do you have to ask? We are talking
> about <u>freedom</u>!! Doesn't anybody know
> what that means anymore?! Doesn't
> anybody realize that if I lose, then
> <u>you</u> lose?!

> (his eyes are getting moist)

> I've been accused of hiding behind
> the First Amendment. Well, you're
> damn right I do! 'Cause I am the
> <u>worst</u>! But if the Constitution
> protects a crazy man like me... then
> it'll protect all Americans.

The reporters are silent. Larry is all choked up.

Our title character in *Psycho Bitch*, as you might guess, is not sympathetic. A ball-busting steamroller, she's a bitch in everyone else's china shop. Accidentally summoned by mousy protagonist, Mary DeLucas, at an assertiveness workshop ("Awaken the Bitch Within"), the foul-mouthed Bitch upsets Mary's bucolic existence. Unrelenting and unrepentant, she's a character we love to hate. We wouldn't want to be in the same room with her, and we don't always condone what she does, but we connect — boy, do we — with that kick-ass-I'll-do-what-I-want-and-I-don't-give-a-fuck-what-you-think energy that we all at times would love to unleash. And in the end, The Bitch does something important for Mary by showing her that she needs to love all sides of her self.

Now don't get us wrong: Your characters can be sympathetic. Many of the best characters are. But like privileged/troubled teenager Nicole Oakley (Kirsten Dunst) in *crazy/beautiful*, they're also complex. Matt Manfredi & Phil Hay created a character we could empathize with, but they were careful "not to sugarcoat her." She's edgy, unstable. They were also careful not to romanticize her instability when scripting her romance with Carlos Nuñez (Jay Hernandez).

"I'm sure it's part of growing up — romanticizing these out-of-control women and trying to heal them and fix them," Hay says. "We were trying to write a story where Carlos could go through that and realize that he couldn't fix her. All he could do is be himself. They'd either be together or not. Just holding true to what he believed was right would, in the end, be what would work."

Whether characters are sympathetic or not, their appeal, as Payne says, comes from truth and complexity. Imperfections. Contradictions. That's what makes them compelling and compels us to write them.

It was the complexity of Pauline Parker and Juliet Hulme, not their sensationalized murder case in New Zealand, that compelled Frances Walsh & Peter Jackson to write *Heavenly Creatures*. The story had been told many times — lurid newspaper accounts, a novel, a play, and non-fiction books — but they wanted to tell it again.

"We didn't really think it had been treated that well," Jackson says in *Scenario*. "Nothing that we had read did we particularly like. And also, the other various treatments all seemed to have a specific agenda, which attempted to make political statements about the murder. What interested us was to show these two fifteen-year-old girls with no other agenda than to be as accurate as we possibly could, and to somehow imagine what was going on inside their minds."

The more Walsh & Jackson explored and imagined the girls' hearts and minds, the more they understood and connected to them, in spite of the crime. "Ultimately, there was a bit of Pauline that I could recognize in myself," Jackson says, "which was very useful."

In the end, that's what matters when you create characters: finding a way to sympathize with them on some level, instead of forcing them to be sympathetic.

"I think it's fair to say that both Peter and I felt hugely sympathetic toward Pauline and Juliet," Walsh says, "and we did start to identify and empathize with them, all the while trying to keep in balance the knowledge of this terrible act. It was that dynamic, of really liking them, but feeling abhorrence at what they'd done, that kept the thing alive for so long in our minds, and gave the film inner life."

RESEARCH

To achieve this level of understanding, Walsh & Jackson did extensive research. They read everything written about the murder, as well as the court records and as many excerpts from Pauline's diaries as they could find. And they conducted interviews all over New Zealand with those who knew the girls and their families. "The more we read, the more we talked to people, we gradually began to formulate who these people were," Jackson says.

If you're creating characters from history or recent events, research is essential. It's not only the path to accuracy and understanding, it's the foundation of a fresh script about people audiences may already know. Before Alexander & Karaszewski write their biopics, they also do extensive research, organizing their findings into notebooks that line the walls of their office.

SCOTT: On our shelves, there are about twenty to thirty books about the Marx Brothers. And then up above are these giant notebooks that say "Marx Brothers." What happened was, we read thirty books, and we highlighted every single thing we thought was interesting in those thirty books. And then we hired a guy to come in and retype everything we had highlighted into a computer. Then it all got organized by chapters.

LARRY: There's "Old Relatives," "Lenny and their Mom," "Childhood," "Chico," "Chico's Family," "Chico and Gambling," "Chico and Piano," "Harpo," "Harpo and Piano."

SCOTT: By this point, that represents six months of work, and we haven't even written a word. And we haven't even figured out the structure of the movie at that point.

LARRY: There's two notebooks for the Marx Brothers, there's two for Larry Flynt.

SCOTT: They all have two. I mean, it's thousands and thousands of collated pages. It's just endless.

The research was exhaustive — and exhausting — but it proved invaluable when they were drafting the script. For instance, if they were writing a scene about Groucho and Ruth, they could go to that "chapter" and have the research at their fingertips. Or if they needed a funny line from Groucho, they could search "Groucho Quips."

Even if you're creating fictional characters, research is essential if they're beyond your own experience and expertise. Unless carefully researched, they might not be convincing. Larry & Andy Wachowski, two heterosexual men, had to do their homework before they wrote *Bound*, a lesbian noir.

"We read a lot of lesbian novels and nonfiction books by people like Susie [Sexpert]," Larry tells *Scenario*. "Dorothy Alyson's *Trash* was a really cool book that we liked a lot, and we also looked at some stuff by Pat Califa. We spent a lot of time in gay bookstores."

"Yeah, people thought we were a couple," Andy adds. "It was right around Bulls time, and we both were wearing a lot of Bulls paraphernalia, and one guy complimented us on our matching wardrobe."

Their research gave them the information and insights they needed to create and relate to their main characters, Violet and Corky. "Once we got into the research, the idea of a butch/femme struck us as being another form of dualism, which is something we both believe in: yin-yang, exchange of energy," Andy says. "They're just reflections of each other and a part of a whole. So they're pretty much the same character, even though on the surface they seem very different."

But their Mafia characters, they insist, did not require research. "We're from Chicago," Larry says, laughing. "That's all we needed."

When CBS asked Carolyn Miller and her former husband/collaborator Daryl Warner to develop a story about child abuse, they started with research, visiting a county institution where young victims are placed after being removed from their homes. "They were good enough, they trusted us enough to let us talk to some of the kids," Miller says. "That is totally invaluable because you get to find out what the kids are really feeling and experiencing, and it's not what you might think at all."

She and Warner took a similar approach when asked to adapt a book about an adopted girl who goes in search of her biological parents. They interviewed a child who had gone through a similar experience, so they would have more than just the book to draw from. "We wanted to talk to a real human being," Miller says. "That was one of the things that was important to us. And that was just a revelation."

And research revealed a wealth of character information to Ramsey & Stone before they wrote *Life*. They'd "never been that into research before" — except for reading secondary material and surfing the Internet — but they'd also never been inside a Southern prison. So they traveled to Mississippi's infamous Parchman Farm, segregated until 1972. For a week, they conducted interviews and toured the facility, including death row.

"We got such incredible stories," Stone says. "Character names that you never could have come up with. And both of us being there, we had the experience at the same time — getting back to the theme of collaboration. It wasn't like one person was, 'Oh, I know all about this world, and I'll tell you about it.' We just really got immersed in it together, and from that point on the script took on a real life."

Ramsey adds, "It never would have had that flavor had we not applied ourselves in that way."

It's extremely beneficial to do your research together. Even though Claudia had been a witness for the trial that inspired *Obscenity*, we spent weeks in the Leon County Courthouse transcribing audiotapes of the proceedings. This helped us co-create many of our characters: lawyers, witnesses, jurors, and judge. We heard their voices together. We knew what they said and the way that they said it. This gave them greater authenticity, richness.

You might not have the time or the money to do much research, but both will be well invested. Research makes your job easier in the long run. Even if you have to hire a research assistant, or a studio hires one for you, do as much research as you can.

"You need to do it yourself because you need to know it," Karaszewski insists. "We have assistants occasionally who help organize it, but it's more about them typing up what we've highlighted and putting it together. I find it impossible to say I hired someone to do my research for me. It's sort of like saying I hired someone to take my test. We need to know all this information by heart, what's in those books, just so in the eight months it takes us to write the script, we don't lose it all."

AVOIDING CLICHÉS & STEREOTYPES

It's not just a cautionary note for script partners. Avoiding clichés and stereotypes is an excellent way to create more interesting, less generic characters.

"They can't just be generic," as Lowell Ganz says.

Generic characters are boring — been there, seen that. Generic means general, so generic characters by definition are not specific, detailed. Or complex. Neither are stereotypes. They're your average mom (bland). Your average dad (dull). Your average teen (surly). Your average professor (an egghead). Your average waitress (no egghead). But imagine a waitress who's brilliant, a true mathematical whiz who can glance at a table for ten and total the bill to the penny. We'd pay to see that.

Yes, you'll need functionaries or flat characters in your script — a policeman, a cabbie — but even they deserve fresh detail (unless you're spoofing). It's not just an exercise in good writing, it's an exercise in humanity. "Writing in generalities and typicalities is akin to bigotry — we only see what's alike about people, not what's unique," Janet Burroway says in *Writing Fiction*.

The same, of course, applies to writing scripts.

When you "studiously avoid the clichés and hackneyed characters," as Brad Anderson says, your characters become unique. They begin to take on a life of their own instead of a life defined by generic convention. "With *Next Stop Wonderland*, Lyn and I wanted to make the anti-romantic comedy heroine in Erin, later played by Hope Davis. So, we made her smart (she hates romantic comedies), coordinated (she never trips in her high heels), and vaguely depressed (she sits at home listening to melancholy Brazilian jazz). This beat down the conventions in my mind to good effect."

If ever two minds come in handy, it's during the difficult process of detecting clichés and conventions. They're so ingrained they're often unnoticed. But what you don't see, perhaps your partner will. Clichés and conventions die hard, but they're more likely to do so with two of you beating them down and creating something fresh in their place.

When the Wachowski brothers wrote *Bound*, they broke the bonds of generic convention by gender bending. "We wanted Corky and Violet to be really cool, the way men always are cool in this kind of film," Larry says. "And conversely, we wrote Caesar as the most hysterical character — the most 'feminine,' in that he's always crying, spitting everything out, up and down, emotional." As a result, the characters and their interactions are fresh and, for all the suspense, often funny. Not your ordinary noir fare.

"We don't much like to write ordinary characters," say *Windtalkers* writers, Rice & Batteer. "We like to write damaged characters, characters that need a movie to happen. Characters who in one sense or another needed to have a festering wound ripped open, giving a chance for the bad blood to spill and the real healing to begin."

Hey, they just wrote a war movie. But festering wounds and bad blood aside, Rice & Batteer offer a valuable insight: Write characters who need a movie to happen. Clichéd characters don't, so why write a movie about them?

Or stereotypes, for that matter. Stereotypes are not only boring to see and boring to write, they're a more insidious form of cliché. Writing in generalities and typicalities is akin to bigotry, as Janet Burroway says, but stereotyping is the real thing. It defines a broad group of people by a narrow group of characteristics. It says all women, men, blacks, Hispanics, gays, (fill in the blank) are a particular way. This is dehumanizing.

Being aware and avoiding stereotypes helped Manfredi & Hay when they created Carlos and Nicole for *crazy/beautiful*.

PHIL: Either of them could easily have degenerated into stereotypes. Guy from Boyle Heights going to white high school. It could have easily been rich white girl/guy from bad neighborhood who gets into the wrong kind of stuff. And that didn't really interest us.

MATT: For us it was interesting to do the opposite and hopefully be a little surprising about it. But then it's really not surprising because that's closer to reality.

PHIL: That's closer to reality. At least I think.

MATT: We didn't want to romanticize how great it was to be a poor kid from Boyle Heights.

PHIL: Right, right. Exactly. We didn't want to create some kind of phony anthropological take on it, you know what I mean? And that's hard to balance.

127

We were well aware of the ugly stereotype of strong women when we wrote *Psycho Bitch*. That's one reason we wrote it. We wanted to say that strong does not equal bitchy, and that society, in subtle and not-so-subtle ways, bottles the bitch within all of us. So we turned the stereotype on its head. Most bitches in movies are pissed-off, unhappy, castrating broads with no sense of humor. So we gave The Bitch a great sense of humor. And made her happy as hell to be out of the proverbial bottle.

Once we'd answered the question, "Who are you?" and created The Bitch in broad strokes (pun intended) by avoiding — or embracing — clichés, we faced the difficult work of creating her voice. We knew it could not be generic. It had to be highly specific, surprising, and hip.

CLAUDIA: I can write dialogue that's specific and surprising, but I live in Tallahassee. I'm not exactly fluent in hip.

MATT: So Claudia turned The Bitch over to me. On one hand, that struck me as ironic, considering my first impression of her, but on the other hand, it was also apropos, since it was Claudia's failure to summon "the bitch within" that inspired the script in the first place.

We let our complementary strengths lead the way. Far more in touch with pop culture, Matt created The Bitch's voice and her look. But hip L.A. guy that he is, he still did research.

MATT: The Bitch was a challenge because in addition to being raucous and venomous and spewing some real zingers, she had to be shrewd, a worthy adversary. So I conjured every caustic, psychotic person I'd ever known and upped them to the Nth power. Plus I tuned into that youthful — dare I say, "edgy" — vernacular to give her a pop-culture sensibility. The whip-smart barbs on Joss Whedon's *Buffy the Vampire Slayer* proved inspirational, as did Daniel Waters' *Heathers*.

From *Psycho Bitch*:

INT. MARY'S BEDROOM - MORNING

Blissfully dreaming, Mary snuggles her pillow.
Then —

THRASH METAL MUSIC!

Mary slaps the clock radio. MUSIC STILL BLARES
through the apartment. Mary bolts upright.
What the hell? She throws on her FLORAL PINK
ROBE and creeps toward —

THE KITCHEN

METAL MUSIC. POUNDING and BANGING.

A figure leans into the open refrigerator.

                    MARY
          Bruno, is that — ?

The figure SLAMS the refrigerator door. And
reveals herself. It's Mary, or rather, the
BITCH VERSION OF MARY — ATTITUDE IN BLACK
SPANDEX AND FOUR-INCH FUCK-ME PUMPS.

                    THE BITCH
          Where the fuck's the coffee?

                    MARY
          Augh! What... what? What are you?
          Who are you — ?

The Bitch BITCH SLAPS her.

                    129

                    THE BITCH
          Get a grip! You're pegging the
          freak meter.

                       MARY
          But, you're...me! I don't understand.

                    THE BITCH
               (pointing to Mary's temple)
          Clickety-clickety... the wheel's
          spinning but the hamster's dead.

Mary still looks at her blankly.

                    THE BITCH
               (deadly sweet)
          I'll be very clear. I'm a bitch,
          it's morning, and as you probably
          noticed, we just got our period.
          So I want some coffee right fucking
          now. COMPRENDE?!

The FRONT DOOR OPENS. The landlord, BRUNO, lets
himself in and turns down the stereo.

                    THE BITCH
               (to Bruno)
          Hey! Hey!

                      BRUNO
          Why the hell you got it so loud?

                       130

>   THE BITCH
> Guess what, Missing Link?   I LIKE
> IT LOUD!   It helps me with my morning
> yoga.

She starts a "sun salutation," narrowly missing
his groin and face with her hands.

>   BRUNO
>   (dodging her)
> Augh!   What the hell's the matter
> with you?

>   THE BITCH
>   (backing him out the door)
> The matter is I don't like fat-assed,
> furry-backed fuckwads coming into my
> apartment without my permission!
> Neither, I don't think, would the L.A.
> Apartment Association. So the next time
> you barge in, not only am I gonna have
> your pathetic little job, I'm gonna see
> what else that key fits — like your
> sphincter!

>   BRUNO
> Okay, okay, the rent stays $1,200!

The Bitch SLAMS the door in his face.

> THE BITCH
> (to Mary)
> That robe sucks ass.

The Bitch's "look" evolved from extreme fashions we saw in Los Angeles — sort of ghetto-meets-goth. During one of Claudia's trips to L.A., we were window shopping on Rodeo Drive when we spotted this fabulous trashy-chic, red-leather, leopard-lined jacket. We both knew immediately that this was The Bitch, the kind of thing she'd kill to wear. This helped us form a mutual mental image of her. And take her to the moon, to paraphrase Tarantino. After all, if you take a stereotype far enough, it just might turn into an archetype.

WRITING FOR ACTORS

If you're writing a role for a specific actor, that person or persona will shape and define your character. Woody Allen's persona shaped Alvy Singer in *Annie Hall* and Isaac in *Manhattan*.

And Eddie Murphy was intimately involved with the creation of his character, Ray Gibson, in *Life*. "We had no boundaries, except for what Eddie wanted," Robert Ramsey says. "The whole development process was to service Eddie. Whatever Eddie wants."

"Oddly enough, whatever we came up with, he wanted," Matthew Stone adds.

Above all, Eddie wanted them to avoid stereotypes.

MATTHEW: He would say, "I'm not gonna pick cotton." Because that's what black prisoners did on these Southern plantations. He said, "You know what? I'm not gonna pick cotton because audiences are gonna see me picking cotton, and their assholes are gonna clench so tight, they're not gonna unclench until they leave the theater. We can't have that. They're not gonna laugh." So we said all right. "And no whipping." It became sort of like no slavery imagery, which was cool.

ROBERT: No watermelon.

MATTHEW: And no watermelon.

ROBERT: He called them "niggerisms." He occasionally coached us in how to write for a black person.

MATTHEW: Like what things would push the wrong buttons, even if it was factually accurate. Can't do it. He is so aware of his audience.

ROBERT: He knew what he could pull off and couldn't pull off.

MATTHEW: It's one of Eddie's absolute best performances. It was so fantastic to hear him saying stuff. The guy is a phenomenal improviser. But there were also times when he flat out did the script. I'm not gonna do Eddie Murphy for you, but it sounded just like the way we would say it here, reading it in front of the computer. It was like, "Oh, my God, he's doing it so perfectly!"

From *Life*:

> **RAY**
> You know what, Claude? This whole
> time we've been down here, you've done
> nothing but think about yourself,
> acting like this whole thing is my
> fault. That plan with your cousin,
> did that include me?

A long beat.

                    CLAUDE
No.

                    RAY
Damn right, it didn't. And now you
want to be my friend? Well, let me
tell you something, Claude-my-shit-
don't-stink-Banks. You got a lot to
learn about friendship.

                    CLAUDE
Does that mean I'm in?

                    RAY
I don't think so, Claude. You'd just
slow me down. We'd have to stop every
five minutes so you could polish your
silverware. There's no way around it,
you're soft.

                    CLAUDE
What'd you say?

                    RAY
I said you're soft.

                    CLAUDE
Don't call me that. You know I hate
it when you call me that.

Ray gets in Claude's face and silently mouths
the word — "soft." Claude throws down his hoe
and sinks his fist deep into Ray's gut.

> CLAUDE
> Damn, that felt good. I should have
> done that the first time I met you.

He knees Ray in the face and sends him sprawling
in the dust. Ray touches the blood coming from
his nose and laughs maniacally. Eyes blazing,
he jumps to his feet. Ray tackles Claude,
dragging him to the ground. The two men roll
around, trying to strangle each other.

Even if you're writing your script with no actor attached, it can be helpful to write with an actor in mind. Imagining the same actor, even putting up pictures (at the risk of looking like a celebrity stalker), is a way to make sure you're both seeing and hearing the same character.

"A lot of times we talk about actors," says Scott Alexander, "so we're sort of picturing the same person. We'll just sort of free associate — 'this is a Steve Martin kind of a guy, and this is kind of a Gary Farmer type.'"

Channeling Tommy Lee Jones helped us both conjure a mental image and voice for State Attorney Wayne Mueller. And imagining William Hurt in the role of Sara's love interest, Joe, made his character come alive for us.

Peter Tolan & Billy Crystal use a similar method when they co-create. "We sit down, and we say, 'What about this character? Who do you think this is based on? Who would play this?' Just so we can get an idea of the rhythm of the character."

For *Analyze This*, before Robert De Niro was even attached, Tolan wrote the screenplay with him in mind. "I went to the producers very early on, and I said, 'Unless you get somebody like De Niro to play this part, there's no reason to do this movie. Because the audience has to fully believe that this guy is a mobster. You get somebody else who doesn't have the same weight, you shouldn't even make the movie.' My job was to write the draft that got De Niro. Which I did."

Billy Crystal isn't credited as co-writer, but Tolan gives him a great deal of credit. "That came directly out of Billy sitting there, and us talking about what the character would do. So actually he worked it out pretty well for us." Tolan improvised all the characters with Crystal, who plays De Niro's shrink in the film. "I'd play a part, and we'd go back and forth, and he'd talk in his character's voice, and I would be everybody else. I would be De Niro. And when De Niro did it, he was really fantastic."

You can also channel late, great actors (just don't count on their being available for production). In an interview in the *Los Angeles Times*, Alexander Payne says he and Jim Taylor thought of Giulietta Masina — Federico Fellini's wife and frequent leading lady — while writing *Citizen Ruth*. And for *About Schmidt* — based on a book by Louis Begley and Payne's solo-written script, *The Coward* — they conjured William Holden. So even seeing dead people can bring your characters to life.

COWABUNGA!

Some collaborators like Olivier Ducastel & Jacques Martineau dive right in. They find their characters as they write the script, not before.

136

"At the beginning, we don't know a whole lot except perhaps their approximate age, their job, the city where they live, their family ties," they say. "Once the first draft is written, we can begin the process of refining them. But, in reality, it's not our major preoccupation, because we think the essential thing will be the choice of actor who will finally give real shape to the character. All we can give in a script is a direction — certain personality traits that are shown by actions and a way of speaking. Next, the actor becomes the character, giving it a body and a psychology. Our job during the filming is to determine whether that's consistent."

Even if you have done the most meticulous prep, your characters will very likely evolve as you write. Ruth did as Payne & Taylor wrote several drafts of *Citizen Ruth*. So did Sara in *Obscenity*. Like Ruth, she became more active as we wrote and rewrote. And like Ducastel & Martineau, we discovered her psychology as we went along. After a half-dozen drafts, we'd defined her character arc — how she changes. A reluctant heroine, she arcs from being deeply ambivalent about her brother's sexuality and his defending gay porn to defending gay porn herself. In the process, she finds her place in the community whose standards she has helped to define.

From *Obscenity*:

SARA ON THE STAND

> ### SARA
> I know what happens in Down For the
> Count makes a lot of people uneasy.
> It did me. I wasn't comfortable with
> it in my life or other people's lives
> or the town where I live... But I
> realized what we do with those things

we don't like or understand — we
ignore them or push them away or box
them up and call them obscene... I saw
what that can do, and I don't want to
be part of that. And I don't want
this community to be like that... It
may not be my cup of tea — or yours —
but who we choose to love is nobody
else's business. And I don't think
that's a crime.

ON JOE — Impressed and proud.

> LINDA
> Your witness.

Linda sits. Mueller stands and walks to Sara.

> MUELLER
> That was very touching. Do you need
> a minute?

> SARA
> No, I'm fine.

> MUELLER
> Then tell me, Miss Mitchell, do you
> honestly believe the men in Down For
> the Count love each other?

> SARA
> I don't know. They're actors.

                    MUELLER
              (snapping his fingers)
          Exactly. So isn't it much more
          likely they were committing these
          graphic sex acts not for love, but
          for money?

                    SARA
          I assume they were paid.

                    MUELLER
              (picking up speed)
          So the actors make money, the
          producers make money, the distributors
          make money, and —
              (gestures to chart of adult video
              rentals)
          judging by these numbers, you store
          owners obviously make money. But you
          want this jury to believe it's all
          about love — the highest, purest form
          of human expression?

          Sara looks over at Linda, who telegraphs <u>keep it
          cool</u>.

                    SARA
          I was just trying to say that gay
          men have loving, sexual relationships,
          just like you and me.

                    MUELLER
                (grandstanding)
        You and me? You and me? You don't
        want the people in this courtroom to
        think that you and me are having a
        sexual relationship, do you?

Sara can't resist.

                     SARA
                (with utter disgust)
            No sir, I don't.

The jury CHUCKLES. Linda LAUGHS. Joe GUFFAWS.

The Judge BANGS his gavel. Reestablishes order.

Mueller reattaches his balls.

Your characters may also change to meet the needs of your story, as Annie did when Brickman & Allen wrote *Annie Hall*. "They say that character is action and that all drama comes out of character," Brickman says, "but that's only partly true in this case, because the character of Annie came out of the needs of the plot rather than the other way around."

In their first draft, Annie was a lot like Alvy — from New York, self-absorbed, and appealingly neurotic. In the second draft, however, she became someone whose background was different from his, "which sowed the seeds for a plausible separation later," Brickman explains.

"It was necessary to give the story some forward motion and developmental potential which it really didn't have in the first draft —

an assembly of rather brilliant and funny and original observations, scenes, and jokes, some of which remained but some of which had to go as the love story between Annie and Alvy took predominance over the more cerebral and literary material."

A love story, alas, that comes to an end because, as Alvy says to Annie late in the film, "A relationship, I think, is — is like a shark, you know. It has to constantly move forward or it dies." So does a story. But character provides the potential for that forward motion.

F. Scott Fitzgerald once said that at the highest level, character is story. Okay, he also said in his otherwise perfect novel, *The Great Gatsby*, that the billboard eyes of Doctor T. J. Eckleburg have retinas a yard high when he clearly meant irises, and he essayed in "The Crack-Up" that there are no second acts in American life, which is clearly a crock, but he's more accurate about character and story. They may not be one and the same — at any level — but they are so closely interrelated and dynamically interdependent that they're almost inseparable. So no matter how fully you've co-created your characters, they won't be complete until you've co-created your story.

SCRIPT PARTNER POINTS

👍 Co-create character by asking yourselves, "Who are our eyes on this journey? Who are they and why are they? What's lacking in their lives that this is going to fulfill? Would they like fries with that?" (just kidding on that last one)

👍 Riff on the kinds of characters you want. Toss in character traits, habits, attributes. If it helps, write bios.

👍 Talk about people — or channel actors — you both know who resemble your characters. If it helps, put up photos.

👍 Remember that your characters don't have to be sympathetic or even likeable (Hitler, anyone?). Just make sure they're complex and interesting. And find a way to connect to them, however sympathetic they may or may not be.

👍 Do as must research as possible to deepen your understanding of characters outside your expertise.

👍 Avoid clichés and stereotypes. Or brainstorm what the character cliché would be and do the opposite.

👍 Your characters will evolve as you write. Be open to the new directions they take you.

"We're only interested in one thing, Bart. Can you tell a story? Can you make us laugh? Can you make us cry? Can you make us want to break out in joyous song? Is that more than one thing? Okay!"

— Jack Lipnick (Michael Lerner), *Barton Fink*

CHAPTER 6

CO-CREATING STORY & STRUCTURE

If you've answered Ganz & Mandel's question, "Who are our eyes on this journey?", you'll need to answer a new set of questions: What is the journey? What is the path that your characters — and the audience — will be taking? What is the pattern of human change? In short, what is your story?

For us, brainstorming — or spitballing — the broad strokes of our story is the most exhilarating part of the process. Anything's possible at this point. And all the advantages of collaboration come into play: greater creativity, confidence, energy, excitement, experimentation, feedback, and laughter — especially laughter — whether it's a comedy or a drama. That's why we always create our story in the same room. We bounce the possibilities back and forth: "The Bitch does this." "And then this!" "Yes, and what about this?" And creative miracles happen.

"Out of one weird spitballing idea comes another idea that is also weird but less so," says William Goldman in *Which Lie Did I Tell?* "And then out of some divine blue, someone is shouting, 'No, no, *listen to me*, I've got it — listen to me — ' And there it is, the spine of the story, with all the sludge ripped away. You can see it, and it's going to be such a great movie you wouldn't believe it. At its best, what spitballing does is give you the illusion that just this once you have slain hunger and beaten death."

An appropriate image, because creating a story, exhilarating as it may be, often seems to require superhuman strength. Consequently, for many teams this is the most challenging and critical phase of the process.

"The story is the hardest part of any writing," Renee Longstreet says. "It is. For us, there's no comparison."

Harry agrees, "If the story doesn't work, nothing's going to work."

To get your story "to work," it's important to consider the materials you have to work with.

"A builder who does not know the material he has to work with courts disaster," Lajos Egri states in *The Art of Dramatic Writing* ("the most stimulating and best book on the subject ever written," according to Woody Allen). "In our case," Egri says, "the materials are *character, conflict,* and *premise.*"

CO-CREATING STORY FROM CHARACTER

When Brickman & Allen gave Annie Hall a background different from Alvy Singer's and "sowed the seeds for a plausible separation later," character flowed from the needs of the story. But story also flows from the needs of the character. These needs are external but also internal, conscious but also unconscious: In *Tootsie*, Michael Dorsey needs an acting job, but he also needs to be humanized. With a lot of help from Larry Gelbart ("I had been writing that show for about a year," Gelbart sighs), Dorsey gets both.

In *Psycho Bitch*, Mary needs to be assertive to win Mr. Right, but she needs to learn to accept herself first. In *Obscenity*, Sara needs to defend Sam's video store from criminal obscenity charges, but she also needs to overcome her own prejudice that homosexuality is obscene. By the end of these stories, both conscious and unconscious needs have been met.

144

At the beginning of their story development process, Matt Manfredi & Phil Hay ask themselves how their characters are going to change, how they'll be different by the end. "It's been ingrained in us," Hay says, "and we understand implicitly that characters have to change and something has to happen. The character should have the capacity to learn. Or else that character is going to be pretty flat."

Unless your dramatic purpose is showing a character incapable of growth — such as Ruth Stoops in *Citizen Ruth* or Jim McAllister in *Election*, also written by Alexander Payne & Jim Taylor. "Jim McAllister is constantly, unconsciously, totally creating the crisis in his own life, so that he can break out of it.... He has to break out and do something new. He just changes his life, but he doesn't grow," Payne says in *Scenario*.

McAllister destroys his life as a high school teacher and creates a new life as a museum tour guide, but he ends up in the same place. "That's our cruel joke," Taylor adds.

From *Election:*

```
EXT. STREET - CONTINUOUS

CLOSE ON JIM AGAIN

                    JIM (V.O.)
          ... when I think about my new life and
          the exciting things I'm doing, and I
          think about what her life must be
          like — probably still getting up at
          five in the morning to pursue her
          pathetic ambitions — it just makes
          me sad.
```

The limousine pulls out of the driveway and onto the street.

> JIM (V.O.)
> I mean, where is she really trying to get to anyway? And what is she doing in that limo? Who the hell does she think she is?

Suddenly Jim HURLS his soft drink at the limo, and it BURSTS against the back window. The limo SCREECHES to a halt.

Panicking, Jim turns and RUNS in the opposite direction.

INT. NATURAL HISTORY MUSEUM - HALL OF MINERALS - DAY

Jim stands before a group of SCHOOLCHILDREN, holding a large rock in one hand.

> JIM (V.O.)
> But that's all ancient history now. I've got a whole new life. That's what's great about America — no matter who you are or what you've done, you can always start over.

> JIM
> So would that make this an igneous rock or a sedimentary rock? What's

```
    the difference between igneous and
    sedimentary anyway?

A BLONDE LITTLE GIRL thrusts her hand in the
air, vaguely reminding us of someone. Jim
notices her but continues to search the group.

                    JIM
         Anybody?
```

Characters in character-based franchises like James Bond and Batman usually don't change, either. Their stories spin out of the hero's external need to overcome the villain *du film*. But when the Batchlers develop a script like *Batman Forever*, they also spin story out of their villain's need. "We really think it's important to plot the villain's story," Janet says, "because otherwise you end up with a villain who basically only does what the hero wants him to do, and not what would make sense from the villain's point of view."

This violates what the Longstreets like to call the "inner logic of behavior."

"I find the biggest fault of writers working in our business is they will try to fudge the story to get a plot the way they need it to go," Renee says. "This is the most important lesson I think we can teach — that the inner logic of behavior must be true."

Following your characters' inner logic is an excellent way to generate story. And if you don't, you risk destroying their credibility and developing flaws in your script.

"Big movies have enormous flaws," Renee says, "because they don't do inner logic. They force the story. You can't do it. You have to have *people*."

At the end of the day — and a movie — it's the people we care about.

"It's hard to come up with a plot that is so clever and so intricate that even if the audience doesn't care about the characters, they're fascinated by the plot," Phil Hay says. "I think that almost never happens. And it's not even a laudable goal. As long as we can look at it and say, 'I care about these characters,' then everything's fixable. Everything can be worked out."

CO-CREATING STORY FROM CONFLICT (AND CONNECTION)

Pick up any scriptwriting book, and you'll be bludgeoned by the importance of conflict. "The basis of all drama is conflict," Syd Field says in *Screenplay*. "Without conflict there is no action; without action there is no character; without character there is no story. And without story there is no screenplay."

So if you need to brush up on conflict as the basis of drama, there are numerous books on the subject (many of them by Syd Field). All we can really add here is a fresh way of looking at conflict: It isn't some magic ingredient you must throw into the mix like eye of newt; it's a by-product.

With all due respect to Syd Field *et al.*, the basis of drama is doing (the word "drama" comes from the Greek, *dran*, "to do"). In the best plays and screenplays, someone is trying to do something important. Lysistrata is trying to stop a war; Michael Dorsey is trying to get a job. But it isn't easy. Their will runs into walls on its way. And when will meets obstacle, conflict occurs. Knowing this, you can create all the conflict you want. You can create wonderful conflict-driven stories. But keep in mind that wonderful stories aren't just about conflict.

"*Romeo and Juliet* is the story of the conflict between two families," the novelist Ursula LeGuin has observed, "and its plot involves the conflict of two individuals within those families. Is that all it involves? Isn't *Romeo and Juliet* about something else, and isn't it the something else that makes the otherwise trivial tale of a feud into a tragedy?"

As Claudia explores in *Crafting Short Screenplays That Connect*, that something else is connection. Conflict is not incorrect, it's incomplete. There are moments of change in our lives that are simply not comprehended by conflict. They're connections, human exchanges, "people taking care of each other in small ways of enduring significance," as Stephen Jay Gould says in "Counters and Cable Cars." However fleeting or small, these moments create ties between us. Connection is just as essential as conflict — to our lives and the stories we tell — but it's been essentially overlooked.

The truth is, the best stories have both: conflict *and* connection. "They're complementary forces woven together," Claudia says, "like strands of deoxyribonucleic acid — the double helix of drama."

The development of our story for *Psycho Bitch* is an excellent example of this interweaving. The very title of the script — the first thing we had — suggested conflict. We knew The Bitch would be trouble for our protagonist, whoever she turned out to be.

As the Batchlers acknowledge, story often flows from an antagonist's intentions. "A lot of the times — with the stories we write — the villains start out driving the story, and the hero has to derail the villain's plan," Janet says.

Our hero/protagonist, as we've said, turned out to be the very mousy Mary DeLucas who wants connection: "true love and a really expensive white wedding." But once The Bitch is unbound, there's no way she's letting Mary bind herself — and by extension, The Bitch

— in the holy bondage of marriage. She must derail Mary's plans, and Mary must derail the derailing, put The Bitch back in the proverbial bottle ("Oh, these metaphors!" to borrow a phrase from Larry Gelbart). Which Mary does — at the altar — and goes off on her honeymoon, where she realizes if she wants to live happily ever after — or live at all — the connection she needs in her life is The Bitch.

Psycho Bitch was always intended as a high-concept script, more commercial and plot-driven than indie-minded *Obscenity*. That's not to say that we didn't work hard to create complex characters, but our approach to the material, our way of unlocking the story, was exploring its potential for conflict and connection. As we did, we found the story's major movements and moments.

"A lot of times we look at our scripts that way," says Scott Alexander. "'What are the big scenes?' We tend to be more plot-oriented in terms of the events of our movies. This probably comes from having written *Problem Child*, which at the end of the day ended up being about six or seven big set pieces strung together, and it was called a feature. So sometimes we say, 'What are the big trailer scenes?' That sounds sort of ridiculous, but we can be writing *Larry Flynt* and saying, 'Do we have the trailer moments? Do we have big moments that sort of define the movie?'"

CO-CREATING STORY FROM PREMISE

Another method of defining your movie is determining what your script is really *about*. What is its premise? Lajos Egri lists different words that mean the same thing — "theme, root idea, central idea, goal, aim, driving force, subject, purpose, plan, plot, basic emotion" — but he prefers premise "because it contains all the elements the other words try to express and because it is less subject to misinterpretation."

Simply put, premise is the proposition that your story will prove. Egri offers examples from Shakespeare: "Great love defies even death" (*Romeo and Juliet*); "Blind trust leads to destruction" (*King Lear*); "Ruthless ambition leads to its own destruction" (*Macbeth*). These elegant propositions contain three elements "essential to a good play": character (loving, blindly trusting, ruthlessly ambitious); conflict (defying, leading to); and ending (death, destruction).

Once you know your premise, you know your story's essence, its purpose, what you're trying to say — powerful mojo when you're creating story. We recommend that you write it down because you can easily lose sight of it in the often-chaotic development process.

Working as a collaborative team helps us keep premise in mind. When we get stuck during story discussions, one of us will say to the other, "What's this friggin' story *about?*" If this tough question is followed by blank stares and embarrassing silence, we brainstorm until we find the answer. Articulating premise is never easy, and we *never* come up with anything as elegant as Egri's examples, but once we've stated our premise, we're that much closer to creating our story.

Developing *Psycho Bitch*, we looked to premises of favorite comedies for inspiration: "A moment of courage can change the course of a person's life" (*Back to the Future*); "An unprejudiced heart can change the course of life in the valley" (*Babe*); "A man becomes a better man by (literally) walking in the shoes of a woman" (*Tootsie*). We decided that our premise would be: "You must learn to love yourself — all sides of yourself — before you can find true love." This gave us Mary's character (mousy), her conflict (awakening and accepting The Bitch), and our story's ending (true love and a very Vegas wedding).

Ultimately, we create our stories by exploring all three of the tools we have to work with — character, conflict/connection, and premise. We bounce from one to the other — creative pinball — until we've developed a clear, complex story. But we explore other aspects of story as well. Setting, for example. Initially, we set *Psycho Bitch* in the corporate world. For three weeks in Florida, we went down this story path, but Matt felt increasingly uneasy.

MATT: We were deep into the story development process, and time was running out because I had to head back to L.A. in a week, but I couldn't muster enthusiasm for the material. Finally, I slumped in my chair on Claudia's porch and groaned, "It's not funny. None of it. It's boring."

CLAUDIA: It was a terrible moment for us. I couldn't stand the thought of scrapping the work that we'd done, and I was furious at Matt for suggesting we should. Because he was right. The story just wasn't funny.

Fortunately, Claudia stifled the impulse to slap Matt silly — or knock Pinocchio off the computer. Both little guys survived unscathed. So did our script idea. We set aside the work that we'd done and tried to figure out why the story wasn't working. We realized that we didn't give a shit about the corporate world. The setting was wrong for the story. We were kicking around other possible settings when we remembered our walks down Rodeo Drive. Why not set Psycho Bitch in a bridal shop in Beverly Hills? Yes! Think of the repeat customers! Mary could hide in Alterations — hemming and hawing! Things started to click, and by the time Matt returned to L.A., we'd worked out our Bitch-in-the-Bridal-Shop story.

There's no predicting what will bring a story to life. For the brothers Alfonso & Carlos Cuarón, the story for their acclaimed road trip movie, *Y Tu Mamá También* (their response to "a lot of crappy teen movies," Alfonso tells IFC Films), took off when they placed their three main characters in an erotic context.

"By adding a little sex and a little fun, the entire project came alive," Carlos says.

And they took their story up another level when, influenced by French New Wave techniques, they added a third-person narrator who would provide layers of context in voice-over.

"The films I did before had a very subjective point of view," Alfonso says. "Everything was seen through the eyes of the main character. In *Y Tu Mamá También*, I wanted to create an objective and reflective distance."

Sex and voice-over. That's a whole lot fresher than sex and violence.

"THE REAL CRAFT OF SCREENWRITING"

Shrek screenwriters Ted Elliott & Terry Rossio did most of their early writing at a CoCo's coffee shop in Orange County. "Big table, no distractions, pretty waitresses refilling our coffee — okay, minimal distractions — all for about five bucks," Elliott says. They sat across from each other, writing in long hand, passing a single pad of paper back and forth.

"While we worked from an outline, we hadn't yet discovered the importance of really nailing the structure before we wrote FADE IN," he says, "so there was a lot of tearing out and crumpling up and staring blankly at each other, wondering how we're going to pay for the coffee on the miserable salaries from our real, full-time jobs."

Gradually they discovered what Elliot calls "the real craft of screenwriting: structure." They started outlining until they got it right, until they set the major story moments, and sometimes until they figured out the structure of individual scenes. "We can now divide up the scenes and sequences and work independently," Elliott says. "Sometimes we're in the same room, on separate computers, sometimes not."

"SCREENPLAYS ARE STRUCTURE," shouts William Goldman in *Adventures in the Screen Trade*. "The essential opening labor a screenwriter must execute is, of course, deciding what the proper structure should be for the particular screenplay you are writing." This, he believes, is "the single most important lesson to be learned about writing for films....Yes, nifty dialog helps one hell of a lot; sure, it's nice if you can bring your characters to life. But you can have terrific characters spouting just swell talk to each other, and if the structure is unsound, forget it."

In *The Screenwriter's Workbook*, Syd Field seconds Goldman. "Structure is the most important element in the screenplay. It is the force that holds everything together; it is the skeleton, the spine, the foundation."

While Goldman is careful to say that your first job is deciding what "the proper structure should be for the particular script you are writing," and describes in great detail his own struggle to find the right one for *Butch Cassidy and the Sundance Kid*, Field tells you flat out what it should be: a strict three-act structure he calls "a paradigm." If you've spent any time on the planet Hollywood, you can probably recite it in your sleep: Act One, setup, thirty pages, then Plot Point I throws the story into Act Two, confrontation, sixty pages, then Plot Point II throws the story into Act Three, resolution, thirty pages.

In Hollywood, first and third acts have gotten shorter, especially in comedies, and we've been down the Green Mile of more than a few three-hour-plus movies, but for the most part, Syd Field remains the industry standard. Many have complained that Field's ubiquitous paradigm has spawned generations of predictable screen stories. They're right, it has. Far too often stories are forced into it whether

154

they fit or not — the narrative equivalent of Cinderella's sisters cramming their feet into the glass slipper. But this has more to do with the write-by-number nature of Field's paradigm and the assembly-line mentality of Hollywood than it does with the three-act structure itself.

"Hollywood is schizophrenic because it is a corporate culture that deals in an art form," Marshall Brickman explains. "Risk is not encouraged, it is frowned upon. If you have a toaster that works and sells, you do try and make as many of them as you can and keep them on the shelves. If you have a formula for a kind of film, or enough elements of a formula (i.e., star) to feel comfortable, then you try and go with that. It's risk vs. investment strategy, and the prudent investment strategy has pretty much won, the irony being that after a while the stuff gets so repetitive and predictable and lacking in originality or personality that what happens is, well, look at the movie section of your local paper and see how many 'mainstream' movies you really want to go and see. Thank God for independent cinema and — God help me — Showtime, HBO, Lifetime, A&E....But don't get me started."

Brickman assures us, however, that there's nothing wrong with the three-act structure per se. "The three-act structure is not a 'formula' any more than a rectangular canvas is a formula for a painting. Just a very general framework into which you can put your ideas."

It's ancient as Aristotle, who said in his *Poetics* that "tragedy is an imitation of an action which is complete and whole," adding that, "'Whole' is that which has beginning, middle, and end."

Movies might be more original and less predictable if we replaced Syd Field's strict paradigm with Aristotle's more organic guidelines. And some of the more original movies like *Citizen Ruth*

155

seem to be the result of writers doing just that. "We never tried to cram this story into some kind of a Syd Field notion of how a script should be, how a story should be told," Jim Taylor says in *Scenario*. "It had more to do with whether it felt right or not: that was really our only criterion — that it had some shape to it, however small."

But Scott Alexander & Larry Karaszewski acknowledge the importance of using the more traditional Hollywood structure, especially when creating less traditional stories.

SCOTT: You can take Syd Field's paradigm and shove it down our *Larry Flynt* script, and it works. You can say, page 10, he starts *Hustler*. Page 30, he gets arrested for the first time. Page 60, he gets shot and paralyzed and goes crazy. Page 90, he gets locked in the loony bin, and Jerry Falwell sues him, and Larry decides to go to the Supreme Court. Climax of the screenplay. And it fits into that formula. Now it's a completely ridiculous movie! I mean, it's dealing with a lot of strange characters and issues you don't normally see in a Hollywood star-driven production. But it has a normal form.

LARRY: We always joke that our form is very studio-friendly; it's our content that tends to be odd. Usually, when you see a more independent kind of movie, the form is odd and the content is odd. We manage to take this strange subject matter you don't usually see in a movie, and by putting it into that Hollywood form — I think that's the reason why our movies have been made by studios instead of independently — they feel comfortable. They do look at that structure.

Because they're "really trying to tell a normal movie," Alexander & Karaszewski look for their structure first. The characters in their biopics are already essentially established, so the challenge is deciding what *part* of that person's life they will tell, rather than telling a ponderous, all-encompassing "cradle-to-the-grave" story.

LARRY: We try and look for what's important. We try and figure out what's the happy ending. I think a lot of biographies aren't successful because they end with the guy dying. *Man on the Moon* ended with the guy dying, but —

SCOTT: But that was the joke.

LARRY: We say, "How do we take this person's life and go out on a victory?" It doesn't have to be a traditional kind of a victory. It just has to be, "What was the success for themselves?" Like Ed Wood — his greatest success is that he made the worst movie of all time. With Larry Flynt, it was that he beat Jerry Falwell in the Supreme Court. With Andy Kaufman, it happened to be his death. His death was his greatest work of art.

By answering those questions — "What part of the whole story are we telling?" and "What events are significant?" — they find their structure.

These are important questions, too, for fictional stories. Matt Manfredi & Phil Hay carefully consider "point of attack" when they're creating the foundation for a script. "It's always in terms of, 'Why are we starting the story here?'" Manfredi says. "'Why didn't this happen yesterday? Why didn't this happen tomorrow? Why is this movie occurring right now? Why are we coming into the story at the point we're coming in at?'"

They acknowledge the importance of structure in their writing ("the first thing after character is structure," Hay says), but they don't follow Field's paradigm as closely as Alexander & Karaszewski. When scripting *crazy/beautiful*, they had firm ideas of what the acts were, but for them and director John Stockwell, it wasn't the kind of movie that falls into the paradigm of turning points punctuated by big events.

157

"The story couldn't exist as a — *Bam!* First act ends! *Bam!* Here's the end of the second act!" Hay says.

"I think it's a movie that takes a little more time getting to know its characters," Manfredi adds, "getting to know this world and setting the tone. I think if you took out ten minutes in the beginning, it might fall into a very conventional structure, but I think it would lose something in that, too. It would seem a little rushed."

BREAKING THE STORY

Whether you've chosen to work in the three-act structure or not (most TV writers don't), you'll be breaking your story, as Andrew Reich & Ted Cohen call it. On *Friends*, the entire room full of writers — "the room" — participates in this process.

Reich explains, "You start out, 'Okay, Monica and Chandler just got married. What's their story going to be this week?' And we come up with that. 'Okay, we've got a Monica/Chandler story. Now we've got the other four. Let's try and do a Joey/Phoebe story.' You have three stories, each broken into scenes, put into order. That episode is now broken. There's an outline, a rough outline. The outline Ted and I write if we're sent off to write an episode will be much more detailed. It'll have much more — like the shape of the scenes, whatever. But episodes being broken means that."

Doing this for your own story gives you the significant moments (often called "action beats") in the order they occur. But creating this order is rarely an orderly process.

"A lot of times it is about looking backwards," Karaszewski says. "A lot of times it's knowing how you're going to end the movie and then figuring out how you're going to get there."

Alexander adds, "With *Man on the Moon*, we always knew the third act was going to be Andy gets sick; people think it's a joke. And he dies; people aren't sure. Closing scene — Tony Clifton sings the song; now the audience isn't sure. We always knew that's how we were getting out."

John Rice & Joe Batteer knew the ending of *Windtalkers* before they knew the rest of their story or structure. "In essence," they say, "the process of writing was flipped a bit on its ear by having an ending, a powerful ending that we considered almost a gift, before we had a beginning." They worked backwards, creating action beats that would lead to the already-known climax of each main character's story. For the bodyguard, Joe Enders (Nicholas Cage), this would be the moment he must decide whether or not to take the life of the Code Talker. And for the Navajo, Ben Yahzee (Adam Beach), it would be the moment when he realizes the truth behind the bodyguard's edict: to protect the Code at all costs. "These structural pylons were the only ones we pounded into place," Rice & Batteer say, "and they proved their salt in endless re-approaches to the material. They never changed. That gave us clarity and focus."

That's the greatest benefit of structure — clarity and focus through the arduous process of drafting and re-drafting — particularly when you're collaborating with a partner, not to mention the parade of collaborators you'll have to work with if your script goes into production. Structure keeps you on the same page.

We craft a meticulous structure before we begin writing. By working backward, forward, or zig-zagging, however the Muse happens to lead us, we find our story's major structural pylons: the inciting incident, turning points, climax, and resolution. It's comforting to have these in place. As Claudia's friend, Mark Spragg (*Everything That Rises*), says, "Before I swim across a big lake, I want to know where the big rocks are."

Next we break the three acts down into eight to ten-page sequences ("chapters," we call them, and we called them that before

159

DVDs). Each has its own dramatic arc and event that throws the story into the next sequence. Last, we decide what scenes we need in each sequence, often blocking out the beats of dialogue for each scene. This gives us a map of our movie and keeps what we call "card-house questions" from coming up as we write — questions about some flaw in character, story, or structure that can cause the whole script to come crashing down. A heap of dusty defeat at our feet — it ain't pretty.

As we co-create this design, our complementary strengths come into play. Claudia is more adept at developing the deep structure, the deeper patterns of connection and disconnection. Matt is stronger at developing the surface structure like acts and plot points. (She's Freudian, he's Fieldian! Just kidding.) Together, we make sure the beats are covered.

Marshall Brickman bristles at the suggestion that he's stronger on structure than Woody Allen. "Somebody decided I was the structure man, but then this person disappeared or died or was killed, so I have never had the chance to confront him on this. *All* you have to do is look at either Woody Allen's movies without me or mine without him to see that probably each of us can do either thing." But it was Brickman's eye for structure that spotted a hole in Act Three of *Manhattan*. There was no confrontation between Isaac/Ike (Woody Allen) and Yale (Michael Murphy) who both are in love with Mary (Diane Keaton).

Brickman urged Allen to include such a scene. "I felt there was some dramatic or comic result to be gained from a showdown between the two characters." Allen tried a scene where Yale and Isaac confront each other over the phone, but when he and Brickman screened the film, they agreed that the confrontation had to happen face to face. "So we did it," Brickman says, "and it stayed in. Whether the picture would have been better, worse, or exactly the same with its omission we'll never know."

160

From *Manhattan*:

>   YALE
> I wanted to tell you about it. I
> knew it was gonna upset you. I —
> uh, uh... we had a few innocent
> meetings.
>
>   IKE
> A few?! She said one! You guys, you
> should get your story straight, you
> know. Don't-don't you rehearse?
>
>   YALE
> We met twice for coffee.
>
>   IKE
> Hey, come off it. She doesn't drink
> coffee. What'd you do, meet for
> Sanka? That's not too romantic. You
> know, that's a little on the geriatric
> side.
>
>   YALE
> Well, I'm not a saint, okay?
>
>   IKE
>   (Gesturing, almost hitting
>   the skeleton)
> But you — but you're too easy on
> yourself, don't you see that?! You
> know, you... you — that's your
> problem, that's your whole problem.

> You-you rationalize everything. You're
> not honest with yourself. You talk
> about... you wanna — you wanna write a
> book, but — but, in the end, you'd
> rather buy the Porsche, you know, or
> you cheat a little bit on Emily, and
> you play around the truth a little
> with me, and — and the next thing you
> know, you're in front of a Senate
> committee and you're naming names!
> You're informing on your friends!

>   YALE
>   (Reacting)
> You are so self-righteous, you know.
> I mean, we're just people, we're just
> human beings, you know. You think
> you're God!

>   IKE
> I-I gotta model myself after someone!

Nick Kazan is quick to concede that Robin Swicord is the structure man, er, woman in their collaboration. "Robin is really quite structurally brilliant, I think," Kazan says. "She seems to know intuitively exactly where actions should fall to set up other actions, how the subplot should work, where this should come in, where that scene should come in, if this action is falling late or early. I don't know. I'm just fumbling through."

Ideally, your complementary strengths will help you create a structure that will keep you from fumbling through and your script from collapsing when you draft or, worse, when your script goes before the cameras. Unfortunately, this isn't always the case, according to Jim Taylor. "Often movies go into pre-production before the script is ready, with the misguided idea that the script will somehow miraculously get 'fixed' before shooting, which almost never happens," he tells us.

Peter Tolan & Harold Ramis didn't realize the structural problems of their screenplay for *Bedazzled* until after the film was finished. And no one was more surprised than they were, since it was a "tremendously easy movie to write," Tolan says. "I told Harold that it would be a monstrous, huge, huge hit."

The scripting went well; the shooting went well. Everything was going *too* well. Tolan began to suspect something bad was going to happen. He was right. "Once we actually got it up and were putting it together, we realized the real problem — it's not an involving movie. Because at a certain point, the audience is going, 'Okay, I understand how this works — he gets a dream, and it gets screwed up.' So the audience is out of the movie trying to figure out how it's going to get screwed up, and they're second-guessing it. So people never really connected to it in the way, I guess, we wanted. So in some ways, it turned out to be a dumb movie with a real big trap."

The trap was predictability — the result, in part, of an episodic structure. Kazan & Swicord had to avoid this structural pitfall when adapting Roald Dahl's *Matilda*. "At the end of every chapter, Matilda basically vanquishes one villain after another," Kazan says. "She humiliates her mother, and she humiliates her father. We had to structure it so that, although we had some of those humiliations at the end of each one, there was an answering threat from the authorities, saying, 'You got me this time, but now I'm really going to make your life miserable.' We had to give the appearance of escalation so that it wouldn't feel episodic."

163

Episodic structures, of course, don't have a monopoly on predictability. Heaven knows we've sat in movie theaters guessing how — and when — the plot would work out. And this isn't just true of bad movies. Sometimes even a vibrant, original film like *Y Tu Mamá También* telegraphs its own ending (plant a lab test in Act One...). Perhaps that's why some teams prefer to write their script without working everything out and let the structure emerge as they go.

COWABUNGA! II

When they wrote *Drôle de Félix* (*Adventures of Felix*), Olivier Ducastel & Jacques Martineau had only a "very vague" structure before they started drafting. "We just discussed it, and then Jacques wrote a first version of the script," they say. "In short, we think that to construct our stories, we do it in the scriptwriting. By that we mean the first building block is the drafted script. It's the only way we've found to do it. All the rest doesn't interest us."

Brother teams Joel & Ethan Coen and Peter & Bobby Farrelly will also start drafting without a structural safety net. Sometimes they don't even know where their story is going. This makes Goldman crazy. "The Coens drive me nuts a lot of the time. Everything I feel you must do, they don't," he says in *Which Lie Did I Tell?* "Example: I cannot explain too often how crucial it is for you to know your story before you start. For me, if I don' t know how a story is going to end, I don't know how to enter each individual scene preceding."

But that's not how the Coen brothers work. "We type scene A without knowing what scene B is going to be," Ethan tells Goldman, "or for that matter, we type scene R without knowing what scene S is going to be.... Because we're doing our own thing, we can get stuck and literally grind to a halt and put it aside for a year even."

The Farrelly brothers have an equally unusual way of approaching their material, purposely writing themselves into a corner. "We think if we can go into a corner where there's no way out," Peter says, "and then we take a week or a few days or a month even, and find a reasonable way out without making it absurd, then nobody in the audience is going to sit there and get it within a minute and get ahead of us."

Don't get us wrong: Goldman's a big fan of staying ahead of the audience, he just uses a well-designed structure to do it. "The audience is so quick, so smart, they grasp things immediately," he says in *Adventures in the Screen Trade*, "and if you give them what they expect, if they reach the destination ahead of you, it's not easy for them to find it in their hearts to forgive you."

OUTLINES AND TREATMENTS AND CARDS — OH MY!

"We used to write into the darkness," Matthew Stone says, "and that didn't really work as efficiently. I mean, it would work, but it would be many, many drafts later that it would work."

So he and Robert Ramsey started outlining. Likewise for Manfredi & Hay. "There have been times when we've worked without an outline and just started working and going," Manfredi says.

"It's been a long time since we've done that," adds Hay.

Like Rossio & Elliot discovering the "real craft of screenwriting," many teams have discovered the advantages of co-creating an outline, especially if they're planning to split up the scenes, acts, or drafts. "We worked out every scene of *crazy/beautiful* in excruciating detail," Hay says, "the beats of the scene, in outline form, then we found that it was easier to take separate scenes and go away and write them."

Usually when they outline, they create a breakdown that Manfredi describes as "more like a term paper outline. It's a little bit more like a narrative with bullet points — Act One and bullet. But each scene has a bullet, and the scenes that are obvious to us are just little sketches." The scenes don't include sluglines (e.g., EXT. HIGH SCHOOL - DAY) at this point but may contain bits of dialogue for a specific beat or comedic moment.

Ramsey & Stone dislike outlining, but they consider it a necessary evil.

ROBERT: It's really an unpleasant part of the process. Writing seems so much more fun than outlining. Outlining is ghastly for us, actually.

MATTHEW: It never gets you all the way where you need to go, but it gives you that light at the end of the tunnel. I like to sit here with my little piece of paper that has the outline on it and start crossing things off when we're done with them.

ROBERT: Matt charts our progress because I've got the keyboard in front of me. He has the notes, and he's always keeping track of where we've been and where we're going.

How closely they keep track of where they're going depends upon the project. "The last two things we did were book adaptations, and we didn't have to outline them so extensively," Stone says. "We would write sort of beat sheets of structural changes." For other projects, they've created detailed outlines including descriptions of scenes. Sometimes they include sluglines and/or bits of dialogue; sometimes they don't. "It varies," Stone says.

The process varies, too, for Payne & Taylor. They wrote only the barest outline for *Citizen Ruth* before they started drafting because they knew "basically where we wanted it to end up," Jim Taylor says.

For *Election*, which had a very strong story that jumped around in time quite a bit, "we had to use some kind of outline to try and get it under control. But once we had decided what the basic structure would be, we put the outline away and rarely referred to it." For *About Schmidt*, they used no outline at all. "The movie doesn't have much narrative," Taylor says, "so we didn't do any outlining and just went where the character took us — as long as he was headed where we wanted him to go, which was Denver. He made it there fine, so I guess we succeeded."

Whether you like outlining or not, it's an invaluable tool when you work on assignment. "Once you're working for someone, if they have an outline in front of them and everyone agrees with the outline, there are no surprises," Matt Manfredi explains. "Everyone knows what they're getting. And it seems to make everyone a lot more comfortable and prepared for what the script is going to be. It could be a better script that they get, but if it's not what they expect, it could be a problem."

"Everyone has to write an outline," Reich says about *Friends*.

"Because it goes into the production people who then use it for costuming and set design and all that kind of stuff," Cohen adds. "It gives them a lead on getting stuff done before the script is done."

After meeting and discussing their thoughts about *Life* with Eddie Murphy, Ramsey & Stone typed up an eighteen-page outline/treatment, with descriptions of scenes and bits of dialogue, to show Murphy and producer Brian Grazer. "It was almost like a short story," Ramsey says.

"We were wondering if we were gonna screw ourselves by actually writing this detailed treatment," Stone adds, "and then they'd say, 'Wait a second, this isn't what — ' You are always taking that chance. But we needed it. We needed it as a communicative tool. It

167

ended up being something Eddie signed on to just based on the treatment."

The one tool Ramsey & Stone don't need or use is the note card.

ROBERT: We never use cards.

MATTHEW: We did try once doing cards; that just didn't work for us because they can move around too easily. Larry and Scott do cards.

ROBERT: Those guys went to USC, though, so they actually learned how to do what they do.

It's true: Larry Karaszewski & Scott Alexander *do* use cards. Lots and lots of cards. When they're starting a project, anything and everything that sounds like a scene gets jotted down on a card. "The biopics have sort of corrupted this process," Alexander says, "because in school I was taught that you want to have thirty-five to forty-five cards on the bulletin board, and *The Marx Brothers* here has approximately 1,200 cards."

1,200? No, no, they're exaggerating. But there is a butt-load of cards on their board. "When you look at note cards, you get a real feel for how the movie is flowing," says Karaszewski, "as opposed to a treatment when you're just sort of reading a big block of words."

They add and subtract cards, move them around, sometimes combining two or more into one. "It's just playing in the sandbox for a while," says Alexander. Often they'll spend as much time working with the cards as they spend drafting the script. "We try to go into it — but we're kidding ourselves — that we know the first, second, and third acts. Particularly, we know what the end of the first act is and what the end of the second act is, so as you're looking at the cards you can just be visualizing the structure of the movie. You can see if the movie is pacing itself correctly. You can see if the first act looks top-heavy."

They sometimes color code the cards for structural purposes, as they did while working on their adaptation of Michael Paterniti's off-beat book, *Driving Mr. Albert: A Trip Across America with Einstein's Brain*. "It's one of the few times we've had a script that has different time periods on a parallel track," Karaszewski says. "And so for each one of those stories we have different color-coded cards, so that allows us to see, 'Oh, my God, we're doing four flashbacks in a row; that might be a mistake.'"

They even put colored dots on cards which correspond to scenes featuring certain characters. "We did that with *The Marx Brothers* occasionally with their father," Alexander says, "where we noticed that he's really a charming character at the beginning of the movie, and then he was just really dropping out, basically because their mother drove the act — their mother ran their lives for many, many years. So we would look at the cards and say, 'Is there a way, every seven or eight cards, to at least have him make a little guest appearance?'"

Using note cards has also been beneficial for Michael Colleary & Mike Werb (*Face/Off*; story, *Lara Croft: Tomb Raider*). "We start by talking for several days about how we see the story, the characters, and the overall shape of the plot, taking notes along the way," Colleary tells the Writers Guild. "Then we scene-card. We'll do a card for every scene, beginning to end, sometimes in detail and sometimes a few words to describe a whole sequence ('museum heist'). Deadline permitting, we'll try to do a detailed step-outline from the cards, filling in more detail as we go. The outline is complete when we know what will happen in every scene."

We've used note cards as well; in fact, we've tried most of the techniques listed above. Part of the evolution of our process has been figuring out which visual tools help us most. For *Obscenity*, we broke the story into acts on Matt's computer, indicating what happens in every scene. But it wasn't the best method for us because huddling over the same computer was awkward — and a ticketable violation of personal space. So for our next script (which shall remain nameless) we tried the scene-card approach. But we soon realized that because we shifted work spaces, this technique was a little unwieldy.

During one work session, the cards snaked all the way across the porch at Claudia's farm, and we "walked the movie," reading and rearranging the scenes. Claudia loves this kind of flexibility, but it makes Matt nervous. Instead of concentrating on the order and emotional flow of the scenes, he kept watching his step and dancing around the cards (and he's a pretty good dancer), which didn't help Claudia concentrate, either. For Matt, like Matthew Stone, the cards moved too easily. They were too high-maintenance.

But for *Psycho Bitch*, because our story development time was so tight, we tried cards again. Matt suggested we keep them in a stack, which we did, shifting the scenes until the order was right. Then he typed a detailed scene-by-scene outline to take back to L.A.

But the method that has helped us the most is what we jokingly call "going horizontal" (now, now, it's not what you think). Once we've created our characters, story, and structure, we lay out our screenplay on paper — *big* paper — a long sheet of butcher paper or several 8 1/2" x 11" sheets taped together. We draw horizontal lines from left to right for the main story and each of our sub-stories, labeling them accordingly: A, B, C, and so forth.

Along each story line, we make vertical marks for major structural beats. We indicate where each sequence begins and ends, titling each so we know its context ("jury selection"), then we fill in the scenes/action beats for each story. This allows us to see how they interweave and how each sub-story intersects the main story.

Last, we make a small Post-it® note for every scene in the movie and put these in order from left to right across the top of the paper. This long row of Post-its lets us read the movie from beginning to end and make sure it's flowing. If it isn't, we make changes.

When we're convinced that our overall structure is sound, and the order and emotional flow of our scenes is correct, we lock it by taping the Post-it notes to the top of the paper. Now it's portable. We can roll it up and take it to the beach or the farm or Los Angeles or Tallahassee, wherever we're working. And we do. We'd be lost without it. We admit it's an insanely elaborate (okay, anal) visual tool, but for us it's an invaluable blueprint, one we refer to again and again as we draft and re-draft our script.

SCRIPT PARTNER POINTS

⊕ Co-create story by asking yourselves, "What's the journey?" Brainstorm ("spitball") your story in broad strokes. Anything goes at this point. Don't forget: Give each other permission to suck.

⊕ Let story flow from your protagonist's needs — internal and external, conscious and unconscious. Decide how your main character will change, or if he or she is incapable of change.

⊕ Try spinning story out of your antagonist's intentions (villains are people, too).

⊕ Avoid plot holes and character inconsistencies by following your characters' "inner logic of behavior."

⊕ Find your story's major movements and moments by exploring the patterns of conflict and connection between your characters.

⊕ Decide what your story is really *about* — what you're trying to say, what proposition the script will prove — and craft it into a premise. Then write it down. If you don't, believe it or not, you may forget it.

⊕ Work backwards, forwards, sideways, however the Muse directs you, to find your story's "structural pylons": inciting incident, turning points, climax, and resolution. There can be real comfort in knowing your structure before you start drafting your script, especially if you're new to the process.

⊕ Experiment with outlines, treatments, and note cards to find the most effective method to co-create your story and structure and to communicate it to others.

"What a feeling having you inside my head....Indescribable — you knew just when to feed me the next thing, just a split second before I needed it. There was a rhythm we got into, like great sex."

— Tom Grunick (William Hurt), *Broadcast News*

CHAPTER 7

CO-DRAFTING THE SCRIPT

Of all the questions people ask us about the collaborative process — and there are many — the most frequent one is, "How do you actually *write it* together?" They can see how two or more writers brainstorm and create character, story, and structure, but how two or more writers put one script on paper is as perplexing as the ending of *Vanilla Sky*.

And no wonder. It's the most intimate part of the process, a shift from foreplay to performance, to borrow Marshall Brickman's marriage-bedroom metaphor: "You never really know what's going on unless you're there in the room."

If you haven't co-drafted a script, it may be perplexing to you, too. Who does what? How do you decide? And how *do* you actually write it together? Do you co-write every word? Divide up the scenes? Divide up the drafts? We — and every team we've talked to — have faced the same questions. And the answers differ for each writing pair and sometimes for each writing project.

"There are several kinds of collaborations, and I've worked in all of them," says Harold Ramis. "At *SCTV*, I was the head writer, working around the big table writing group pieces. And I've worked with one or two others — what I call the Dick van Dyke mode — you know, one person types, one lays on the sofa, and one paces. And then you switch. I've done Sectional Collaborations. With *Animal House*, first we did the Dick van Dyke for three months to write the treatment: We sat in the room, made each other laugh, talked it

173

through; one typed, and the other paced. And then we did this kind of Sectional Collaboration where we divided up the treatment in thirds, and we each wrote a third and then swapped thirds. Someone wrote the first, someone wrote the second, someone wrote the third, switched them and rewrote each other, then switched them the third time, so we'd each written on each third of it. And then there's what I would call the Sequential Collaboration, where one person writes and then goes away and you rewrite. So it's collaborative in the sense that you're starting with something that they've done and rewriting it. They may or may not come back into the process and rewrite you. That's what Peter [Tolan] and I do — kind of sit in the room and outline and brainstorm, and then I let him do the ice breaking, which is probably the coward's way out." He laughs. "I let him do the heavy lifting. Then I rewrite him."

"Deciding the process is part of the process," says Nick Kazan. When we ask how he and Robin Swicord decide how they'll co-write each script, he laughs, "I don't know!"

Well, that's honest.

One thing he does know — they could never adopt the method used by Ramsey & Stone and Alexander & Karaszewski, the "nine-to-fivers" who work in the same office at the same computer and co-create every word. "Their work exists together, and it's a real symbiotic relationship," Kazan says. "I don't mean that they would be lost without the other person, but they certainly are accustomed to thinking in that way so that being in the same room makes sense."

Kazan admits that unless he's alone at his computer, his words won't flow. "When we sit and brainstorm a scene, Robin will brainstorm it. Basically, I don't know what to think — unless she shuts up, and I'm at a keyboard! I exist in a practical realm. It's what the characters say and do. Robin can see what they *ought* to say and do and get them to say and do it in an organic way, which would never lead you to believe that they were being nudged into saying and doing these things. But if I try to force them to do something, it's like they're being forced to do it, and they object! I work in a much more improvisatory way. It's like I have to have some freedom to be a bull in the china shop, and then I go, 'Oh, God, that didn't work.'"

Again, there's no right answer, no recipe to follow.

"Everybody has to work in the way that they work," Kazan says. "We don't have a lot of choice."

In the end, you must work in the way that you work, but in the beginning, it may be helpful to know how other teams do it and how they answer the question...

WHO DOES WHAT?

Whether you co-write every word or divide up the scenes or the drafts of your script, deciding who does what can be fairly simple — go with your gifts. As we've said many times, one of the great advantages of collaboration is complementary strengths.

Lee & Janet Batchler got lucky — the life partner they chose turned out to be a complementary writing partner. His yin to her yang. "It just happened that way, that our strengths were complementary," Janet says. And they divide up their script work accordingly: The more visually-oriented of the two, Janet writes, well, the visuals. The scene descriptions. The action. Not only is it her strength, it's her love. "I really care about the visuals," she says. "I really care about the transitions from one scene to the next. I'm passionate about how you get from one scene to the next scene."

Understandably, she finds great satisfaction in seeing her carefully-crafted descriptions translated to film exactly as written —

175

like the scene in *Batman Forever*, when Harvey Two-Face (Tommy Lee Jones) is introduced:

From *Batman Forever*:

```
EXT. FOREST ROAD - NIGHT

The Batmobile picks up speed.

OVERHEAD

The Batsignal in the sky.

INT. SECOND BANK OF GOTHAM, 22ND FLOOR — NIGHT

A spinning SILVER DOLLAR flips up into frame,
blocking out the Batsignal.

A hand catches the Coin and flips it again.

PAN UP THE ARM TO

the RIGHT HALF of a face: the rakishly handsome
profile of HARVEY "TWO-FACE" DENT.  The other
half of his face is hidden in deep shadow.

                    TWO-FACE
          (speaking to someone at his feet)
     What do you think, sport?  Are you
     counting on the "Batman" to rescue
     you?

Two-Face is talking to a middle-aged SECURITY
GUARD, tied up on the floor.
```

                    GUARD
     Are… are you gonna kill me?

                   TWO-FACE
     We might. Or we might not. You
     might say we're of two minds on the
     subject.

JANET: In the script, it's written exactly the way you see it on the screen. I remember at the premiere, going, "That's my shot! They used my shot. That is exactly what that shot looked like!"

LEE: And unfortunately, the director and DP will get credit for it way before you do!

JANET: And that's fine, that's fine. That's the stuff I love to do. I love to do that. Lee is much more the dialogue writer.

They admit their breakdown of duties defies most people's expectations of a male-female collaboration. "People think it's the guy who writes the action," Janet says. "*I* write the action!"

"I'm the romantic," Lee says. "I'm more of a feelings-driven person." The emotional component of a script interests him most — how the writer can grab and move the audience and even change the way they think. "You get to the head through the heart," he says. "So I'm much more attracted to the emotional life of the character. That's how someone comes to life."

He finds himself becoming very absorbed in his characters' inner lives, basing them on people he knows or reads about or just imagines. Consequently, he confesses to being a much slower writer than Janet, taking as much as two hours to get in "the zone" of character connection. "I'm sort of in that world," Lee says, "and then good luck for Jan trying to communicate with me!"

In our collaboration, we both become absorbed in the characters and the emotional flow, which is one reason it takes us so long to finish a script when we co-write every word. And because of our background in theater, we're both strong at dialogue. But Matt is more visual, and Claudia is more verbal, so when Matt envisions an image or a bit of behavior, he describes it to her as well as he can and barks, "Write that!" (Code for "Please spin this into evocative, economical scene description.") When we're drafting a down-the-page action sequence, Claudia asks Matt to do it because he's more skilled at this style of screenwriting.

Still, keep in mind Ted Elliott's warning: "Don't think that finding a partner who's good with action means you don't have to write action anymore. You had both better be thinking constantly about solving the problems, clarifying the characters, sharpening the dialogue, making the story work. A partner doesn't make writing a script easier. But a partner can make the script better."

And these complementary strengths begin to blend over time. That's one of the beauties of a long collaboration like Alexander & Karaszewski.

SCOTT: I probably come up with things more left-brain than he does.

LARRY: Yeah. That would probably be the way it comes out.

SCOTT: Left brain — and no brain. (Laughter.)

LARRY: We sort of do everything together, so I don't know if it's really broken down that easy. And after working with each other for so long I'm not quite sure if it's even left brain/right brain anymore. In the old days, I'd definitely say Scott was more the structure guy, and I was more the wild card kind of a guy. I don't know if it's even that anymore. We just sort of come in and do the job.

The longer we write together, the better Matt gets at scene description, and the better Claudia gets at down-the-page action sequences. So be careful not to pigeonhole yourselves. Yes, it's wise to capitalize on your individual talents, but you don't want to burden yourselves with all the work that taps into your strengths. And you don't want to curtail your creative growth by avoiding the work that taps into your weaknesses. Skills increase over time.

"When Daryl and I started working together, he definitely was the master at dialogue," Carolyn Miller says. "He was far better at it — he's a wonderful dialogue writer — so I had some learning to do. But I got much better at it with time."

The same proved true for Lee Batchler. Before he met Janet, he was training — with the Lehman Engel Musical Theatre Workshop — to be a composer in musical theater. He was told he couldn't write lyrics. But he persevered. And the more he struggled, the better his lyrics became. When at last he could write lyrics, he was told he couldn't write dialogue. Same story, more struggle. And now, with Janet, what he does for a living (in part) is write dialogue. "A lot of people are victims of snap judgments," he says. "'This person is talented, this person is not talented.' Sometimes it takes a while for someone to get it. There are people who get it right away like Orson Welles, but very few of us are Orson Welles. It takes a long, long time to learn a craft."

A supportive collaboration is the perfect place to take some creative chances and strengthen your weaknesses. In the long run, this will strengthen your collaboration as well — and the scripts that you write together.

THE FIRST DRAFT

The terror inspired by the blank page is well known. Fortunately, collaborating "takes the terror out of being in the room with that sheet of paper and typewriter and not one word is there," as Aaron Ruben says.

But diving into a script can still be daunting, even for the most experienced writers like Larry Gelbart et al. when they wrote *Caesar's Hour.* Each week was truly a blank page because it was a variety show. There was no long story or "bible" to tell them what was coming in the season to come.

"There was no season to come," Gelbart says. "It was six o'clock to come." Which made the number of pages they had to fill every week even more daunting. "*Caesar's Hour* really meant Caesar's *hour.* In those days you were only allowed six minutes for commercials so already we're talking about fifty-four minutes, and there was very little on the show that was not comedy. Perhaps you would have a soloist do something, so say that was three minutes, so the rest of it had to be comedy comedy comedy. And there were thirty-*nine* weeks, not twenty-two. So you wrote *hundreds* of hours of comedy material."

We confess we can't imagine.

"I can't imagine because I don't have to," he laughs.

Whatever form you've chosen — TV hour, half-hour, or feature-length film — you have to fill it. Write that damn first draft — good, bad, or ugly.

"You can write something terrible," Matthew Stone says. "If you're writing it, you can rewrite it the next day. God bless the computer — just get something down. You can rework it."

Lee Batchler agrees. "Your first passes at stuff — you write stuff that's garbage, and you know it's garbage. But there's a kernel of something there, and you go and try and discover it and enhance it and make it better."

"It's really about getting down something to work from," says Ted Cohen.

During his many years in radio and TV, Aaron Ruben co-wrote one film, *The Comic*. His writing partner was the film's director, Carl Reiner, who was working like crazy one morning when Ruben arrived at their office on the Columbia lot. "There he is pounding away on the typewriter," Ruben recalls. "I say, 'What are you doing?' He says, 'I'm writing something so we'll have something to rewrite!' That's what you have to do. Get something on paper so you can say, 'That stinks. Let's come up with something better.'"

"Screenwriting is rewriting," quoth conventional wisdom, but you can't rewrite until you have a first draft. And though it's fashionable, freeing, and frequently true that "all first drafts are shit," as Hemingway said, it's also freeing and true that "there's usually something pure and forceful or surprising and funny about a first draft," as Nick Kazan puts it, "and one of the things that can happen to screenplays is that they become perfected, and in being perfected they lose their eccentricity and humanity."

Larry Gelbart makes the same point. "I don't agree completely with Hemingway's edict that all first drafts are shit. Very often he's right, but it overlooks the fact that there's a certain kind of energetic innocence in a first draft. You're coming at it the first time, and you're not daunted or you are daunted. And it's hard to retain that because as you polish, you do grind things down. But there's no question that you make things better."

So when you write your first draft, you've got all the freedom you want — to stink or swim. But first you need to decide which drafting process works best for you.

CO-WRITING EVERY WORD

The co-creation of every word, line, scene, and sequence is a complex interplay of aesthetic forces. A creative jam session.

Gelbart employs the oft-used jazz analogy ("on behalf of those people too fearful to be clichéd," he laughs). "It is like improvisational jazz. It is. The idea is sort of the melody, the line that you want to follow. Then a soloist will take a line and go up and down and under and around and create another melody based on the original melody. You feed off one another." He and other great "soloists" co-created hundreds of hours of comedy material during the run of *Caesar's Hour*. "It was like a jazz session with people bouncing off one another, and each with his own style and voice, which made such color for the scripts, I think."

Gelbart offers a jazzy description of what a *Caesar's* session was like, once the writers had locked the idea. "We'd say, 'All right, let's start with Sid calling home and saying, "Hey, I got six tickets. This is the hottest show you can get." And then we would pitch in sequence, you know, 'Sid says this,' 'Sid says that,' and, 'Nah, that's no — yeah, that's good, no, nah, okay, fine.' We'd throw jokes, and Sid would nod he liked that one. If he didn't like one, Sid had a way of *uh-uh-uh-uh-uh* machine-gunning the joke as it flew out of the room, and you knew that joke was dead. So you pitch you pitch you pitch you pitch you pitch, and pretty soon you're saying, 'Okay, now they all know they're going; they all know they want to have dinner first.' Then you start making jokes about 'Where shall we eat?' 'Where shall we this?' 'What shall we that?' 'What are you going to wear?' 'What are *you* going to wear?' 'What are *you* going to wear?' 'Oh, mine's in the

182

cleaners.' You know, you just take reality and heighten it or diminish it by replacing it with silliness. And before you know it, you'd have fifteen, twenty pages."

He stops and looks across the table at us. "Sounds simple, huh?"

We laugh. Yeah, right. Co-writing every word is anything but simple. And if this is your first time trying this method, don't expect the warp speed of *Caesar's Hour*. Writing *Obscenity* together was slower than rush hour — hell, *any* hour — in L.A. traffic. Working from our detailed scene-by-scene, we drafted the script from beginning to end. We lovingly labored — nay, agonized — over every line and even some punctuation.

The Batchlers had their worst disagreement over one *word*. "We just remember sort of looking at the clock and going, 'We spent an hour on a word,'" Janet says. (They do not remember what the offending word was.)

We bogged down so often we created a comic routine, pretending to be in the rest home still arguing over the same damn comma. That got us laughing and out of the bog. We also made a small sign — DON'T MICRO! — and put it next to Pinocchio on top of the computer. Don't get us wrong — we loved the process. It was one of the most satisfying creative experiences in our co-writing life, *but it took eighteen months!* People started asking, "What is this you're having, a rhinoceros?"

Like women (and rhinoceroses) forgetting their labor pains, script partners tend to forget their painful labor co-writing every word.

"It's a strange thing," Matt Manfredi says, "because when I think about writing any script that we've written, you kind of forget the hours that are spent typing."

If we'd stayed on the same side of the country and continued working this way, we would have written our next script much faster, but this was our first co-written script, and as Claudia's dad used to say, "The first olive is always the hardest to get out of the bottle."

So if this is your first time trying this method, and you're not facing a deadline, allow lots of time. You're not just co-creating a script, you're co-creating your process.

WHO TYPES, WHO PACES?

"We were always asked, 'Well, which of you really did the writing?'" Fay Kanin says. "Oh, you get that a lot — 'Which one of you was really the writer and which one just did the typing?'"

Now there's a question that ticks a writing team off! Of *course* you're both creating, no matter who's typing or pacing or sprawled on the couch.

Hal Kanter tells a wonderful story about co-writing an Edgar Bergen/Charlie McCarthy routine for an Academy of Television Arts & Sciences benefit. His partners on the project were *I Love Lucy* writer/producer Jess Oppenheimer and *Gomer Pyle/Get Smart* writer Norman Paul. The trio worked in the den of Oppenheimer's home — Hal sitting, Jess typing, and Norman pacing. "Norman always paced," Kanter says. At one point when the writers got stuck, Norman kept pacing and pacing and eventually paced out into the garden and all the way around to the front of the house. "A moment or so later the doorbell rang in front. Jess's wife opened the door and said, 'Norman! I thought you already came in.' And he came in and said, 'A great line occurred while you guys were out of the room!'"

Like many teams we've polled, we don't work in the type/pace paradigm. Wherever we work together we sit across the table from each other. Matt tends to do more of the typing because we usually use his computer, but we switch when his eyes start to look like pinwheels. We only pace when we're stuck and need to find a solution — the magic of motion again.

Robert Ramsey & Matthew Stone sit at desks facing each other with the monitor between them so they both can see it.

ROBERT: I'm the typist. Matt's on the mouse. That's how collaborative we are — I'm on the keyboard, and he's on the mouse. You've never seen someone get so much work out of a mouse.

MATTHEW: *Whoosh, whoosh!*

ROBERT: He rules the screen with that mouse.

MATTHEW: I'm editing as we go.

ROBERT: It's like playing music. It's like he's on drums, and I'm on piano.

MATTHEW: I find that Rob can talk or think and type at the same time. I can't. If I'm typing then I'm not adding anything to the process. I'm just typing what he's saying. Once in a while, he goes to the bathroom, and I commandeer the keyboard and I write a few things in.

ROBERT: Early on I had a competitive advantage with the keyboard, just because I had gone through four years of journalism school where I had to sit in news labs and write a story in half an hour. And I worked at the newspaper, and you pound out copy. That created a habit that exists today.

MATTHEW: We co-write every word.

ROBERT: Every sentence. Every sentence is collaborative. It's pretty wacky.

MATTHEW: Some people say, "You take home this scene, and I'll take home that scene, and tomorrow we'll switch" or whatever. That's just never worked for us. We just have to be together in front of the computer.

ROBERT: We have one of most meshed relationships you'll probably ever encounter.

Scott Alexander & Larry Karaszewski work in the sit/sit — or sit/lie — paradigm.

LARRY: Scott's got to be on the keyboard. I sit over here.

SCOTT: I never leave this chair. I do all of the typing. Larry lies on the couch. He's very comfortable over there.

LARRY: Zen writing.

SCOTT: We never switch.

LARRY: Except when I'm looking at porn on the Internet. He'll read *Variety*, and I'll click around. (Laughter.) It's the way we've worked since day one. Back in college Scott had a computer. So we'd go to Scott's room, and Scott would be using his computer. I had no idea how to use one.

Matt Manfredi & Phil Hay prefer the sit/slouch-on-the-couch paradigm. But they do trade places, depending on who's in a better mood that day.

PHIL: Less crabby has to type.

MATT: Yeah.

PHIL: Less crabby is *willing* to type. Crabby's just sitting on the couch complaining.

MATT: We decide at the beginning of the work day, but our greatest arguments of all time were all about who's saying, "You're in a bad mood," "No, *you're* in a bad mood," "No, no, you *put* me in a bad mood, so you think I'm in a bad mood." (Laughter.)

Generally, Alexander Payne & Jim Taylor always work "with one of us 'driving' at the keyboard, while the other one observes or comments or dictates or dozes off," Taylor tells us. They've also used the rare type/type paradigm. "I'm kind of a Macintosh fanatic, so I end up being 'tech-support' most of the time when we're writing," he adds. "When we were working on *Election*, I hooked up an extra monitor and another keyboard to the same computer so we could both work on the same document at the same time without having to crowd around the keyboard. We don't always use this setup, but sometimes it's helpful." This interlocked Mac method allows them to *Think different* and write same.

Now and then they'll unlink their minds, as Payne tells *Scenario*. "Every once in a while, Jim or I will say, let me just have a half hour, because every once in a while you have to be in a writer's place, silent, and just write and not have to say it first and explain it or justify it. But 98% of the time, it's together."

Occasionally, we do the same thing. One of us will say, "Give me five minutes — I'm onto something!" You never want to stifle that impulse. It's the Muse talking to you, and heaven knows her visits are infrequent enough. Sometimes these brief solo sessions produce your best work. Struck with inspiration, Matt took a whack at a scene in *Obscenity*, and we hardly touched it through all the rewrites.

DIVIDING UP SCENES

Matt Manfredi & Phil Hay co-draft every word when they write comedy, but they find it difficult to do this when they write drama. For *crazy/beautiful*, they divided up scenes and wrote them alone.

PHIL: We just felt you get closer to the truth in a more comfortable way, doing it yourself and then turning it over to the other person — as opposed to the two of us trying to be like, "Okay, the next line, as she's sobbing..."

MATT: There are certain times when you want it all out there before you have feedback. You don't want to filter yourself or the other person. You just want to get it out there and see how it looks. I think for some reason with a drama it seems especially this way. Whereas with a comedy, it's just, "Is this funny?"

PHIL: You're more vulnerable. And even though we still talk, and we aren't afraid of what the other person thinks — we know each other so well — it still is vulnerable. No matter how close you are with a person, that stuff is much more vulnerable, and you try to protect it more. That's not what you should be doing.

From *crazy/beautiful*:

INT. MOTEL BEDROOM - LATE THAT NIGHT

In bed, Nicole rests her head on Carlos' chest. He strokes her hair. A long, peaceful moment.

> NICOLE
> I tried to do it too.

Carlos is silent.

> NICOLE
> I tried to kill myself.

Carlos nods. He keeps stroking her hair, waiting.

                    NICOLE
It just happened. It... I'd thought
about it, a lot, and one night... one
night it started. I just went for the
pills. I kept daring myself to go
farther. Not daring, just asking
myself if I could. Open the bottle.
Put the pills in my hand. Take one.
Then... take them all. And it wasn't
like I wanted it to happen, but it was
happening without me. It just started
happening. I was watching it.

                    CARLOS
How did...what happened?

                    NICOLE
I stopped it. I woke up. Long enough
to spit the pills out.

A pause.

                    NICOLE
I feel like it's inside me. This
thing. From my mother. My dad thinks
so, too. That's why he's so freaked
out about me. He thinks I'm like her.

                    CARLOS
Did he say that?

                    189

                    NICOLE
No way. He doesn't talk. And I'll
never talk to him. He's not a person
anymore. He's a ghost. It's like we
live in a grave. We have since my mom
died.

                    CARLOS
How do you feel right now?

                    NICOLE
Good. I feel much better when I'm
with you.

He looks away but keeps stroking her hair.

You may decide, too, that dividing up the scenes is the best way
to work on a particular script. Or like the Kanins, the Longstreets, the
Batchlers, and Reich & Cohen, you may prefer drafting all your
scripts this way.

For the Kanins, dividing up scenes was essential because of their
different work styles. "I am a *slow* writer," Fay Kanin says. "Because
I diddle. I mean, I take all this time before I get down to the
typewriter. Oh, my God, my drawers get very clean. I do all the
things, just *anything* to not do it. Wild horses couldn't get me to the
typewriter until the very last moment."

Michael, on the other hand, was very structured, writing
everyday with his yellow pad and paper — usually from ten in the
morning till about 3:00 or 4:00 in the afternoon. "Then he stopped,
he did what he wanted to do, and he slept well," she says. "Me, I'm
sweating — *errrr!* — I don't want to get to the typewriter. But once I
got to the typewriter, you couldn't get me away because then I

began to fall in love with the characters and the whatever it was, and then I was a really terrible wife. I wanted only to write at that point. At the beginning I was a good wife." She laughs.

For Andrew Reich & Ted Cohen, dividing up scenes is essential because of the tight deadlines they face on *Friends*. "We have five days to write a script," Reich says. "We'll write the outline on the first day, split up scenes, so we have two days to write it on our own and then two days together to put it together."

The days writing alone can be "kind of torturous," so they're always tempted to start working a little earlier, but they know they can't. "It would just take forever because we would agonize over every line," Cohen says. "At least at the beginning, if you can get down some kind of shape, it's easier to do on your own. Because you're not sort of fiddling with 'this *well* should be a *so*' and everything."

The key to this method is careful outlining, "really nailing the structure," as Ted Elliott says. This means establishing the beats of your story and, if possible, the beats of your individual scenes before you divide them up to draft.

Before Manfredi & Hay could divide up the scenes for *crazy/beautiful*, they outlined them beat by beat, in "excruciating" detail. "Then we found that it was easier to take separate scenes and go away and write the dialogue," Hay says.

Once your scenes are outlined, you'll need to decide how you'll divide them. Again, each team has a different approach.

"We have our sort of arcane way of doing that," Reich says. "We don't say, 'You write the first act, I'll write the second act.' We try and find a fair way. We divide the scenes up: These are easy, these are medium, these are hard. If there are four hard scenes, we each take two hard scenes. We try and make it so we both have an equal amount of work to do."

After working alone on their scenes, they come back together for those last two days to create a draft they both like.

From *Friends* ("The One With the Stripper"):

INT. ROSS'S APARTMENT — A LITTLE LATER (NIGHT 2)
(Ross, Dr. Green, Mona)

THEY ARE PRETTY MUCH WHERE WE LEFT THEM.

> DR. GREEN
> So, explain yourself, Geller. You
> get Rachel pregnant and now you
> don't want to marry her?

> MONA
> You got Rachel pregnant? Are you
> guys together?

> ROSS
> No. Oh, no. It was just a one-night
> thing. It meant nothing.

> DR. GREEN
> Oh, so my daughter means nothing to
> you?

> ROSS
> No, no. She means a lot to me. I
> mean, I love Rachel.

                    MONA
What?!

                    ROSS
Not in that way. I mean, I'm not
in love with her. I love her like
a sister.

                    MONA
Ew! You'd sleep with your sister?

                    ROSS
Okay, maybe not like a sister.
Like a friend.

                    DR. GREEN
And that's how you treat your friend?
Get her in trouble and then refuse
to marry her?

                    ROSS
Hey, I offered to marry her!

                    MONA
You offered to marry her?!

                    ROSS
(PLACATING) Yes. But I didn't
want to.

                    193

> DR. GREEN
> Oh, you didn't want to marry my
> daughter? Why not? So you could
> be with this tramp?
>
> MONA
> Tramp?
>
> ROSS
> Oh, I'm sorry. (DYING) Dr. Green,
> Mona. Mona, Dr. Green.

With fairness and passion in mind, the Kanins divided their workload based on individual preference. "I would say, 'Well, I want to write that one and that one and that one because I like those,'" Fay says. "Michael said, 'Okay, then I'll do that and that and that.' So we wrote scenes separately and then alternated, took that mix and put it together in a screenplay, and the other one looked it over. That seemed to us a good way to work. We helped each other a lot."

Harry & Renee Longstreet work in a similar manner, letting individual preference — or resistance — dictate who writes what.

RENEE: We say, "You want to do that? Okay."

HARRY: Occasionally, though, it's, "Ugh! Blechh! *You* do the first act!" Sometimes.

RENEE: Right. And I don't think we've ever had an argument over who does what.

After they write their scenes solo, the Longstreets trade, reading each other's work and making copious notes for the rewrite.

Carolyn Miller & Daryl Warner preferred alternating the scenes. "He'd do scene one, three, five, something like that, and I'd do two, four, six," Miller explains. "And then we'd exchange what we did. We'd go over each scene together line by line. The first act was always the hardest because you're establishing the tone, the characters, and all that. Act One is harder for collaborators because I might have a concept for a character that was different from his. So there was a lot of discussion. For the rest of the acts, it was easy because by then we knew the story and characters so well."

Lee & Janet Batchler write and rewrite as they go, usually working sequentially through the screenplay. One of them writes the first draft of a scene or sequence, and the other follows behind and rewrites. "Lee tends to do more of the 'blank page' work," Janet says, "with me taking the first rewrite most commonly."

But, because of complementary strengths, sometimes Janet will write the first draft of a scene, especially if there's plenty of action. "It varies from script to script, depending on the content of the scene involved and the deadline we're working under," she says. "We then rewrite each other to death, until finally we can sit down in a room and read to each other our most recent changes, deciding on final phrasing together. And by that time, there are rarely any substantive changes left to discuss. We're just tweaking the actual language."

Michael Colleary & Mike Werb use a different approach, usually dividing the work up by acts and writing on separate computers.

"We talk throughout the day, solving problems, trying out dialogue, proposing set-ups and pay-offs, making sure we are being consistent, etc.," says Colleary. "When the first draft is complete, we'll trade pages, make notes on each other's work, discuss and incorporate the changes. Then we start over. Usually we'll do four to five passes on every draft before we're ready to submit."

DIVIDING UP DRAFTS

"Woody Allen mostly creates his own dialogue, and who better than he?" says Marshall Brickman. But they'd done extensive preparation together before Allen began drafting scenes. "What we created was the story — ideas for scenes, ideas for jokes, the structure (if any) — the characters (except for Woody Allen, whose character is pretty much fully formed outside the project — that is, we were aware of what the audience's expectation was and what he could plausibly portray, i.e., not the head of Interpol, except in a broad comedy), what the people do, where the story is going, etc."

After a few months of those kinds of discussions, Allen would pound out the first draft — "on his old Royal typewriter, which he probably still has," Brickman says. "Then we'd kick it around and do another draft."

Like Allen, Billy Crystal often stars in the film versions of his co-written scripts, and he brings his improvisational gifts to the process as well — but after his initial brainstorming with Tolan, Crystal stays out of the process until the second draft. Tolan tends to do much of the "heavy lifting" — getting the first draft down on paper. Then the pages are passed to Crystal.

"Billy does his thing then," Tolan says. "He goes in and tweaks and fixes and moves things around, and gets it more to what he thought it was going to be. He says, 'Well, this is good,' or 'Why don't we do this instead?' — chop, change — and at the end of that whole process, we get a screenplay. And it seems to work for us. We don't get into situations where it's, like, 'What the hell is that?' Billy's a very good collaborator and a very funny guy, endlessly entertaining."

We've worked in similar ways since we've lived on different sides of the country. After we created and outlined the stories together, Matt wrote funny but bloated first drafts ("loose-and-baggy monsters," we affectionately called them) of *Behind the Eight Ball* and *Psycho Bitch*. Brevity is the soul of wit, even in soulless Hollywood, so comedies tend to be short (as do studio readers' attention spans), and Claudia had to take out her "chainsaw" and cut them down to size before we could rewrite them.

Just remember that this approach only works if one of you *wants* to write the first — and frequently the most challenging — draft alone. Otherwise, it may feel like a burden, sparking resentment and possibly ownership issues. If that's the case, you'd be better off dividing the scenes or the acts, or co-writing every word.

Or, like Urban & Addis when they wrote *Poor White Trash* and Tolan & Ramis when they wrote *Bedazzled*, you could split the difference. And the draft.

"Harold and I sat together two or three times," Tolan says, "and we chose what we felt were the best choices that we had. Then we split the screenplay in the middle."

"Because structurally *Bedazzled* was so episodic — it was a series of wishes — it was easy to split," Ramis says. "And once we sort of knew where the overarching story was going, it was just convenient. Peter literally wrote sixty pages and sent it to me, and I wrote the second sixty and sent it to him."

"It took me about — I screwed around — it probably took me two or three months to do my half," Tolan says. "So then he did his half and married the two together. He made some changes in my half to make them agree with what he had done, and he sent me the script. I read it, and it was really funny."

The danger of this approach is a possible tone shift in your script. "In Harold's half, it does sort of get spiritual, 'cause Harold's a really spiritual guy," Tolan adds. "He's always looking for the underlying spirit of a piece, no matter what he does. And that's just where he's at."

197

ACTING IT OUT

There's an additional reason Matt does the typing. No, he's not a better typist — Claudia's fingers fly at hummingbird speed, an impressive 105 wpm — but he is a better actor (Claudia makes no claim to being an actor at all). Sitting at the computer allows him to read the lines aloud while Claudia listens (and applauds appropriately). This method works wonderfully for us as we write a scene. It allows us to hear the characters' voices and connect to their emotional flow. It also helps us identify clunky lines (put a little English on that sentence!) or super or superfluous ones, as well as any beats of dialogue that may need to be cut or rearranged.

"Acting out the dialogue and hearing it out loud is a key advantage to writing with someone," Brad Anderson says.

Larry Karaszewski agrees. "The dialogue thing is probably the biggest reason for a collaboration, because you basically have to audition the lines. If they make someone laugh, or someone thinks it's a good line, or they seem fairly amusing, that helps. You have to say them out loud."

But do they *act* them out?

"Oh, yeah," Scott Alexander says. "We're both hams, so we act out the lines. If the line is trying to be funny, then we'll try to deliver the line to make it funny. Then Larry gets to kick back on the couch, and I get on the computer for a few minutes and type it all in."

Robert Ramsey & Matthew Stone also stretch those thespian muscles as they co-write.

ROBERT: We use accents and stuff.

MATTHEW: That's sometimes what comes out, and we write it down that way.

ROBERT: I'd never want to see that. I'd never want anyone to see that.

MATTHEW: We don't stand up and — well, every once in a while we do, but we're not like Carrot Top with the props and the bag of things. We just sort of sit here.

ROBERT: It's the kissing that's the hardest part. (Laughter.)

If lips are off limits, ad-libbing may not be ("You're allowed to add things — it's called *ad-libbing!*" shrieks Jennifer Tilly in *Bullets Over Broadway*). This approach proved beneficial for David Sonnenschein & Stuart Geltner as they drafted *The Knife and the Rose.*

"Stuart and I are both very fluid with becoming the characters," Sonnenschein says. "And sometimes — if it went one direction, but we didn't feel quite like this is really it — we'd switch roles and become the other character, just to see what would happen with that dynamic." With a tape recorder on, they ad-libbed in character to create new dialogue and refine what they'd written.

When Milos Forman agreed to direct *The People vs. Larry Flynt*, he helped Scott Alexander & Larry Karaszewski with their script revisions. Their process of what they call "finessing the moments" involved Forman's performance of the dialogue.

SCOTT: Here's the problem with working with Milos — Larry and I are two fine actors as you can clearly see. And when you work with Milos, he insists on playing all the parts. You know, let's get real — he's Czechoslovakian. I can deliver that line; I can sell that line to the back of the theater. And then you got Milos stumbling over it, and like, I don't know if it's a good line.

LARRY: Aw, I disagree with that. Milos is great. He's even better than the actors at the end of the day. There were times when we'd sit in his room, and he would just read the script of *Larry Flynt.*

199

SCOTT: Milos doing Larry Flynt's Kentucky accent, that was something. That was priceless!

LARRY: It was awesome. It was a great performance.

To "finesse" your dialogue, you may want to cast actors or bribe friends to perform your scenes for you. Listen closely and take notes — or better yet, turn on the tape recorder. You'll be surprised how much you want to tweak.

Fortunately for Brad Anderson, his writing collaborators are frequently his lead actors as well. (Lyn Vaus played the main role in his first film, *The Darien Gap*, and appeared in *Next Stop Wonderland* and *Happy Accidents*; Steve Gevedon performed in *Happy Accidents* and *Session 9*.) After Anderson writes the "first pass of the dial," he relies on his collaborators' acting skills for subsequent revisions. In a series of writing sessions, he takes notes as they "riff off" his script. "Each person inputs his ideas," he says. "Lyn and Steve, more than myself, both have a way with jokes and clever quips. I write down what I find funny and ignore the rest. There is a lot of acting out."

There's a lot of wrangling as well. "It can get pretty brutal and self-effacing," Anderson admits. "These are less writing sessions than they are mild brawls."

And hearing the script can help you clarify more than just dialogue.

Part of ad-libbing was to discover what was really going to happen in the scene," Sonnenschein says. "Sometimes the characters themselves would actually define what direction the scene would take."

Anderson agrees, "You often get ideas for how the characters behave, what they do. At this stage, direction can be added to the script that helps bring it to life."

REWRITING THE SCRIPT

"Hopefully, rewriting just makes things better and better," says Jim Taylor. "Sometimes it makes things worse, but if you have the time and energy, I think it's good to revisit your script as many times as you can."

It's clear that a great deal of rewriting is done as teams draft their scripts — one of the major advantages of collaboration. Your "first draft" is rarely just a first draft.

"We've usually done three to six drafts at least by the time we've put the words 'First Draft' on something," Janet Batchler says, "because we rewrite each other so much." But they did nine passes on *Smoke and Mirrors* to get to the "First Draft."

Even if you rewrite each other along the way, you'll probably have more work to do when your first draft is finished. If you're like us, you'll have a loose-and-baggy monster on your hands. That's fine; in fact, that's just how Alexander & Karaszewski prefer it.

LARRY: We're different from other people — we like these absurdly long scripts.

SCOTT: We're like that 800-pound guy in *The National Enquirer* who lost 100 pounds and is calling up all his relatives.

LARRY: "I just lost 100 pounds, and I feel great! I'm down to 700!"

Revising is a hefty task, especially when massive cuts are involved. Because their scripts often run 200 pages, Alexander & Karaszewski are faced with cutting upwards of eighty pages (except in the case of the Marx Brothers script, which was so long they excised the equivalent of an entire motion picture). Once this scriptendectomy is over, they spend months polishing, "trying to perfect lines, trying to shorten things," says Alexander.

201

LARRY: You come up with ideas of how to do it: "This scene has this idea, and this scene has that idea. Why don't we just have one scene that has those two ideas in it? And this scene has eight good lines, but ten mediocre ones. This scene has five good lines." Every single word has got to fight for its life.

SCOTT: It's like reducing a stock — hopefully the soup gets richer.

Or, if one of you is a crackerjack editor, you may decide to defer to that complementary strength. That's the case with the Batchlers, whose "unshowable" first drafts are usually 140-150 pages. "I do more of the editing because I'm a really good cutter," Janet says. "I can edit very fast. I go in and say, 'We have a half page of dialogue, and we can do it with one visual. This speech could actually be cleaner if it was only one sentence long.' I'll say, 'We can go from this point in the middle of the scene to the next scene, and let the audience fill in the gaps.' Let the audience do the work, and we can just go there!"

That's why she loves transitions; the right cut between scenes can make your script read more like a movie, throwing the story — and the reader — forward. If script length allows, Janet also crafts something compelling at the bottom of every page. "Something really provocative, where you go, 'Oh, my gosh, I have to see what the next line is' — to make you turn that page and keep reading."

Either editorial approach — making cuts together or separately — can get sticky. Inevitably, each of you will be trimming something the other one wrote — and possibly loves. At tough times like this, check your ego at the door and remember William Faulkner's reminder that, in writing, you must kill all your darlings. Keeping in mind the common good — a good script — can also ease the pain. But it still ain't easy.

"We try not to take offense if one of us writes something that fails," says Phil Hay.

"Sometimes we fail to not take offense," adds Matt Manfredi. They laugh knowingly.

Surrendering ego is mandatory for television writers, who revise their scripts countless times — not just with their partner but with "the room." As Ted Cohen explains, "the revision process starts with presenting our draft to seven or eight other writers and producers, then having general discussions about what changes are needed."

"You go through it and you make the jokes better," Reich adds. "You tighten scenes, all that kind of stuff."

After the table-read with the entire cast, the writers revise again. This process continues as the actors rehearse. "After seeing it up on its feet, we go back, do another rewrite, then see it again the next day, go back, do another rewrite," Reich says. "Then there's a day of camera blocking where typically we just send one or two writers down to the stage to see if things are still funky. Do a little more rewriting. And then it's the show night."

But the rewriting doesn't stop there. During the taping, if a joke doesn't make the studio audience laugh, the writers "huddle" to come up with one that will.

ANDREW: That's the *most* pressured part of the job. You're on stage and the audience is waiting, and the actors are waiting, getting impatient, and it's probably an area or a joke where you've tried two or three things throughout the week already. It's probably going to be one of your problem jokes. It's just like, "Okay, we're going back to this." Or it'll just surprise you. Something's been funny all week. Dead silence. And then it's figuring out, okay, why?

TED: There's safety in numbers, which is nice. Usually there's six or eight people, and you know you're all working on it together, so I think it makes each person feel freer to just pitch something even if it's not necessarily fully-formed because maybe it will lead to something else and something else.

ANDREW: It's absolutely on the spot.

Looking back on his many years of writing — and rewriting — in television, Aaron Ruben laughs, "Sitcom stars have often looked upon collaborating writers as the enemy. Fat Jack Leonard once asked, 'Who you guys writing against this week?' But, boy, they sure depended on us."

TOO MANY NOTES!

"It used to be that there wasn't such a thing as studio notes," Nick Kazan tells us. "They'd say, 'You know, I think you should have more of the girl in there' — and that was it! They did have writers on the lot, and they did have some people who just did story and some people who did dialogue, etc. But there was an integrity to the work, and you felt like, when you went to see the movie, you were seeing your work."

That environment changed in the late 1970s after William Goldman's spec screenplay for *Butch Cassidy and the Sundance Kid* sold for a record $400,000.

"People said, 'This is way too much money to pay for a screenplay. We should be hiring people to write screenplays and get them to do what we want,'" Kazan explains. "So staff started to come on. And then there was a lot of money, and that allowed for more staffs, and people started getting their own little pet projects. Then Paramount began writing voluminous notes, and they started publishing these note sessions. Everybody would get together with the writer, and they would have a huge session, and everybody would say whatever they wanted. Then somebody would transcribe the notes and send them out, and you'd get these documents that were thirty pages long! One friend of mine, a producer, who was then dealing with a subsequent regime (because these people from Paramount spread out all over to various studios), would habitually go in and say, 'These notes are very interesting. Could we just go over them? What does this one mean? And what about that one?' Half of them would get crossed out because no one knew what they meant, so then there were only fifteen pages instead of thirty! But it's ludicrous to think that anyone could execute that many notes and still stay inside the scenes and characters. Obviously, you can't do that. God bless 'em, most studio executives are very smart. They're very nice people. They obviously mean well, but they feel as though they're not doing their job unless they're telling you how to change what you've written."

And if you've been hired by the studio to write — or rewrite — a script, you have to listen.   "You are the writer at the beginning," Matthew Stone says, "but by the end of it, suddenly the guy who was cutting the checks wrote it."

Robert Ramsey nods. "It's a steady process of being co-opted."

Mark Twain once said, "Glacial epics are great things, but they are vague, vague." So are studio notes. This is one of Ramsey & Stone's biggest complaints.

MATTHEW: We've learned one thing about taking notes from the studio, which is you must butt heads with them to some degree just to get them to explain themselves. It's not about disagreeing with their notes. If you don't press them, they get lazy and they say these by-rote things that could apply to any script.

ROBERT: The dialogue is very consistent between studios. There's a rule book. I haven't seen it, but I can see the evidence of it constantly in my interaction with creative execs around town.

MATTHEW: To get a note that says "the main character is not pro-active enough." I'm not being argumentative when I say —

ROBERT: "What the fuck do you mean?"

MATTHEW: "What do you mean? Where? Are you talking about this scene?" You've really got to pull it out of them. Taking notes is a whole art unto itself.

So count your blessings that you have a partner to help you decipher what has been said.

"When we come back, we've taken notes," Stone continues. "'Yeah, I heard him say that; I thought he meant this.' And Rob will think the executive meant something else. We get to sort of say, 'Oh, you thought that? I see. Maybe they meant *this.*' And it actually helps us. It's like, 'You were there, you saw the accident, too — what did you see? What happened?' If I was on my own and I was taking these notes, I'd be a lot more confused."

For this reason, Lowell Ganz values having Babaloo Mandel by his side during their "creative negotiating" with producers, directors, and actors. "It's always very wonderful either during the meeting or afterward in the parking lot to know there's somebody that was actually there the whole time," Ganz tells *Creative Screenwriting.* "Not your wife when you come home later who doesn't understand why you're so upset, but somebody who's actually there, who you can just look at and go, 'We're not crazy, right? I wasn't talking nonsense — I mean we both heard the same thing, right?' So that's a good thing."

Once you both agree what was said, the trick is to apply it as you rewrite.

"Try and give them what they want," Ramsey says, "without building a house for them that will fall down."

And try to maintain perspective, even though you may have to go through a staggering number of rewrites.

"I can say safely that I rewrote the last scene in *America's Sweethearts* thirty-five times," Peter Tolan says. "Thirty-five different attempts at it — just endless! Every imaginable pitfall. Without getting specific, a lot of things happened. I felt, right around twenty-eight, that I had it. And then an event happened that caused that to go down the toilet, and I had to start all over again. On and on it went. It was actually pretty funny."

Renee Longstreet has to laugh, too, when recalling a particular script note that came from the head of a television network. "I won't say his name, but he said to Harry, 'I don't care if it is bad structure, I want the climax up front.' That's one of my favorites. I said, 'Oh, God, I don't want to be married to *him*!'" She and Harry crack up.

So maintaining your sense of humor can be a big help.

For Ramsey & Stone, it also helps to remember that they're being paid. "You are an employee of sorts," Ramsey says. "You hope that they're hiring you for your point of view, but at some point their point of view is absolutely as valid."

And stay open. Sometimes even the *worst* studio note can be helpful.

"We got some notes from a CBS show that were *insane*," says Carolyn Miller. "We wanted to kill them! I said, 'Ugh! This is just going to change everything. It's a major re-conceptualization of the story.' It was a terribly painful process, but it forced us to rethink a lot. And we came up with what I think was a much more interesting script."

There are times when radically rethinking your script is exactly what's needed, but you're too close to the story to see it — the forest for the trees and all that. When a friend who teaches at the Sundance Filmmakers Lab read *Obscenity*, she loved it. "I found it a page-turner from Sam's murder on," she told us.

Terrific, we thought, except Sam doesn't die until the end of Act One.

Act One was too "bucolic," as our friend poetically — and diplomatically — put it. She suggested that we might want to think about starting the script with the murder.

From our earliest conversations about *Obscenity*, we'd thought of the gaybashing as our first turning point, but after getting these thoughtful notes, we saw what a powerful opening scene it could be. We also realized that opening with the murder would give us more time to explore the emotional impact of Sam's death on Sara and to explore the events leading to her decision to continue his controversial court case. We were able to see the story — and structure — anew. That's what revision means — re-seeing.

Okay, we'll be honest — redesigning the script was a bitch. Since our old Act One bit the dust, we not only had to rebuild the act, we had to find ways to embed essential scenes that happened before the gaybashing. To help us visualize this new structure together, we "went horizontal," as we described earlier, and co-created a badly-needed blueprint that allowed us to "read" the new screenplay before we wrote it. Once we were sure of our structure, rewriting was exhilarating. Everything seemed to fall into place. We had such unexpected and amazing new insights, we jokingly called them "cosmic transmissions." And once we were finished, thanks to our friend's notes, we had a much stronger script.

So be open to all notes, whoever may give them — friends, family, writers groups, managers, agents, agents' assistants. Even studio executives. As Janet Batchler says, "The person you think is never going to offer anything of value can come up with a solution to a problem."

And speaking of cosmic transmissions — and people you'd never expect to be helpful... We'd heard of spirits from the afterlife dictating manuscripts (specifically the Seth books by Jane Roberts, who went into trances and spoke as a personality named "Seth"), but we'd never heard of spirits dictating screenplays. Until we spoke to David Sonnenschein.

The Knife and the Rose is based on the true story of a Brazilian healer named Arigo who "channeled" spirits to make medical diagnoses and prescriptions. Sonnenschein had extensively researched Arigo's life, conducting numerous interviews with the living, but for the revision process, he and Stuart Geltner, both trained in transchanneling, wanted to get a sixth sense about their subject.

They pulled out the Ouija board. Face to face, the alphanumeric board between them, the writers placed their fingers on the planchette and asked Arigo's spirit their questions. They relaxed and waited for something to happen. "Our question really was, 'Is there anything that you, Arigo, in this spirit realm, would like to convey to us that may contribute to this script and our efforts in portraying your life in cinema?'" Sonnenschein explains. "So it was really a direct question to a deceased real person."

The planchette moved in response to that and several other questions. When Geltner saw one letter being pointed out, he was able to hear the whole word, and Arigo began to "speak" rapidly to them. They dictated his comments into a tape recorder. "We went for about half an hour, forty-five minutes, a lot of stuff coming."

209

Obviously this method has limited application, though Sonnenschein says, "For other writers, it might be worth trying out just in general to tap into their intuitive nature."

For their specific script purpose, it was perfect. And they found Arigo's guidance invaluable. "It corroborated much of what we'd already been doing, but there was an extraordinary emotional connection for us as writers directly to this source. That really helped define and refine our intention as writers to go really, really deep into this and throw away things that didn't matter or that were not on track."

They used some of Arigo's own "words" from the channeling session as dialogue in the final scene of their film. And thanks to his comments, they focused their story, trimmed a superfluous subplot, and refined his voice in the script.

Which just goes to show you — everyone's dying to give you script notes. Even the dead.

SCRIPT PARTNER POINTS

🐸 Decide which drafting process works best for you (and you can only decide by doing):

    Co-writing every word together
    Dividing up scenes
    Dividing up acts
    Dividing up drafts (or dividing them down the middle)

🐸 If you co-write every word, find a comfortable and productive way to work together — e.g., one types/one paces. Try to avoid one types/one sleeps.

🐸 Tap into complementary strengths when drafting — e.g., one of you may be better at writing action, one may be more proficient at writing dialogue.

🐸 Faced with the blank page, the daunting task of writing your first draft, remember that collaborating takes the terror out of it (or at least it's a collective terror). Just get something down.

🐸 Throw caution (and pride) to the wind by acting out your dialogue — especially if you're writing comedy — while writing your first draft.

🐸 When you've finished a draft that you're proud of, have friends or actors read it aloud. Listen closely and take notes. Or turn on a tape recorder. Ask for feedback and maintain perspective (and a sense of humor) when others say what they think.

🐸 Be open to all rewrite notes, whoever may give them. Listen for consensus — but also for the random, brilliant suggestion.

"What the hell are we gonna do? Just because our relationship is in the toilet doesn't mean we can't work together, does it?"

— Richard Babson (Burt Reynolds), *Best Friends*

CHAPTER 8

THE CREATIVE RELATIONSHIP

An agent told a filmmaker friend, "There should be therapists for writing teams because it's the hardest relationship in the world."

It is. It's harder than friendship. "It's harder than marriage," as Gelbart says. But not just because there's no sex. The creative relationship is the hardest relationship in the world because it's really two relationships — a professional and a personal one.

When the personal relationship isn't working, chances are you won't be, either.

"As Daryl and I developed problems in the marriage, we were writing together less and going in our own directions more," says Carolyn Miller.

And when the professional relationship isn't working, the personal relationship will be adversely affected.

"You know, Daryl and I had a good run for a while, and then we had some things that didn't go so well," Miller says. "We had a movie at Disney Television that was a very sour experience, and it just impacted our relationship so much. Believe me, I wasn't happy about it either, but it became clear that for him, unless his writing career was going well, he wasn't going to allow himself to be happy about any other part of his life. And I thought there was more to life than that. It was kind of a turning point for us, I think, as a married couple."

So Andrew Reich was right to be concerned when he and Ted Cohen started writing together. "My worries were not, *Is this going*

213

to get us a job? It was, *We're friends, and now we're working together — are we gonna be able to make that work?*" Reich says. "I think that was a process that we were both luckily mature about all along, and we realized there are gonna be different issues when you're writing together than when you're just friends. You disagree with each other more than you would if you're just hanging out. How do you get past those moments, and how do you really listen to and respect the other person?"

"Strangely, you're the only friend that I have left," Ted deadpans. They laugh.

This doesn't mean your personal relationship has to be close.

"I have always thought of Woody Allen as a friend," says Marshall Brickman, "although I would not expect him to bring me chicken soup if I were in bed with a cold, nor, I assume, would he expect that of me. The relationship has always been cordial but not intimate. We do not discuss personal problems. But I feel he has my best interests at heart, as I have his."

That's the key. Cordial or close, you must have each other's best interests at heart. You must care about each other as a person and as a writing partner. If you don't, you won't write together for long.

The creative relationship is also the hardest in the world because of the enormous time commitment, especially if you're "nine-to-fivers" like Alexander & Karaszewski.

SCOTT: What we do is like being locked in a prison cell with one person. You can just see that one person every day of your life, and you don't see anybody else. It's a very strange formalized relationship. There are probably very few analogies to it except prison.

LARRY: (sarcastic) The glamour of movies. We'll just say it once in a while — "Isn't making movies great?" Ha! We're usually locked

214

in some anonymous office building, looking at each other, having to deliver pages at the end of the day. Some runner will show up at the door and knock, and you have to hand him something! That's what making movies is.

SCOTT: But it seems to work.

LARRY: Yeah. We like the material. You know, we're very proud of what we do. And strangely enough, we're still friends. But we don't socialize that much anymore, simply because I see him all day. So it would be ridiculous if I said, "Hey, so what movie do you want to see tonight?" It just doesn't happen. When we get out of here, we head for the hills.

SCOTT: I mean, I see you more than I see my wife.

LARRY: Scary.

SCOTT: You just do the math.

The creative relationship is the hardest in the world because writers are headstrong mules, some of the world's worst control freaks. We want things the way we want them. That's one of the reasons we turned to writing — to create universes where we *do* have control. Still, to succeed as a collaborative pair, you must learn to let go.

"What you have to do is compromise," Fay Kanin says. "That's the word of collaboration — compromise."

Compromise is essential but also humbling, so some writers are covert about it, like Jacques Martineau. "Jacques always starts out by grumbling and saying that he'll never *ever* do what Olivier is asking, and then he does it, but in his own way."

Compromise is also humanizing.

MATT: When I was directing this short film several years back, my nickname on the set became "Mr. Control." It was kind of funny

215

but also very telling — I had this need to oversee and control every aspect of the production. But collaborating with Claudia has made me more relaxed and flexible, open to compromise.

Andrew Reich describes a similar evolution. "I was used to directing things and just forcing, and I think working with Ted has been a good process of learning how to work together — which no one can do instantly."

And the creative relationship is the hardest in the world because, whether we admit it or not, writers are competitive. Granted, a healthy competitiveness can be a good thing. It can bring out the best in each partner. We know. We often write better because we're trying to impress one another.

CLAUDIA: When I write a joke, I want Matt to guffaw. He's the funniest person I know (outside my own wacky family), so if I crack him up, I know an audience will laugh, too.

When Ted Elliott writes a scene, he doesn't just want to impress Terry Rossio, he wants to *floor* him. "I want him to be jealous," Elliott says. "Just a little, but jealous all the same. And that prompts him to write a scene that impresses me, floors me, makes me jealous."

But competitiveness can corrode your creative relationship if you start keeping score about your respective contributions to your scripts.

"There are some real dysfunctional partnerships out there," Matthew Stone tells us. "People keep tabs on what their contributions are. This and that. 'That person said no to my line.' We've fortunately not done that."

The truth is, the longer and better you work together and the more you meld your voice and aesthetic, the harder it is to know who wrote what. When we ask Marshall Brickman about his and Woody Allen's individual contributions to the scripts they co-wrote, he says,

216

"It's not really possible to answer with any accuracy or insight. One person moves the conversation in a direction in which the other person can have an idea or think of a joke or plot twist that would not have been possible without the conversation. So who takes credit for what?"

Or, as Stone says about working with Ramsey, "I think that by the time the thing is finished, it's so completely both of ours that I would be hard-pressed to remember who came up with a certain moment, a certain scene, even. It just doesn't matter because that's not the point."

The point is to co-write the best script you can. And to do that, you have to set your human frailties aside and find productive strategies for working together.

KEEP IT FAIR

We interviewed twenty script partners or teams for this book, which made transcribing the audiotapes a formidable task. Before Claudia left L.A., she sifted through the tapes and started choosing the ones she wanted to transcribe.

"Hey," Matt said, "why do you get to choose?"

Claudia started to counter with a quote from Annie Savoy ("Actually, none of us on this planet ever really choose..."), but she knew Matt was right — we both needed to have a say in the matter. So we tried to think of a way to divide up the cassettes that would be fair to both of us. The answer was right there in the interviews — Reich & Cohen divide up scenes based on difficulty, and the Longstreets and Kanins pick and choose based on preference. Inspired by their examples, we sorted our Everest of audiotapes by length and difficulty and took turns choosing the ones we'd transcribe.

It's crucial that teams keep it fair, though how they accomplish this differs. Like Woody Allen and Peter Tolan, Matt prefers writing the first draft of a script once we've co-created our characters, story, and structure. But we both know what a bitch it is to get a first draft down on paper, so when we'd finished transcribing the tapes, Claudia offered to write the first draft of most of these chapters.

Nick Kazan, on the other hand, considers one partner writing the first draft a risky approach. "Those partnerships are really fragile because one person is doing all the writing essentially," he says. "The other person is certainly contributing but not doing the writing. So then it comes to divvying up the credit and the money, and you say, 'Well, maybe you should just get story credit with me.' 'No, no, no, I'm used to getting screenplay credit. I don't want to just get story credit,' and 'That's not fair,' and so forth." But Kazan acknowledges that a lopsided workload is less risky when both partners have successful independent careers. "The people I'm collaborating with by and large are extremely successful, so if that turns out to be unequal, I don't care what my credit is. If it's unequal, and I'm doing more of the work, I don't care either. That doesn't matter. It's the fun of doing it with a friend and being able to tell this story."

Fair, in short, does not always mean equal. But however you decide to divide up the work, both of you need to feel fairly treated. Resentment caused by a sense of unfairness will corrode or even end a creative relationship. To prevent this, you and your partner will need to agree on what equal and fair mean to you.

You want to be able to say, as Renee Longstreet does after decades of writing and fighting with Harry, "I feel we've kept it fair. Oh, yeah, I'd say we have. And it's been pretty damn fun."

DEALING WITH DISAGREEMENT

When we talk to solo writers interested in working collaboratively, their chief concern is how to deal with disagreements. "How do you keep the creative relationship going when you and your partner argue?" they ask us. "How do you avoid hurt feelings?" "How do you resolve disagreements?" They're right to be concerned. Even in the most long-lasting and successful collaborations like Alexander & Karaszewski, disagreement is inevitable. How often do they argue about creative issues?

"All the time," says Alexander.

"Yeah," Karaszewski says, "all the time."

How often and how intensely partners argue will vary from team to team — and sometimes from project to project — but even the most compatible, peace-loving partners will argue occasionally as they co-create scripts. And that's not a bad thing. As we said in Chapter Two, disagreement is an integral and invaluable part of the collaborative process.

Our fiercest fights, in fact, have led to some of our greatest breakthroughs.

CLAUDIA: When we were rewriting *Obscenity* for Sundance, we were bogging down because I was trying to preserve one of Matt's jokes.

MATT: Usually I love it when Claudia wants to leave in my jokes, but we had a tight deadline, and I was beginning to panic.

CLAUDIA: Matt argued that we should just cut the damn joke and move on. I argued we shouldn't. And Matt was getting pissed off (and he's rarely pissed off) because I was going to incredible lengths to justify keeping it in. To me, it was more than a joke. The script is such a serious story, and the joke is a lovely connection beat between Sara and her love interest, Joe — the first time they laugh together. So I wouldn't budge. Then somehow, don't ask me how, in the midst of this argument, I had one of those cosmic transmissions, a blazing out-of-the-blue insight that deepened the whole script.

That's one reason Peter Tolan says a mouthful (as we say in the South) when he tells us, "In a good collaboration, you've *gotta* be able to argue. I mean, you gotta really be able to say, 'I don't like this and here's why. Here's why this doesn't work,' and you gotta hope, too, that that person is open to hearing that."

That is why Andrew Reich recommends writing with "someone you've had arguments with or you know you can settle things with without throwing tantrums."

David Sonnenschein admits that creative disagreements with Stuart Geltner sometimes get "really nasty and ugly." But they both understand these fights are necessary and temporary. "We know that neither of us is right," he says, "and that we'll find a third solution that neither of us has seen that will attend to both of our points of view. And that's a very beautiful kind of exchange because we trust each other. We trust the process that we can really fight in the middle of it. We trust that it's for the higher good, that we are in battle, and if we don't find a solution within a couple of minutes, it's okay — we will find it. We'll go on to something else, and then we'll come back, and it will work out."

Like so much else in collaboration, trusting the process and each other requires respect.

"It has to do with being able to listen and to respect the other one's opinions," Fay Kanin says. "And to fight. When it's necessary, to fight. But we never fought about the basics of the project. It was about, you know, whether the scene should go this way or that way, whether she should feel like this or she should feel like that. We would argue, but we never fought physically. The worst thing physically that Michael ever did was he went out once and slammed the door. That was shocking!" She laughs. "But aside from that, we worked it out. We had great respect for each other. I think that's important in a collaboration."

"You really have to respect the person you're working with," Carolyn Miller says, "and you have to appreciate that if they don't agree with you, they're catching something that you're not. You have to hear what that is and work through it. It can be a painful thing, but it really makes you stretch."

As Ed Solomon says about creative disagreements with Chris Matheson, "If Chris feels adamant about something, we go with that. I respect him enough to know that it's right, even if I can't see it."

"You have to get the fact that your partner is not trying to sabotage the movie," says Larry Karaszewski.

If your collaboration is new, it's reassuring to know that this trust and respect will increase as you work together. "For the first couple of years," adds Karaszewski, "when you're working with somebody you don't know, you think, *Oh my God, that guy's an asshole! He doesn't know what he's talking about!* At a certain point you realize, *Well, he does sort of know what he's talking about.*"

But disagreements will still occur, and if they aren't sensitively and successfully resolved, they can be downright destructive. So finding ways to resolve your differences is all-important. That is why, as we interview writing teams, we ask how they resolve their creative disagreements. Their answers are illuminating and instructive, offering us the following insights and strategies:

DON'T TAKE IT PERSONALLY

Harry & Renee Longstreet have their worst fights when they co-create stories.

HARRY: We kill each other on story. Verbally, in fact. One show we were on, our office was right next to someone who is a very good friend of ours now, and we'd be in there hacking out a story for the series and fighting and screaming obscenities at each other.

RENEE: She didn't know us. That was when we met her.

HARRY: And she'd say, "Oh, my God, they're gonna kill one another!" And then — oop! — lunchtime, and we'd walk out holding hands, and she'd go, "Huh?"

How did they manage to go from sixty to zero, from hurling obscenities to holding hands?

RENEE: We never get personal.

HARRY: It's business. It has nothing to do with who we are or our relationship.

RENEE: We both had bad marriages. That's all I can say.

HARRY: Two bad marriages behind us. That helps.

RENEE: Both of us have an aversion to confrontation.

HARRY: Oh, yeah, we had all the confrontation we'll ever need.

RENEE: Right. Sometimes I get really mad at you, but I've never said anything in twenty-five years that I've had to take back. Ever. We've never said to each other such hurtful things that we can't get past them. I once said "Fuck you" — on the stairs — and you still remember it.

HARRY: But it wasn't about creative —

RENEE: No. I've never said anything mean to you, and I don't think you've ever said anything mean to me. That's the best advice we can give — don't be mean.

HARRY: Keep it about the work and not about the people.

RENEE: Right. And if it does get about the people, don't be mean to each other. Don't say things you'll regret. Ever ever ever. Because that would have cleaned us out. We never would've been able to come back to the work.

Alexander Payne & Jim Taylor "never take any criticism personally," Taylor tells us, but he concedes that this isn't easy. "You have to have a certain sense of self-confidence — or very low self-esteem, take your pick — not to be insulted when someone doesn't like what you've written." And he agrees that the level of insult is greatly reduced if they argue about the work, not each other. "I'm happy to say that our collaboration is very amicable. I think we're both good at keeping our disagreements focused on what's best for the story."

But even arguments focused on the work can get personal, according to Matt Manfredi & Phil Hay.

PHIL: Our arguments genuinely are about creative issues. They're about, "I think this is a wrong choice for this character." That kind of thing.

MATT: So it's productive. You just consider it part of the process, and it doesn't get personal —

PHIL: Yeah. Some of them — It gets personal. (They laugh.)

MATT: It gets very personal.

PHIL: But a lot of them are creative, and a lot of them are just venting, you know, frustration and rage. It's a very frustrating business.

We ask Alexander & Karaszewski how they've kept the peace, kept the friendship.

LARRY: What peace? What friendship? (They laugh.) I don't think either of us takes it personally anymore.

SCOTT: I'm here, ain't I?

LARRY: I'd say that was a problem during the first few years. I mean, we had these fights that were just insane! People would storm out, and there was "Fuck you!" and this hateful, hateful, dirty fight.

Nicole Yorkin & Dawn Prestwich have also mellowed over the years. "When we first started writing," Prestwich tells *Written By*, "we would be very sensitive if the other person didn't like our idea, and now that's just a blip on the screen. It's a given that if the other person doesn't like it, you've got to find something better."

CHECK YOUR EGO AT THE DOOR

Not taking it personally is easier said than done, especially when you consider that "everybody's neurotic and writers are *more* neurotic than most," Gelbart says. Still, if your creative relationship is going to last, you and your partner have to find a way to set your egos aside.

"Ego is the great destroyer," Nick Kazan says.

"We try to take the ego out of the relationship, and that's the Cash/Epps way. That's the third ego," Jack Epps tells *Written By*. "The partnership has got to be the thing."

Ramsey & Stone agree.

ROBERT: You don't have to surrender your ego to everybody on earth, but you do have to, to some degree, surrender your ego to that person.

MATTHEW: I hear a lot of people say that — well, not a lot of people — mostly I hear novelists say, "I could never work with somebody else. The purity of the voice." Well, if you can subjugate your ego to the partnership, it is your voice. It's your voice as a partnership.

ROBERT: Our goal professionally is really to create a voice — that Ramsey & Stone voice. It's a harmony.

Subjugating one's ego is never more difficult or important than in the heat and potential hurt of an argument. For that reason, Ted Elliott & Terry Rossio have created a strategy they call "egoless arguing."

"Simply enough," Elliott says, "it means that the ideas do battle, not the people." When one suggests an idea, they each point out pros and cons, so even the partner who came up with it is no longer ego-involved. The idea must pass muster on its own merit.

"I've always believed in the hierarchy of good ideas," says Harold Ramis. "When you're right, one proof of being right is that everyone recognizes it. Particularly in comedy. You can't stand there and say 'this is funny' if no one else agrees with you. You know, argument is not an inherently negative thing in the pure dictionary sense of argument. It's just disagreement and discussion. There's no emotional component attached to it, but if you have to make a point by somehow browbeating the other person or screaming, chances are you're not right anyway."

Phil Hay describes creative arguments "that have to happen, that have to be resolved, but it doesn't matter who's on what side." Ego isn't what matters. What matters is getting the work done as well as they can. He uses pitching as an example: Often when he and Matt Manfredi are preparing a pitch, they'll disagree on how much pre-planning they need to do.

"Someone has to take each role in the argument," Hay says, "and there are a lot of times where we switch in the middle without really realizing it. One person thinks we don't have to prepare that much, and the other person says, 'No, no, we have to plan the whole thing; this time it's important to have everything completely scripted.' And then halfway through, the person who wanted it scripted is like,

'Look, we've done enough.' And the other says, 'We don't know what we're doing.'"

Your personal stake is not in your individual ideas or what side you're on but in the overall script you're co-writing. We might all be better off — and better at setting our egos aside — if we made a small (or big) sign that said: IT'S THE SCRIPT, STUPID.

SHOW DON'T TELL

When we're disagreeing about the way a scene should be written, one of us will occasionally say, "Let me play a minute," and type out the scene. Then the other can see that person's vision — and version — on paper. If it works, terrific. The proof's in the pudding, or in this case, on the page.

Nick Kazan & Robin Swicord use this strategy, too, to avoid or resolve arguments. "If Robin tells me that she wants to change the scene that I've written, I don't like that," Kazan says. "I don't want to hear that she doesn't like it. Whereas if she just rewrites it and shows me the new scene, okay, fine! Sometimes I may object and think it was better before, but more frequently I say, 'Well, great. I liked it the other way, but I like it this way, too!' Again, it's showing. So we'll get the script back and forth, not discussing it, because discussing it gets into ego. Once you say, 'No, I don't like what you did,' they say, 'Well, fuck you!' In fact, I just changed something back in the script we're working on, and I don't know what Robin's response is going to be. She was shortening it, and I thought it lost its value. So I put it back because I think it's funnier in the original form, that the rhythm works better."

Not that they won't discuss script problems they're having.

"If you anticipate a problem, if you're having difficulty, you want to brainstorm," Kazan says. "Or if you don't know where the next section should go. You obviously have to talk about that. Robin likes to talk out stuff because she wants to know where she's going. I like to be surprised by whatever happens, so I like to talk about things less. We just kind of work that out."

BARGAINING

Sometimes, however, showing your partner how you see the scene can still lead to disagreement, as it has with the Batchlers.

"We hand each other pages, and we don't really talk about them," Janet says. "We do draft after draft, and we label at the top what scene it is or what sequence it is, and rewrite each other, until it comes to the point where I'm taking out his changes and putting mine back wholesale, or he's taking out my changes and putting in his wholesale — and then it's clear that we've got to discuss it. And then we get the kids out of the house, and we lock ourselves up in a room and we scream at each other."

We ask how they resolve these screamfests.

"We strike bargains," Janet says. "'I'll give you that incredibly bad line *if* you'll let me cut this, this, and this.'"

"I won't say it's an incredibly bad line," Lee objects. "It's brilliant, and I'm right!"

They laugh.

When we ask Alexander & Karaszewski if they strike bargains to resolve disagreements, they disagree.

SCOTT: We yell at each other, and we cut back room deals.

LARRY: We have never cut back room deals.

SCOTT: Oh, sure we do. That's baloney.

LARRY: Even though you always shoot that down, we've never — I would love it. A lot of times that's the more civilized way of doing it.

SCOTT: There are back room deals like, "Okay, you can have that, but I get — " There are. He just doesn't want to admit it. They are unspoken. There are unspoken deals.

LARRY: Yeah, I wish there were.

SCOTT: There are plea bargains.

LARRY: I would *recommend* back room deals for people who want their collaboration to live. Here's the thing — our scripts are so long that when he's saying, "I love this scene, it's never getting cut," I'm thinking, *All right, I'll let him keep that scene today, but tomorrow I'll bring it up again.* And then he'll beat me back down, saying, "Oh, that scene's gotta be in the movie." After a month of doing this, and we're still on page 160 as opposed to 120, the scene goes.

We've struck similar bargains as we've co-written this book. Claudia has loved and woven into the first draft many lengthy quotations from our interviews; Matt has frequently recommended we trim them, which is ironic considering it's usually Claudia who gets out the "chainsaw." We've traded places, which proves Phil Hay's point that some creative arguments just have to happen, and it doesn't matter which side you're on. We've done some horse trading, too — "You get this if I get that." But like Alexander & Karaszewski, as we've watched this manuscript get longer and our time get shorter, we've agreed that some of the pieces just have to go.

WEARING YOUR PARTNER DOWN

"Actually," says Scott Alexander, "I have a completely brilliant way of driving Larry crazy, which is I'll walk in with a big fat agenda, like, 'I've figured out a way we can cut out pages 48 to 63. Don't even need them anymore.' Larry is like, 'What are you talking about?' 'We should just lose this whole subplot, this whole thing.' He'll say, 'Oh, my gosh — this is so amazing, this is so great, because the movie's running so long.' And I'll say, '*Nah*, I don't like it. I wanna keep it the way it is.' I'm backing off my own case."

Does this accomplish anything other than wearing his partner down?

"No," says Karaszewski, "it accomplishes nothing whatsoever. It's frustrating."

Alexander laughs. "So it's a good technique."

"Wearing your partner down" evolved from a prehistoric practice invented by the adolescent female whose parents wouldn't let her go steady, so she walked in the door and announced, "Mom, Dad, I'm pregnant!" When her parents freaked out, she grinned, "I'm kidding. I'm just going steady." This exploitive technique (a.k.a. Mind Fuck) was picked up by parents and other partners, and perfected by politicians. But should you decide to resolve disagreements this way, just remember that in all stages of its evolution, this method has been most effective when conducted with humor.

That's how Harry Longstreet convinced Renee to change her title for a screenplay.

RENEE: The title of the movie was *The Adventures of Molly Revere*. Harry didn't like that title.

HARRY: It sounded like a real period piece.

RENEE: He wanted to call it *Lady Under Glass*, which was pretty damn good, but I wouldn't do it. This was the first of our arguments. He started a lobbying effort. I couldn't go to the bathroom without lifting the toilet seat and finding a sign that said "*LADY UNDER GLASS* SHOCKS BOX OFFICE!" I'd find it in my cigarettes — there would be a slip of paper that said "*LADY UNDER GLASS* OPENS TO SOCKO REVIEWS!" You remember that?

HARRY: Yeah. (He chuckles.)

RENEE: So that's how we changed it. I was worn down. "Okay, okay, just do it your way. I can't fight with you any more. I can't fight with you any more."

HARRY: We both know we're right so that's how we resolve arguments. One of us wears the other one out.

But we only recommend this technique if you and your partner are very close and enjoy enough good will that you can wear each other down without wearing your relationship out.

DEFERRING TO THE ORIGINAL WRITER

Over the course of their collaboration, the Longstreets have developed a less exhausting way to resolve disagreements. Like the Batchlers and Kazan & Swicord, they pass scenes back and forth, making notes and rewriting each other, but they also keep track of who wrote the scene first.

RENEE: The original writer of a scene is Writer A. The reader, the one making notes, is Writer B. If it's really a staunch disagreement, Writer A prevails.

HARRY: The original writer will always prevail.

RENEE: You have to defer to the original. Except in cases when I did all the typing.

HARRY: She cheats. She cheats. She slips in stuff. (Laughter.)

RENEE: I admit it. I admit that I've done that.

HARRY: And I've caught her at it, too.

RENEE: Yes. But, you know, I do the final pass because I'm the English major, so my spelling is always right —

HARRY: And I'm still dyslexic after all these years, so she'll fix all that stuff.

RENEE: I get final cut. But you've won lots of times. You've won as much as me.

HARRY: Sometimes I've —

RENEE: More!

HARRY: Right.

RENEE: Sometimes. (They laugh again.)

DEFERRING TO PASSION

This is one of the most common and successful peacemaking techniques.

"The way we make decisions is: Who has the most passion?" Jack Epps says.

We often do the same thing, but we don't just defer to passion. We discuss it, exploring the reasons behind it. This can lead to cosmic transmissions or at least convince you the passionate partner is right.

Gene Wilder was wild about his "Puttin' on the Ritz" number in an early draft of *Young Frankenstein*. He expected co-writer and director Mel Brooks to love it, too, as he tells *Scenario*: "I said to myself, now Mel's going to smile! And he said, 'Are you crazy? It's frivolous, it's self-indulgent. You can't just suddenly burst into Irving Berlin and "Puttin' on the Ritz"!'"

More than a painful moment for Wilder. "He took a chisel and cracked my heart," Wilder says.

So he and Brooks had their first big disagreement. "First I argued. And we never argued. But... I argued softly. Then, I started arguing vehemently. Maybe for thirty, forty minutes. I had done research on this — I had gone to psychiatrists and everything — research about nerves and reflexes and how you could test them, and what kinds of movements would help, and then I translated that into comic behavior. And Mel just said, 'Okay, it's in.' I was stunned. I said, 'Why didn't you just *say* that?' He said, 'I didn't know! When you gave it to me and I read it I didn't know. So I thought, let's see how hard he fights for it. Because if you had said, "Yeah, well, maybe not... " then — out! But when you argued that much for it, I knew it must be right.' Well, it was a great relief, but boy, did he pull a fast one. I'm glad he did it. I knew it was right, but when he gave me such a jolt, I had to tell him the reasons *why* I knew it was right. Not just, 'Oh, it's wonderful, it'll be funny.' I had to start telling him all the reasons why, structurally, it was right, scientifically it was right, and theatrically it was right. So, that was a big hurdle, and we got over that one."

Thank heavens. It's difficult to imagine the film without the now-classic top-hat-and-tails number (and even more difficult to discuss it without someone imitating the hysterically inarticulate rendition by The Monster/Peter Boyle).

DEFERRING TO THE DIRECTOR

Though Mel Brooks deferred to Gene Wilder's passion, often in writing teams with one partner directing the project, the director's vision prevails.

"I think another thing that helps in our collaboration is that Alexander is going to be directing what we write," Jim Taylor says, "so the final say has to be his. He will be the one who is on the set trying to make the scene work, so he's the only one who can really say if the scene is working. I'll fight him on certain things up to a point, but then I have to defer to his opinion."

This is the advantage of the "unequal dynamic" that Marshall Brickman insists is necessary for a successful collaboration. "What is desirable above all is a consistent, unique, original tone, sensibility, world-view, or point-of-view," Brickman says, "and if the two people are always deferring to each other — or fighting over choices — then you either get television or a very bland and unoriginal piece."

There were times in their collaboration when Brickman prevailed (like adding the confrontation between Isaac and Yale in *Manhattan*), but usually he deferred to Allen. And they never had confrontations themselves when they disagreed. "No," he says, "it never got testy."

"Experienced writers recognize that the director is gonna be the guy out there on the line, the one who has to make the call about whether something's working or not," says Harold Ramis, who has directed many of his co-written scripts, including *Caddyshack, Groundhog Day, Bedazzled, Analyze This,* and *Analyze That.* "That's the tension between writers and directors creatively that you see expressed in the Writers Guild's frequent complaints about the increasing power of directors and the disrespect shown to writers. It's always going to be William Shakespeare's *Hamlet* no matter who directs it. But on the other hand, movies are so collaborative, and the director does end up being the arbiter. So when I'm directing, I invariably write the shooting script. It doesn't mean I change everything, but I decide what stays in and what doesn't."

CREATING RULES TO REPAIR THE RELATIONSHIP

If it does get testy between you and your partner, and — in spite of your best intentions — you both say things you regret, you'll need to find ways to repair the damage. This is especially important if you're not lovers or spouses because "there's no way to kiss and make up," Gelbart says. So non-conjugal collaborations like Ramsey & Stone follow relationship rules recommended for conjugal couples.

ROBERT: I always use marriage metaphors when talking about our partnership, which is actually longer than either of our marriages.

233

MATTHEW: Well, with the marriage metaphor, we have a couple of little rules that aren't really written down. We don't really leave the office mad. (Laughter.) Seriously, if we've had an argument that day, usually we solve the problem anyway by the time we go. But we'll say like, "I'm sorry, Matt; I was out of line when I said that," or "I didn't mean that," or whatever. It's not just by rote because you want to come in the next day and work, and you know you're gonna have these problems.

ROBERT: I'm probably not as good at marriage as I am at being a partner.

MAINTAINING PERSPECTIVE

Last but not least, don't lose perspective.

"It's just a screenplay," says Scott Alexander.

"It's just a screenplay," Larry Karaszewski agrees.

Harry Longstreet says, "There's an old joke: 'We're not curing cancer. It's not brain surgery. It's more important than that.' But that's bullshit. It's not more important."

It's certainly not more important than your creative relationship or your relationship as friends, lovers, or spouses, as Kazan & Swicord realized when they collaborated for the first time.

"Before we did *Matilda*, I was extremely apprehensive," Kazan says, "because Robin and I both have very strong opinions, very strong and different voices. And we fight — we hope in a pleasant way — to retain whatever aesthetic is in our material. So, I just thought, well, if this collaboration goes south, it's going to be okay. I'm going to say, 'Look, the marriage is more important than this. You're a wonderful writer, you finish it — go with God!'"

After Kazan completed the first draft, they began passing their rewrites back and forth. If Kazan changed one of Swicord's revisions back to his version, he wrote her a note explaining his reasons. In response to one of his changes, she wrote Kazan a note of her own. "It said, 'Yes, I understand what you're saying, but I completely visualized this scene, and this is the way I've seen it.' And I got insulted. The implication was that she had visualized it, and I *hadn't* — or that was the implication that I saw. I said, 'It's a movie — don't you think I visualize it also?!' And she said, 'Look, you finish the screenplay. The marriage is more important,' and she gave back to me almost word for word this speech that I had prepared four months earlier. I burst out laughing because I had prepared the same speech but never said it to her! She was taken aback, like, 'Why are you laughing?' And I explained. I don't even remember how we resolved that sequence, but that was the only awkward moment."

WHAT TO DO IF IT DOESN'T WORK OUT

"You know, collaboration means that you have to give in to the other person," Fay Kanin says. "And marriage means that, too. When you do that for a long time, you find that. Though we worked it out, we had the usual argument — *hiss!* — argument, 'No, I think that,' 'No, I think that,' and one would yield to the other. But at a certain point we said, 'Enough already.' We talked about it, and we said, "You know, the marriage has to go or the collaboration."'

They chose the marriage.

"That didn't mean we didn't still help each other and advise each other," Kanin says. "I read all his stuff when he wrote alone, and he read mine. And when he did *Woman of the Year* — he wrote that with Ring [Lardner Jr.] — Kate [Hepburn] and Gar [Kanin] and I were all part of that."

Carolyn Miller & Daryl Warner made the opposite choice. As their personal and creative relationship headed south, they decided it was best to divorce, a metaphor often used by script partners when they split up.

"People that we know who have been in partnerships and dissolved those partnerships speak in terms of divorce metaphors," Robert Ramsey says.

And divorcing your writing partner can have similar consequences, Manfredi & Hay explain.

MATT: There are a lot of people we've developed relationships with. Down the line maybe we want to do something with these folks, and if Phil and I decide we aren't going to work together anymore, do they want to work with me or do they want to work with Phil?

PHIL: Or neither? Which spouse do you invite to Christmas dinner?

MATT: It's exactly that on a grand scale.

PHIL: It really is. So the best way to do it is to not split up.

MATT: There are certainly examples of amicable splits, but those seem to be people who have been working together for thirty years.

Like the Kanins. Theirs was a mutual decision based on mutual respect — for each other and for the work. But often the decision is *not* mutual. One partner wants out. That's when it really gets tough.

"It's a very hard admission," Gelbart says, "as it is in any relationship — a friend, a sweetheart, whatever. Oh, let me say *lover.* I want to be more modern. It requires a lot of courage to say, 'We're busting up.'"

Aaron Ruben agrees. "It's like telling your wife or your husband, 'Honey, it's over. I've decided I want a divorce.'" And Ruben knows. When his agent offered him a solo shot at writing for George Burns and Gracie Allen, he had to end his collaboration with Phil Cole.

"It was difficult for me," Ruben says, "because there was something very sad about him. He always had a very lugubrious look on his face anyway. And he smoked a curve-stemmed pipe. We'd come up with funny stuff, but always that sad look. And I said, 'Phil, my agent has offered me *The Burns and Allen Show*, but he can only bring one writer on.' And Phil sat there for a while. I could see he was very unhappy. And he said, 'Well, you should never have started the collaboration to begin with.' I said, 'Phil, what have you lost? You got nine weeks of work out of it. I'm sorry, I guess I just have to move on. My agent says it's time to move on.' Well, that was over with. I went to work for Burns and Allen, and it was great."

Larry Gelbart had to do the same thing — twice.

"Both men took it hard," he says. "I was kind of like Shirley Temple. I realize that now. When I was sixteen, seventeen, eighteen, I thought, *What's all the fuss about? This is what I do.* But now that I look back and see what a person is at that age, I think that must've been quite a thing. And for me to say that to men older, to whom money was much more important — because I could always get an allowance if I lost a show — they were pissed. It's not that I was so ambitious. I wasn't doing a Sammy Glick thing where I'd found another rung higher than the one I was on. I just wanted to get out of the relationship — in one instance because we weren't contributing equally, and the other because the personal relationship fell apart. And so it became impossible to do the working relationship."

Which is where we came in — if the professional or personal relationship doesn't work, your partnership won't. And it's probably best to move on. If so, end it as amicably and as honestly as you can.

"Honesty is very important," Gelbart says. "You can't fake a working attitude if you're disenchanted."

Peter Tolan agrees. "It's the same as any real relationship — be honest and say, 'Look, I've outgrown you,' or 'I feel like I'm doing more than my share of work,' or whatever it is."

As you talk it out, you may even discover that your partnership is worth saving. Then you'll need to find ways "to feed it and keep it running," as Tolan says, "to evolve with it as opposed to evolving apart."

SCRIPT PARTNER POINTS

❹ Whether your personal relationship is cordial or close, keep each other's best interests at heart to help make the professional relationship work.

❹ Compromise (it's not a four-letter word).

❹ Don't keep score of your respective creative contributions.

❹ Figure out ways to keep your workload fair, whatever "fair" means to you both.

❹ Check your ego at the door.

❹ Keep in mind the greater good: a good script.

❹ Don't forget, disagreements are a necessary part of the process. But keep them constructive, not destructive.

❹ Try some or all of the ways that other writers resolve disagreements:

> Don't get personal with your criticism (and don't take criticism personally).
> Show how you envision a scene by writing it down (the proof's on the page).
> Bargain ("*Quid pro quo*, Clarice").
> Wear each other down (humorously).
> Defer to the original writer (if you divide up your scenes).
> Defer to passion (but explore the reasons behind it).

❹ Don't go away angry. Unlike love, collaboration means always having to say you're sorry.

❹ Maintain perspective. The relationship is more important than the script.

❹ If the creative relationship doesn't work out, there must be fifty ways to leave your partner, but the best way is honesty.

"Rough business this movie business. I may have to go back to loan-sharking just to take a rest."

— Chili Palmer (John Travolta), Get Shorty

CHAPTER 9

THE BUSINESS RELATIONSHIP

"I used to say, 'Don't write with a partner; I don't like teams,'" confesses Brooke A. Wharton, a Hollywood entertainment attorney and author of *The Writer Got Screwed (but didn't have to)*. "But that's changed now as I've seen really mature teams that have come together, where they've taken two careers that were good and made a career for both of them that was great."

While that great career certainly depends upon a strong creative relationship, a strong business relationship is essential as well. "You have to think of your collaboration as a small business," she says, "and the basic principles that happen in any small business apply."

Having represented a number of top teams in the industry, having seen "the good, the bad, and the drug-addicted ugly," she's able to list quickly those qualities that are crucial to successful collaborations:

• There's complete honesty in the partnership.

• The representation — agents, managers, lawyers — recognizes both partners and doesn't think one partner speaks for the other. All information is passed uniformly and quickly and clearly almost at the same time to both.

• There are no issues ever about money. All expenses are split 50-50. Always. There are never any fights about that.

• There's a sense of helping between the partners, the acknowledgment that maybe at one period of time, one person may

241

not be feeling as well or may be going through something. There's an understanding that the other will pick up the slack instantly.

• There's an understanding that no meetings will be taken with any studio person or any producer or for any potential project if both partners are not there.

• There's a genuine respect in terms of what both parties contribute.

• Both parties equally share whatever business relationships they have. For instance, "I just spoke with this agent; I want you to also come over, if this is something you want to do."

It's clear that many of the same qualities that feed the creative relationship and keep it running apply to the business relationship as well — respect, honesty, trust, and communication. The absence of any of these, Wharton warns, could destroy the collaboration. So could the following:

• Failure to communicate about who's called about what project. One person taking off in a direction with a piece of work without communicating that to another. Or taking off with a piece and trying to represent it as their solo piece.

• Money issues such as not sharing profits and expenses.

• One of the parties trying to present themselves as superior in the relationship; that will destroy it instantly.

• One person thinking they're hot stuff and bringing a partner in just to help them write — the "I'm doing you a favor" kind of relationship. I've seen these teams work for a certain amount of time, but eventually that attitude drives the recipient away.

INDUSTRY PERCEPTION

If your collaboration is on the rocks, but there's a will and a way to stay together, it may be best to do so for business reasons. This is especially true if you're part of a team that has written for years and achieved some success in the biz. Why? Because the industry perceives you as "a unified one," as Wharton says.

"If you've been a team for any length of time, you have almost no reputation anymore as an individual," Lowell Ganz says in *Creative Screenwriting*. "The only reputation you would have is with people who know you very well and very personally and would be willing to take a chance that you might not be a total dunderhead as an individual. The business is littered with halves of teams that decided they were going to start over and were stunned to find out that anything they did was going to be judged more harshly."

"You get labeled as a team," agrees film/literary agent Dave Brown. "If I offer producers one of the writers, they say, 'Why do I want 50%?' Because they're thinking that the whole was two, so now they're only going to be getting half."

Your abilities and contributions to the former collaboration may even be called into question. "When the team breaks up, everyone always assumes that the other guy's the talented one," says Matt Manfredi. "If they have a meeting with me, as soon as I leave it would be, 'I bet Phil's the guy with all the skills.' And it would be vice versa when Phil leaves."

The same is true for television writers, according to TV/literary agent Jennifer Good with Anonymous Content. "This town is used to teams splitting up, but it can be rough," she says. "Execs and show runners [those who hire writers/staff to create a TV show] seem to be very skeptical about 'who was the real talent in the team.'"

Many producers and others in the industry will insist on seeing solo work before they'll hire a past collaborator for future gigs.

"You have a problem when you're trying to put somebody up for an open assignment with a great writing sample that has both writers' names on it, and the producer or executives are only going to be getting one of those names for the job," Brown tells us. "You can say, 'Hey, listen, he really did 90% of the work.' They're saying, 'Yeah, but we don't know that.'"

So if you have to break up with your partner, and the only scripts you have are co-written, you'll have to write new spec scripts and build a reputation as a solo writer.

"The only way a team that breaks up can start new careers is if they can show what they can do on their own," says Alan Gasmer, Senior Vice President of the William Morris Agency, where he has spent his entire seventeen-year career. "For example, I represented a team of women writers who broke up, and one has gone on as a successful executive producer in television, and the other became a successful feature writer. So you never know. But you have to be able to demonstrate in a script by yourself what you can do to be able to forge a new career."

Jennifer Good agrees. "If both writers have new, fresh material they should eventually be fine, but it can take a lot of work and reinvention."

After her divorce, Carolyn Miller had to reinvent herself as a solo writer. "Credits are everything in Hollywood, and for so many years my credits were tied to Daryl's," she says. "I was really worried nobody would listen to me seriously because I had no solo script. So I had to re-establish myself. That's one reason I went into writing for new media — it was a brand new arena."

Okay, so what if, even knowing the disadvantages of going it alone, you and your partner decide you just can't work together? Brooke Wharton advises that you keep your decision under wraps until the movie's a wrap.

"In every contract a writing team signs with a studio there's a section which says the studio has the right to yank the project if one member of the team is incapacitated," she explains. "So if there's something going on with a team, you don't want it to get exposed. I think partners should generally try to resolve their differences. Until the project is finished. Think about it. The studio's invested, let's say, hundreds of thousands of dollars for a draft and set of revisions from a writing team. From their point of view, if half of the team is down, they wonder if they're gonna get the project that they paid for."

Again, it goes back to industry perception. You and your partner are a unified one, not two separate talents. In the eyes of most producers, agents, and managers, two brains aren't better than one, they *are* one.

This may explain why they don't have a preference for taking on teams — two writers for the price of one — when it seems like such an obvious bargain.

"I don't think they think that way," says Beverly Hills entertainment attorney, Eric Weissmann, partner in Weissmann & Wolff, LLP. "The industry cares about the work product and the success. And if a writing team composed of a nymphomaniac and a gorilla has a hit movie, they don't care!" He laughs.

Now there's a combo we'd love to see — and knowing Hollywood, we probably will.

"I think they encourage anybody," says Scott Alexander. "It's about whether you can deliver or not. If you can deliver solo, they're fine with that."

Phil Hay agrees. "As a writing team, you're just an entity in that you're responsible for doing the work."

"With studios, agents, managers, *everyone*," adds Matt Manfredi, "it's just a given that there are teams and there are not teams."

On the agent front, Gasmer confirms this perception: "I have two cousins that are a team. I have husbands and wives who are teams. I have friends that are teams. I've handled teams in TV. I've handled teams in motion pictures. But the bulk of my clients are individuals." When we ask Gasmer if he prefers to represent solo writers or teams, he says, "It doesn't matter."

"To me, the word on the page is what matters," Dave Brown says. "I don't care how it gets there as long as it isn't stolen!"

The same attitude prevails in the very collaborative world of television writing.

"It's a wash on the team thing," Jennifer Good says. "For each time I hear that a show runner wants a team because they want more bodies in the room, I hear that a show runner doesn't want a team because there may be too many bodies. When I first started out as an agent four or five years ago, I saw more teams being staffed at the low level as 'staff writers'; however, in the past year or so, it seems that there have been more single writers at that level."

Among television executives, the preference for writing teams also goes in and out of fashion, according to Gasmer. "It depends if half-hours are more 'in' this year than one-hours," he says. "The team concept seems to work better in the half-hour because comedy is more collaborative, because it's more about being in the room and being funny and playing off each other. So sometimes they'll call and say, 'We're looking for a team,' or 'We're looking for a male-female team,' or 'We're looking for a female team.' For a while there, I was representing two female teams for television, and I knew that it would be easy, that I could get them a job, just because that was in vogue at the time. I think the half-hour comedy team is an interesting concept. I would always look to sign a half-hour writing team."

DEALING WITH AGREEMENTS

New writing partners seldom anticipate problems in the creative relationship, much less imagine that it might end. Like newlyweds, who wants to think about dismal endings when the romance is beginning? They'd rather devote their energies to their new partner and project — a kick-ass script that actors, directors, and producers will kiss ass to attach themselves to!

But in the business relationship, there's no honeymoon, as several experienced insiders tell us. Most business issues surface when teams are new.

"The immature bickering stuff happens with people who are in film schools or just taking courses or just starting out," Wharton says. "That's where you get the fights and the nastiness and the *this* and the *that*. 'I've got a contact, and I'm gonna take it, and I'll never talk to you again.' That kind of thing which is like, 'Oh, please. Go home, leave me alone. If you really think it works that way, I'll see ya later.'"

For this reason, Wharton recommends that new script partners anticipate these problems and protect their respective rights by signing an agreement that lays the groundwork and goals for their collaborative project. "The written agreement is important for that early stage — the first five years, first ten years, something like that. Because in the first five years of a career, everyone is sort of learning how things work. And people tend to be a little more aggressive and unrealistic at that point."

Eric Weissmann is more emphatic. "I recommend *most firmly* that they sign an agreement that defines exactly what it is that they're collaborating on and exactly what it is that they have rights on," he says. "Particularly if they're friends because sometimes friendships end. People have different recollections of what happens. It is a very frequent problem, almost in every non-professional collaboration, because the people don't have the money for a lawyer. They don't think about it, and they're friends, and they're all excited about what they're writing."

You may be thinking, *What's the big deal? What could go wrong?* Unfortunately, lots of things. Consider this scenario:

> *Joe comes up with an idea for a script and asks Bill to collaborate with him. Bill ends up writing most or all of the screenplay because Joe is too busy with his job (or he's lazy or loses interest). After the script is finished, Bill tells Joe, "Hey, I did all the work, so when this sells, you only get a quarter of the money instead of half." Joe balks because the story was his idea in the first place.*

Sound familiar? We've heard this one several times. As we've said, it's the kind of conflict that can happen when partners haven't defined what fair means to them. And it's the most common fight Wharton sees. In addition to demanding more money, a partner who did most of the work may also insist upon an exclusive "Screenplay by" credit, with only a "Story by" credit for his (we predict) soon-to-be-ex-partner.

"This is ridiculous," Wharton says, "because if it's actually going to be a studio movie or a movie with a Writers Guild signatory [a company adhering to fees/working conditions as set by the Guild], the credit would be determined by the Writers Guild."

Consider this variation:

> *Paul and Carol collaborate on a script. Feeling that she's contributed more to the project, Carol starts shopping the script around as her own. An agent shows interest in representing her and the project, so Carol offers to pay Paul to "just go away."*

"I've seen this happen a million times," Wharton tells us. "The common thing with these situations is there's an ego sort of fight about who did all the work and who was more influential in getting it done and who deserves more money. The problem is one person tries to take all the credit and all the money without acknowledging the other person."

Then there's this possibility:

> *Erica and Donna write a script together. Meanwhile, Donna's career takes off, leaving Erica still waiting tables. Donna thinks,* Hmm, that was a good idea we had, but I can do it better solo, *so she writes a new screenplay loosely based on that idea.* "That's my idea," *Erica objects, and Donna counters,* "No, it's different."

You might think, as we did, that if you copyright the script under both of your names, you're protected from this kind of thing. Not according to Eric Weissmann.

"Having joint copyright owners just means that each person can make a deal for the property, give rights to a third party on a non-exclusive basis," he explains. "But it doesn't say who gets what and who gets what credit, etc."

Still, both of you should *always* copyright your co-written work. For more information, call the U.S. Copyright Office at 202-707-3000. To request materials, call their "hotline" at 202-707-9100. You can also visit their Web site at *www.copyright.gov*. And for a full discussion on copyright law, see Wharton's *The Writer Got Screwed (but didn't have to)*.

Another common issue is control, not just over who makes the decisions about the sale of a script but also what form it will take:

> *Hal and Marcia start writing a script, but they decide to go their separate ways. They have different visions for the project. Hal wants to turn it into a comedy and potentially a TV series. Marcia wants it to be a feature*

with the lead character dying at the end, nixing its potential as a series. Who gets to decide?

"All that happens when this happens is neither of them can do anything because they've just held each other up," says Grace Reiner, Senior Director of Negotiations and Policy Planning for the Writers Guild of America, west. "And that doesn't solve anything for anyone. It's so much easier if they'd agreed, for instance, that Writer A should go and sell it and do it however he or she wants to. And if Writer A is going to try and sell it, it's only going to get sold if there's approval from Writer B. That should be put in some kind of document, that Writer A, in fact, has the authority to do this."

With all these possible problems (and this is hardly a comprehensive list), it's no wonder the experts recommend putting your agreement in writing, especially if you're a new writing team. If you have the money to run it past an attorney, that's even better. But at least get something down on paper and each keep a copy. And do it before you start work on the project.

"That's the most appropriate time and the easiest time to anticipate and pinpoint potential problems," Reiner says. "The writers should try to figure out at the time when they're still getting along, 'What would we want to do with this property if we weren't together?'"

Weissmann seconds the motion. "During the romance, it's very easy to get things signed. Once they're pissed off at each other, it's not so easy."

Think of it as a prenuptial agreement — the paperwork is there in case the partnership sours.

"Pre-nup. That's a perfect description," Weissmann says. "Except there's a little bit less of a romantic aura in the collaboration agreement. And part of the pre-nup agreement generally is not that she has to have sex three times a day," he adds, laughing. "There's not a performance clause, whereas in the writing agreement there can be one."

Reiner draws a further distinction between a prenuptial agreement and a collaboration agreement. "A prenuptial agreement is 'What happens to our property if we break up?' But with collaboration, the piece of property is the *result* of the partnership. It's not just, 'Who owns the car when we're done?' It's more like a child and two people saying, 'This will be the product of our relationship. How are we going to raise it and nurture it? Who's going to get custody? Let's try to resolve those things while we still like each other. And hopefully we will *always* like each other.'" (So scripts *are* babies!)

All this being said, we have to admit that in all the years we've been writing together, we've never signed an agreement outlining the terms of our partnership. We're like Phil Hay & Matt Manfredi, who tell us, "We have a gentlemen's agreement."

The same is true of most of the writers we've interviewed.

"Alexander and I don't have any formal agreement," Jim Taylor says. "But all our contracts stipulate that the money will be split 50-50."

Ours do, too, including the one for this book.

When we ask Ed Solomon if he and Chris Matheson have ever had a written agreement, he says, "Honestly, it's never crossed my mind, but I can see how for some people it would be a good idea."

So can we. So can Jim Taylor. "It's probably a good idea to have something in writing before you begin a spec script," he says, "so there are no questions later on."

So do what we say and not what we do, especially if you and your partner are just starting out.

"Professional people are less likely to have a problem," says Eric Weissmann, "even when they go their separate ways. I've represented a number of very important career collaborators, and there's never been a problem. But I still advise it."

According to Wharton, legal wrangling occurs less often with experienced teams because "they're so grateful to have discovered a formula for their success that they don't want to mess with it." As a result, they tend to steer clear of the ego issues that lead to fights in the first place. But she still recommends an understanding between the parties. "*Some* sort of understanding, whether it's oral or written," she says. "As an attorney, of course, I'd like to see it written. But that never happens."

And splitting up does.

Carolyn Miller & Daryl Warner never signed a formal collaboration agreement, and that became an issue when they divorced. At the time of their split, they had several outstanding projects in various stages of completion. Some were still circulating in the industry. "Then there was another project that we had written — I think we had gotten through one rough draft," Miller says. "And the question was, 'What do we do with that script and who has ownership?' So, we worked out an agreement. We actually went to a mediator for the divorce, rather than a divorce attorney, and he suggested that each of us have a two-year period to finish the script. I think we would share story credit, and the one who finished it would get the screenplay credit." But neither of them ever followed up on the script. "It's old business," she says, "and we've moved on."

AGREEING ON THE AGREEMENT

So what should you include in a collaborative agreement? Eric Weissmann recommends that you address four basic issues:

• Define what it is that you're collaborating on, specifically saying, "It's the story of Santa Claus on roller skates" or whatever it is.

• Say who is to do what, like if one of you just has the idea and the other is supposed to put it down in writing.

• Say what each partner's share of ownership is — Is it 50-50? Is it 75-25? — or whatever.

• Say who has control of the script.

When David Sonnenschein first started developing television projects with Stuart Geltner, they created "a very simple written agreement" that laid out the specifics of their relationship. "It set us up as equal partners," Sonnenschein says. "We made choices together — that we would receive remuneration 50-50 and share credit. The actual writing collaboration was extremely balanced. The agreement was project-specific, and we let it transfer over to the second project because it's just so simple. No agents involved. No risk and no money exchanged."

But the setup for their next project was more complicated. Sonnenschein had written the original draft of the screenplay for *The Knife and the Rose,* which he planned to produce and direct. He asked Geltner to take a pass at the script based on his notes and their conversations, and he raised development money to pay Geltner for his time. "It was much, much different than the other way with the TV projects," Sonnenschein says. "I was in charge, and he was for hire in this kind of legal-business sense. It's like having director's final cut; in this sense, the writer's final cut is mine on the screenplay. He had to listen to me a lot talking about my vision as a writer/director so that he would be able to be free to create yet be within the realm of my vision."

Sonnenschein set up their new agreement in writing, pulling pieces from other contracts and drawing upon past experiences as a producer/director/writer. "We actually took a little while to negotiate it," he says. "Stuart will get a full writing credit with me. We will be co-writers on this, and he will receive more money when the financing is in place. We both showed the agreement to lawyers

253

because this was something that's a piece of a big project, and we definitely wanted to be clear on it."

As any writer should be.

Dave Brown has seen similar agreements among his clients. "What's common is somebody has written a script, and they say to another writer, 'Hey, can you come in here and rework this with me?' And it's not a whole lot of work — it's really a polish. But the original writer says, 'I'm gonna put your name on it, so it's "Co-written by," and we agree you'll only take, like, 30%.' So that'll happen. Or maybe one's a director/writer and one's a writer, and they say, 'All right, let's write this project together. You're gonna direct it.' So there's a financial agreement that he's gonna be attached to direct, as well as receive 30% or half of the purchase price or whatever."

To help you set up the terms of your business partnership — whatever they may be — the Writers Guild of America has created a document called the "Writer's Collaboration Agreement," which the Guild has kindly allowed us to reprint here (see page 256).

You don't have to be a WGA member to use it. "It's for everybody," Grace Reiner says. "Because it's not mandatory, we have no problem with anybody using it. If it can reduce conflict, that's better for the world. And it's intended to do that."

You may want to complete and sign the WGA form as is or use it as a guide, tailoring it to suit your needs. "Change it, modify it, delete, add," Reiner adds. "It's just a template that addresses the kinds of things that you may be talking or thinking about later if you were not to do this together. It makes things a million times easier than the times where we [the WGA] have had to tell a writer after the fact, 'We can't really do anything for you.' Because the Guild doesn't get involved between team members. It's not as though there's an avenue of recourse if you don't have a collaboration agreement through the union, because there isn't. So it's immeasurably easier if the parties agree up front on what their expectations and plans are. We don't care what your agreement is; we just think you should write it down."

WRITER'S COLLABORATION AGREEMENT*

AGREEMENT made at _____, California, by and between _____ and _____, hereinafter sometimes referred to as the "Parties".

The parties are about to write in collaboration an (original story) (treatment) (screenplay) _____(other), based upon _____, hereinafter referred to as the "Work", and are desirous of establishing all their rights and obligations in and to said Work.

NOW, THEREFORE, in consideration of the execution of this Agreement, and the undertakings of the parties as hereinafter set forth, it is agreed as follows:

1.   The parties shall collaborate in the writing of the Work and upon completion thereof shall be the joint owners of the Work (or shall own the Work in the following percentages: _____).

2.   Upon completion of the Work it shall be registered with the Writers Guild of America, west, Inc. as the joint Work of the parties. If the Work shall be in form such as to qualify it for copyright, it shall be registered for such copyright in the name of both Parties, and each Party hereby designates the other as his attorney-in-fact to register such Work with the United States Copyright Office.

3.   It is contemplated that the Work will be completed by not later than _____, provided, however, that failure to complete the Work by such date shall not be construed as a breach of this Agreement on the part of either party.

4.   It is understood that _____ (both writers) is a/are/are not "professional writer(s)," as that term is defined in the WGA Basic Agreement.

(It is further understood by the Parties that _____ (and _____), in addition to writing services, shall perform the following additional functions in regard to the Work:

5.   If, prior to the completion of the Work, either Party shall voluntarily withdraw from the collaboration, then the other Party shall have the right to complete the Work alone or in conjunction with another collaborator or collaborators, and in such event the percentage of ownership, as hereinbefore provided in paragraph 1, shall be revised by mutual agreement in writing.

6.   If, prior to the completion of the Work, there shall be a dispute of any kind with respect to the Work, then the parties may terminate this Collaboration Agreement by an instrument in writing, which shall be filed with the Writers Guild of America, west, Inc. [new mediation arbitration procedure in Constitution]

7.   Any contract for the sale or other disposition of the Work, where the Work has been completed by the Parties in accordance herewith, shall require that the Work shall be attributed to the authors in the following manner:

8.   Neither party shall sell, or otherwise voluntarily dispose of the Work, or his share therein, without the written consent of the other, which consent, however shall not be unreasonably withheld. (It is agreed that _____ is authorized to contract on behalf of the Parties without written consent of the other, on the condition that s/he negotiate no less than _____ for the work.)

9.   It is acknowledged and agreed that _____ (and _____) shall be the exclusive agents of the Parties for the purposes of sale or other disposition of the Work or any rights therein. Each such agent shall represent the Parties at the following studios only:

        X agent   Y agent

        The aforementioned agent, or agents, shall have _____ period in which to sell or otherwise dispose of the Work, and if there shall be more than one agent, the aggregate commission for the sale or other disposition of the Work shall be limited to ten percent (10%) and shall be equally divided among the agents hereinbefore designated.

        If there shall be two or more agents, they shall be instructed to notify each other when they have begun negotiations for the sale or other disposition of the Work and of the terms thereof, and no agent shall conclude an agreement for the sale or other disposition of the Work unless he shall have first notified the other agents thereof. If there shall be a dispute among the agents as to the sale or other disposition of the Work by any of them, the matter shall immediately be referred to the Parties, who shall determine the matter for them.

10.   Any and all expenses of any kind whatsoever which shall be incurred by either or both of the Parties in connection with the writing, registration or sale or other disposition of the Work shall be (shared jointly) (prorated in accordance with the percentages hereinbefore mentioned in paragraph 1).

11.   All money or other things of value derived from the sale or other disposition of the Work shall be applied as follows:

        a.   In payment of commissions, if any.

        b.   In payment of any expenses or reimbursement of either Party for expenses paid in connection with the Work.

        c.   To the Parties in the proportion of their ownership.

12.   It is understood and agreed that for the purposes of this Agreement the Parties shall share hereunder, unless otherwise herein stated, the proceeds from the sale or any and all other disposition of the Work and the rights and licenses therein and with respect thereto, including but not limited to the following:

a.   Motion picture rights
b.   Sequel rights
c.   Remake rights
d.   Television film rights
e.   Television live rights
f.   Stage rights
g.   Radio rights
h.   Publication rights
i.   Interactive rights
j.   Merchandising rights

13.   Should the Work be sold or otherwise disposed of and, as an incident thereto, the Parties be employed to revise the Work or write a screenplay based thereon, the total compensation provided for in such employment agreement shall be shared by them (jointly, in the following proportion):

If either Party shall be unavailable for the purposes of collaborating on such revision or screenplay, then the Party who is available shall be permitted to do such revision or screenplay and shall be entitled to the full amount of compensation in connection therewith, provided, however, that in such a case the purchase price shall remain fair and reasonable, and in no event shall the Party not available for the revision or screenplay receive less than _____% of the total selling price.

14.   If either Party hereto shall desire to use the Work, or any right therein or with respect thereto, in any venture in which such Party shall have a financial interest, whether direct or indirect, the Party desiring so to do shall notify the other Party of that fact and shall afford such other Party the opportunity to participate in the venture in the proportion of such other Party's interest in the Work. If such other party shall be unwilling to participate in such venture, the Party desiring to proceed therein shall be required to pay such other Party an amount equal to that which such other Party would have received if the Work or right, as the case may be, intended to be so used had been sold to a disinterested person at the price at which the same shall last have been offered, or if it shall not have been offered, at its fair market value which, in the absence of mutual agreement of the Parties, shall be determined by mediation and/or arbitration in accordance with the regulations of the Writers Guild of America, west, Inc. if permissible pursuant to the WGAw Constitution.

15.   This Agreement shall be executed in sufficient number of copies so that one fully executed copy may be, and shall be, delivered to each Party and to the Writers Guild of America, Inc. If any disputes shall arise concerning the interpretation or application of this Agreement, or the rights or liabilities of the Parties arising hereunder, such dispute shall be submitted to the Writers Guild of America, west, Inc. for arbitration in accordance with the arbitration procedures of the Guild, and the determination of the Guild's arbitration committee as to all such matters shall be conclusive and binding upon the Parties.

DATED this _____ day of _____, 20_____.

_____

_____

*   The Provisions herein are not mandatory, and may be modified for the specific needs of the Parties, subject to minimum requirements of the Writers Guild Basic Agreement.

As you'll notice, the WGA agreement is set up for one venture, so you can complete a new agreement for each project or change the language to include several or all of your collaborative scripts.

"Certainly the team can modify the agreement to be all-inclusive, to say something like, 'This will be the template for all of our deals,'" says Grace Reiner. "You can certainly do that. And just add, 'Until we both agree mutually that some deal is different.'"

If one or both writers are members of the Guild, Reiner recommends filing a copy of the completed "Writer's Collaboration Agreement" with the WGA. Non-members may also submit a copy, but "we don't necessarily recommend it," she says, "because it's harder for us to file it for non-members. We can keep things for safekeeping, but that's about all we can do with it."

MONEY MATTERS

As Eric Weissmann said, your agreement should specify the percentage of money you both will receive, and the WGA's template above has a section to do so. With occasional exceptions, as we've mentioned, professional partnerships — especially career collaborations — split the money 50-50, even though the creative contribution of the partners is not always equal.

"In terms of division of work, it's not always a 50-50 type of thing," Brooke Wharton says. "Sometimes one person has the ideas and the inspiration, and the other is really more of the labor. It's a fluid kind of thing as to how it creates a unified whole."

In all her years working with professional collaborations, Wharton has witnessed only two situations where the money was not split in half. The first involved a team that came together for one project — one person on the team was a director, and the other was the writer. "The money was split so that the director actually only got what would be considered half of the story fee," she says, "so about 13.5% of the total money."

The second involved a team that had worked together "for a long, long, long, long long, long time," Wharton says. "One of the partners got very sick and was unable to complete the project or participate in any way. So both writers came up with some sort of understanding about how much work had been done, and the writer who was ill was paid a certain amount. Then the other writer completed the work and got the majority of the money."

For Wharton, when it comes to specifying who gets paid what, the paperwork that's most important to professional teams is the contract created for their writing assignments or spec sales with the studios or buying entities. "That's where things are reduced to writing," she says. "The studios are always cautious about teams in terms of the paperwork, in making sure that everything's going to be 50-50 between the writing partners. Especially if the teams have their own loan-out companies [personal service corporations created by the writers]. There's all the paperwork in terms of 'this is a bona fide corporation, and you won't be coming back and suing us.'"

For some partners, however, seeing only 50% for themselves on the bottom line can become an issue.

"In television, I worked with a lot of teams, and they would always complain about the fact that they were getting half the money everybody else is," says Peter Tolan. "That's your choice, though. Clearly, in a lot of team situations, your partner brings to the table the things that make you successful. But maybe you shouldn't have a partner. And a lot of people go off on their own and are successful — or they're not."

Andrew Reich & Ted Cohen tell us that many script partners working for *Friends* have split the sheets over splitting the check. "These were all teams where both people were equally strong and equally valuable and totally necessary," Cohen says. "So they were teams where people wanted to have more pay and respect."

But those partners who have stayed together have done so because, for them, the advantages of collaboration outweigh any financial disadvantages. "Others are making twice as much money as we are," Reich says, "but we don't want to split up."

Matt Manfredi & Phil Hay claim there's even an emotional reward for sharing the bottom line. "Because you're a team and you literally split every paycheck, you have the same kind of livelihood," Hay says. "It's really nice to have someone who is going through exactly the same peaks and valleys of their career as you. You're on the same level. You're going through the same stuff."

"And since Phil and I get a 75-25 money split," Manfredi adds, straight-faced, "it's good that I always know there's someone who can loan me money. I appreciate that." They laugh.

Robert Ramsey & Matthew Stone have made that long financial climb together, building a career "slowly, steadily," as they say, from their first job writing a movie for $3,000 ("we were twenty-three and twenty-four; our needs were miniscule at that point") to writing major Hollywood releases like *Big Trouble*. And all along the way, they've managed to avoid the money squabbles that have dissolved other teams.

ROBERT: It's been a very progressive living. Over time, we've made more and more. We're doing just fine now. We have no complaints.

MATTHEW: You get a raise if you do a good job, and then you get another one, and you get another one. We're those guys that didn't make it overnight.

ROBERT: I meet so many people who think, *Oh, God, if this thing sells, we'll be millionaires!* It's a lottery mentality. It's foolish. It's fostered by the media, and it's just never been our experience.

Their frustration with the media extends to the Hollywood "trades," which publish the financial details of script sales and other industry deals.

MATTHEW: We don't read the trades. That stuff is just poison.

ROBERT: When we were young, we read the trades. It was like, "Who are these people? How are they getting paid?" It's agitating to read about others' good fortune. (Laughter.)

MATTHEW: Because you also know after you've been in the trades that what they're printing is such complete gobbledy-gook most of the time.

ROBERT: This industry deserves a much higher level of media analysis.

MATTHEW: We've never said this explicitly to our agent, but if an article is ever written in which they publish my salary, I'm going to be very pissed off. Why should people know? What is the compulsion with talking about how much money people make?

ROBERT: Why does it have to be in *Variety*?

SHARING THE EXPENSES

Bickering about money (or comparing your paychecks to others') can cause big trouble, so it's important to keep the financial stuff fair. Make sure you share the expenses incurred by your projects. It's usually best to split them down the middle so neither of you feels financially burdened. Then again, keeping track of every cent can be a bookkeeping burden. You'll have to decide what works best for you.

We're fairly relaxed on the subject. Inevitably, one of us incurs greater expenses on a particular project, but we've found that over time things even out. Since we live on opposite sides of the country and value our writing time together, we frequently fly back and forth. This can get pricey (thank heavens for frequent flyer miles!), so we take turns. We put each other up and divvy up the cost of groceries or treat each other to dinner/drinks to balance things out, but we don't nickel and dime each other to death. We'd resent that as much as lopsided expenses. However, if one of us runs up a big tab, we'll keep track of those costs and settle up with a check.

Like other long-distance teams, we call each other almost daily, often talking for two or three hours (thank heavens for cheap minutes!), so we take turns calling each other. But some teams don't sweat it. When we ask Ed Solomon how he and Chris Matheson shared long-distance calls while they wrote *Automatons*, he tells us he doesn't remember it ever being a concern. We aren't quite that *laissez-faire* about phone bills, but we don't itemize charges either. If we find ourselves talking longer than we expected when it's our turn to call, we'll stop in mid-conversation and say, "Hey, this is costing a fortune. Call me back."

The key again is keeping it fair. If one of us feels financially burdened, we say so (nicely), and we discuss ways to keep our expense balances more fairly balanced.

SHARING THE CREDIT

In its *Screen Credits Manual*, the Writers Guild of America defines a "team of writers" as "two writers who have been assigned at about the same time to the same material and who work together for approximately the same length of time on the material."

The WGA also has specific guidelines as to how script partners receive credit: "When credit is accorded to a team of writers, an ampersand (&) shall be used between the writers' names in the credit to denote a writing team. Use of the word 'and' between writers' names in a credit indicates that the writers did their work separately, one usually rewriting the other. This distinction is well established in the industry through custom and practice."

So if you see credits which read "Writer A & Writer B and Writer C & Writer D" (which looks like the front end of a — *shudder* — word problem from math class), the translation would be, "Writers A & B worked together on the script, and Writers C & D worked together on the script, but the two teams did not work together." In television, according to the WGA, the team that contributed more to the script is listed first; in film, there is "no given rule" for the order of credits.

If disputes arise about the assignment of TV or film credits, the Writers Guild may be asked to intervene with Credit Arbitration. The WGA also automatically conducts an arbitration any time a director or a production executive requests writing credit on the project. The process involves the selection of three Guild members to serve as the arbitration committee. Working anonymously and independently, the three arbiters review copies of all available material (scripts, stories, treatments, source material, etc.) as well as any statement of position by the participating parties. The majority rules; if two of the three arbiters make the same decision about how credit should be awarded, that decision stands.

Having served as an arbiter, Carolyn Miller admits that assigning credit can be a challenging process. "You receive this document that explains how you gauge credit," she says, "and that's really interesting because — Is it dialogue? Is it structure? Is it story? To sort it all out is not an easy thing. Very often it gets sort of subtle. For instance, it may be that writers ask for shared credit, and you may think, *No, I want to give teleplay credit to one person and story credit to this other person.* And you can do it any way you want."

But Miller believes the process works, that it protects writers, especially in cases where production executives ask for writing credits they haven't earned. "There was a time when producers were gobbling up credits to get more money from these episodes, which is ugly," she says. "It happened to me once. They claimed credit they did not deserve. All they had done was change some character names and changed a little bit of dialogue."

But the Guild's arbitration process doesn't sit well with some of its members. "The Guild has confusing and unfair guidelines they use to determine writing credit on features," says Peter Tolan. "And despite regular legal actions taken against them by members, actions which are eventually dropped, they don't seem willing to entertain more realistic guidelines. I am not part of a writing team except sometimes in the eyes of the Guild. They'll go, 'Clearly you were working with this person, and so we're going to treat you as a team.' But no, I certainly don't go into anything as part of a team. I come out of it that way a lot of the time with the Writers Guild. They'll make that determination, and so that affects me sometimes financially."

For financial reasons, Reich & Cohen have negotiated separate producer credits on *Friends*. "Two separate contracts. Exactly the same. Everything," Reich says. But they've continued to share writing credit. "When we *write* a script we have an ampersand — it's written by Andrew Reich & Ted Cohen — but our *producer* credits are separate, and we're paid as two entities."

"And that's strictly for money purposes," Cohen adds.

When they were hired to write for the popular series, they were "story editors." As Reich explains, "The ranks of writers on sitcoms are: staff writer, story editor, executive story editor, co-producer, producer, supervising producer, co-executive producer, and executive producer." They've risen through the ranks to executive producer, but they insist that their way of writing together hasn't changed.

"Our relationship as collaborators has been the same whether we were staff writers or the way it is now," Cohen says. "It's just sort of how we present ourselves. We've always been a team business-wise, and I think we always will."

MORE THAN ONE AGENT

Every career collaborative pair that we've talked to has one agent representing both partners. But script partners who are also established as solo writers or only occasionally write scripts together may have different representation. Nick Kazan & Robin Swicord have different agents, so do Ed Solomon & Chris Matheson.

Because we'd both written solo before we met, we had different agents. When we finished our first co-written script, we asked how they'd like to shop it. They said they'd call each other and work out a game plan, but to the best of our knowledge, they never even spoke. We weren't surprised; they weren't all that communicative with us, either — that oh-so-common cry of the writer — but it was clearly time to move on and find representation as a team. We now share the same management company and entertainment attorney, and we have the same literary agent for this book.

If you and your partner remain with different agents, you can clarify their respective roles by using the "Writers Collaboration Agreement." Item Nine allows you to specify where each agent may shop your co-written script, how long they have to sell it, and that they must divide the commission equally.

But in co-agenting, as in co-writing, the workload may not be equal. "Sometimes one person is just a stronger agent," Dave Brown says. "He's got more energy, more connections. I think it's a good agent who says, 'You understand this project better. Maybe you were more involved in the development process. I got your back. Let me know what you need. You take the lead.' And I don't have a problem with that."

Some agents might. "There may be a little bit of a problem if one is a major agent, and the other one is a smaller one, and the major agent wants to be able to run with the package," Eric Weissmann says. "Then the smaller agent may be a little scared that the major agent may steal the client."

And neither may be crazy about splitting commissions. Would this deter them from taking on a co-written script?

"Well, that *could* be a problem, but agents are whores," Weissmann laughs. "As long as they have something to sell."

"Listen, it's Hollywood," Dave Brown says. "There are egos galore and only so much room for them. So you'll have an agent who feels like, *I have to do this with another agent? I can do it myself and not split my commission and take the whole pie. Is it worth my time, or can I pass it off?* I think there are agents who will pass the buck. Some agents out there we all know are really looking at the bottom dollar and nothing else."

Though some agents balk, splitting commissions is becoming more commonplace because of the increasing number of writers also represented by managers. "While the majority of TV writers just have agents, managers seem to have become more prominent the past few years," Jennifer Good says. "We've gotten used to it."

Sticky or not, having different agents can be beneficial to you as a team.

"It can be helpful because you have two agents who are two different levels of contacts," says Brooke Wharton, "and who are gonna be out there and be representing the work."

"Half the time I've worked with another agent, it's gone very smoothly," Brown says. "Ideally we're on the same page. We've put together a submission list. We go through the list of producers and studio executives. Basically like, 'You take this one, I take this one, you take this one, I take that one.' And then *boom*, we're also gonna make calls and we're gonna have a pick-up time for, say, a spec script. It has worked."

Good agents will want to make it work because they've made a commitment to their clients and want to keep them satisfied.

"My agent is a great guy," Nick Kazan says, "and he believes — correctly — that if I'm happy and working hard and doing what I want to do, then I'll continue to be productive. If I'm not, then I can burn out because so many people burn out. There are certainly enough horrible experiences to make anybody burn out."

And speaking of horrible experiences…

PITCHING

For most script partners, pitching ranks right up there with studio notes.

"I hate pitching," Renee Longstreet says. "I hate it."

"Nobody likes it," says Harry.

Carolyn Miller explains why this is often the case. "Pitching is just so alien to writers. I mean, why do you write? You don't want to be an actor. Performing isn't something I would want to do. But that's what you have to do — get yourself in character and tell a story orally that really is engaging and sort of get the structure down and try to do it quickly and look like you're comfortable doing it."

Still, professional teams understand it's a necessary evil. There are times in this biz when they spend almost as much time pounding the pavement as they do pounding the keyboard.

"There are so many other factors that go into being a Hollywood screenwriter," Robert Ramsey says. "Besides the writing, there are these meetings you have to take and pitching and that whole other side of the partnership."

"We still take general meetings all the time," Matthew Stone adds. "When you're between gigs, your agent still wants you to meet new people. There are about 150 people in town we haven't done business with."

"It really is a work-a-day kind of grind," Phil Hay agrees. "Grinding it out and going to meetings and coming up with pitches."

The most common meet-and-greet venue is the pitch meeting — the presentation to studio executives, producers, staff writers, and/or others, of the script or the series you hope to sell.

According to Alan Gasmer, a team has an advantage because "they can play off each other. One starts and then jumps in, and the other finishes and sums. It varies the pitch, and it allows the person they're pitching to to focus on each different person at different times, so it's a little bit more fluid and more — Showbizzy is the way to put it."

Scott Alexander & Larry Karaszewski use the same word when they describe pitching together.

SCOTT: To use the vaudeville analogy, we've created this creepy showbizzy act that we can perform on command. I don't think they get that if it's one nervous guy coming into their office.

LARRY: It's a tag-team match. Someone once referred to one of our pitch meetings as a World Wrestling Federation tag-team match.

SCOTT: And when we're both on the phone, they say it's like "The Morning Zoo" on AM radio.

Each team, we've discovered, has a different approach.

"That's the strange thing about pitching," Phil Hay says. "No rules apply. Everyone does it so differently." He and Matt Manfredi benefit from their background in improv because, as Hay says, "Pitching is such a weird piece of theater."

But sometimes weird theatrics are just what it takes to get a producer's attention. According to *Absolutewrite.com*, when Jeffrey Price & Peter Seaman were shopping their TV series *Johnny Bago* (a recently-paroled hustler drives an RV around the country to evade the feds and his parole officer/ex-wife), they rented a Winnebago and invited executives onboard for lunch and their pitch. The stunt worked. The television series aired on CBS in 1993 (Ramsey & Stone also wrote for the show).

Manfredi & Hay, however, prefer a less elaborate approach. A pitch, they've found, can bog down in detail or become sidetracked. Big believers in brevity, they usually give only a broad outline of their story and characters. "Less is always more," Manfredi says. "We've learned the hard way sometimes that if they want to hear more they'll ask. No one wants to sit through half an hour or forty-five minutes of a pitch."

But that's exactly how long Alexander & Karaszewski presented one of their scripts.

SCOTT: With *Larry Flynt*, it was a forty-five minute pitch, and we worked out an extensive outline just for Larry and me to refer to. You know, flash cards. But we didn't actually work out, "All right, you're gonna say this, and I'm gonna say this." Both of us were familiar enough with the material that we could just go in and do a song and dance.

LARRY: If you have that little outline, while one person is talking about something, you can quickly glance and get what's next. It might only be three words, but "Oh, yeah, yeah, yeah — and then he gets shot!" And while I'm doing that, he can very quickly look at the cue cards, so he's preparing what's next.

SCOTT: I'm not sure that if a person is solo, he could do that as well. Because then it's like watching the president give a bad speech where he keeps looking down.

Working from a detailed "pitch sheet," Nick Kazan & Robin Swicord pitched *Loco for Lotto* for "forty-five minutes or an hour," Kazan says. "It was a long story. We had it worked out on the microscopic level."

Lee & Janet Batchler also write out a "pitch chart" of their entire story. "We tend to pitch pretty long," Janet says. "Sometimes up to twenty minutes. We're not five-minute pitchers."

They may also use photos and illustrations, as they did with one particularly visual project requiring numerous special effects. "If we have something we know they're not going to be able to grab a visual image of," Janet says, "we'll say, 'Here, this is what we're talking about. Think *this*!'"

The Batchlers also tell us that their respective strengths affect their pitching dynamic. "I do most of the talking," Janet says. "I can stay on the story line, and Lee will sort of wander off. So I do the play-by-play, and he does the color. Or he'll do the visual aids."

"Or if we have to set an emotional context," Lee adds, "I'll set that, and Jan will keep driving it through the plot. She's better at pitches than I am."

Carolyn Miller says Daryl Warner "hated pitching more than just about anyone." She doesn't love it, but she knows preparation is the best defense against stage fright, so they would rehearse their pitches again and again. "We'd probably over-prepare," Miller says. "We'd figure out what we needed to tell them, then we'd figure out which of us would say what. If we were going in to pitch several ideas to a production company, we'd give each story five minutes or so. The network pitches are worse — they could be twenty minutes long. It feels like an eternity. You're watching everyone in the room to see if they're paying attention or dozing off."

Or catatonic, as it seemed to Harry & Renee Longstreet when they pitched *We Interrupt This Life* to the new head of development for CBS and her two assistants.

"They're seated across from us, and we're doing our tap dance, and they're stone-faced," Renee recalls, laughing. "I mean, there's not a smile. There's not an eyebrow that moves. Nothing. And we're doing our whole *la-la-la-la-la*. We walk out and we go, 'Oh, my God, if anything ever fell on deaf ears, that did.'"

But when the Longstreets got home, they found a message on their answering machine — CBS asking them to write the pilot.

For all the fear and loathing — and a lot of work for free — that writers endure when they have to pitch, there is the rare team that likes it.

"It's something that we always enjoyed, found useful in finding and refining the emotional moments that sell the project," John Rice & Joe Batteer say, "not just to a buyer but to an audience as well." They presented their *Windtalkers* pitch — "a thirty-minute, highly-choreographed live telling of the events, characters arcs, and rising drama" — fourteen times without luck. Then they pitched to John Woo. When they were finished, the acclaimed director, moved to tears, stood up and clapped. "We loved the applause," they say, "still cherish the words of Mr. Woo that helped get our picture launched, 'It is my kind of movie.'"

But in the midst of all the different opinions we've heard about pitching, there is a consensus about the real reason to pitch with a partner: moral support.

"That's helpful any way you look at it," Dave Brown says. "You're in the damn room with a bunch of these people looking at you, and you're saying to them, 'You've got the checkbook to make my dream come true. I hope you like it.' So it's cool when you've got a friend next to you."

This moral support is important not just when you're selling your scripts but when you're writing them, too. In the end, that may be the single greatest advantage of working together. Because this business, this "terrible business, this intersection of art and commerce and science and opinion and intuition and rules and contempt for rules," as Brickman describes it, is usually harder than anyone thinks.

"We thought it would be like those guys you see who get Academy Awards at twenty-seven and all that stuff," says Robert Ramsey, "and it hasn't been like that at all. We've realized that our careers require a lot more patience than our early ambitions."

"But we really like the writing," Matt Stone adds. "This is really fun. We do enjoy it. I'm sitting here with my best friend. We laugh all day long. It's a great job."

SCRIPT PARTNER POINTS

❀ Avoid potential problems by completing a collaboration agreement that lays out the terms and the goals of your business relationship, especially if you're new partners.

Make sure the agreement covers at least four points:
A description of the collaborative property
Each partner's creative contribution
Each partner's share of ownership
Who has control of the script

❀ Keep track of expenses and figure out ways to keep your expense balances fairly balanced.

❀ If you have different agents or managers, discuss with each other and with your reps who will do what and for what duration. Consider spelling this arrangement out in your collaboration agreement.

❀ Keep in mind that pitching — weird theater though it may be — is a necessary evil in the industry.

❀ Play with different approaches to pitching (long, short, rehearsed, improvised, tag team, weird theatrics...) until you find a presentation style that works best for you.

❀ Whether your pitch hits or flops, take heart that there are two of you in the room. Offer each other moral support. In the end, this may be the greatest advantage of working together.

❀ When we started this book, we toasted each other with a bottle of Dom Perignon, which we bought at a local sub shop and drank out of plastic cups (another story...). And when we finished the book, we shared a nice bottle of Pouilly Fumé. While we'd never endorse drinking, we do endorse doing something ceremonious — and fun — at the beginning and the end of your project. It seals the deal and celebrates the commitment you've made to each other and to your script.

"Deep in most of us is the potential for greatness, or the potential to inspire greatness."

— Jean Brodie (Maggie Smith),
The Prime of Miss Jean Brodie

CONCLUSION

"How long is it going to take you to write this book?" Fay Kanin asked when we interviewed her.

We told her our deadline was ten months away.

"That's fast," she said. "You better rent a house in Malibu."

We laughed. She was right. Ten months was fast.

And looking back, we know this book wouldn't have happened if either of us had tried writing it solo. During those ten months, while we were writing the book, we dealt with war, unemployment, dementia, and death (and, of course, taxes). It's amazing that the book's here at all, but here it is — because we wrote it together. When one of us had to stop and deal with a crisis, the other "picked up the slack instantly," as Brooke Wharton put it. Or, to paraphrase Brian Helgeland & Curtis Hanson, when one of us ran out of wind, the other one rowed. And we always gave each other moral support.

So this book isn't just an exploration of the collaborative process; it's a testament to the process itself, the way that "two personalities can accommodate each other to achieve a result," to quote Marshall Brickman.

We hope the book has brought you closer to understanding — and trying — this remarkable process. And making it your own. As we've said all along, there's no right way to write together; there's only the way that works for you and your partner. And we hope, with the experience, wisdom, and advice of the writers we've interviewed here, you'll write a very good script. Maybe one that will sell and become a movie you love.

"It was beyond our wildest dreams to get a movie made and to get a movie made that actually reflects what we wrote, and it feels good," Phil Hay said. Still, he and Matt Manfredi know they can't rest on their *crazy/beautiful* laurels. "I don't think you ever get to the point where you can relax," Hay said. "But you just keep going, and if you're having a good time doing it, you just keep doing it and try to do good work."

That's the *real* Script Nirvana for script partners — enjoying the process of writing together. That's the real satisfaction, reward, and success. It is a cold world out there. It's a tough business that keeps getting tougher. And in writing, as in life, it's nice to have someone by your side. As every successful script partner knows, writing is a lonely profession, but it doesn't have to be.

In this cold, troubled world, it's no small cheese to write well together. To inspire greatness in each other. To co-write a great script. We agree with Brickman that it "speaks well not only of the medium, but gives one hope for the very future of the civilization."

Co-write and enjoy.

AFTERWORD

Andrew Reich & Ted Cohen
Executive Producers and Head Writers of *Friends*

Andrew's Top Ten Reasons for Working with Ted

1. He's funnier than I am.

2. He's better at story than I am.

3. He wrote my favorite *Friends* line of all time (Rachel: Joey has a secret peephole! He takes naked pictures of Monica and he eats chicken, and he looks at them!)

4. He never says, "I told you so."

5. He's patient with me when I'm cranky and say things like, "This all sucks. We suck."

6. He's less lazy than I am.

7. He's always willing to come over to my house to work, which is good, because I'm really lazy.

8. When I'm writing on my own, I have the urge to call him about once every ten minutes.

9. If he hadn't had the idea to write together, I'd probably still be an agent. (God help us all.)

10. When I give him this list, he'll have notes that will make it better.*

---

* He did. He told me my original number 6 — "He's not a stupid jackass like everyone else" — made me sound too hostile.

Ted's Top Ten Reasons for Working with Andrew

1. He's funnier than I am.

2. He's better at story than I am.

3. He knows the best places to eat heavy ethnic food that forces you to take a nap after lunch.

4. He has a comfortable couch on which to take aforementioned nap.

5. He has the best library for jump-starting a writer's-blocked brain (including a twelve-volume Victorian hardcore pornographic novel).

6. He has a sweet doe-eyed dog who makes us feel loved even when we're convinced we're no-talent frauds.

7. He actually likes doing the computer-related things — like formatting — that make me want to kill myself.

8. He knows when I need to be told that an idea is good even if he knows it's no good.

9. He doesn't care if I have terrible, earth-shattering gas.

10. He has unerringly good judgment, and is an unswervingly good friend.

FILMOGRAPHY

The following is a list of credits (some edited by the writers themselves) for collaboratively written scripts by our interviewees, though many have impressive solo credits as well. The year indicated is the date the film was released or the television show first aired, not necessarily the date the script was completed.

SCOTT ALEXANDER & LARRY KARASZEWSKI

Movies

Problem Child (1990)
Problem Child 2 (1991)
Ed Wood (1994)
The People vs. Larry Flynt (1996)
That Darn Cat (1997)
Man on the Moon (1999)
Screwed (2000)
The Marx Brothers (in development)
Slushy (story, in development)

BRAD ANDERSON

Movies

Next Stop Wonderland (with Lyn Vaus, 1998)
Session 9 (with Stephen Gevedon, 2001)

LEE & JANET SCOTT BATCHLER

Movies

Batman Forever (1995)
Modesty Blaise (in development)
My Name is Modesty (in production)
Smoke and Mirrors (in development)

MARSHALL BRICKMAN

Movies

Sleeper (with Woody Allen, 1973)
Annie Hall (with Woody Allen, 1977)
Manhattan (with Woody Allen, 1979)
Simon (with Thomas Baum, 1980)
The Manhattan Project (with Thomas Baum, 1986)
Manhattan Murder Mystery (with Woody Allen, 1993)

OLIVIER DUCASTEL & JACQUES MARTINEAU

Movies

Jeanne et le Garçon Formidable (Jeanne and the Perfect Guy) (1998)
Drôle de Félix (Adventures of Felix) (2000)
Ma Vraie Vie à Rouen (2002)

LARRY GELBART

Movies

The Notorious Landlady (with Blake Edwards, 1962)
The Thrill of It All (story, with Carl Reiner, 1963)

A Funny Thing Happened on the Way to the Forum (play, with Burt Shevelove, 1966)

The Wrong Box (with Burt Shevelove, 1966)

Ruba al promisso tuo (with Virgil Leone, Francesco Maselli, Luisa Montagnana, 1969)

Movie Movie (with Sheldon Keller, 1978)

Blame It on Rio (with Charles Peters, 1984)

TV Series

Caesar's Hour (1954)

M*A*S*H (1972)

FAY KANIN

Movies

Sunday Punch (with Michael Kanin, 1942)

My Pal Gus (with Michael Kanin, 1952)

Rhapsody (with Michael Kanin, 1954)

The Opposite Sex (with Michael Kanin, 1956)

Teacher's Pet (with Michael Kanin, 1958)

The Right Approach (with Michael Kanin, 1961)

Lo Spadaccino di Siena (with Michael Kanin, 1962)

TV Specials

Rashomon (with Michael Kanin, 1960)

HAL KANTER

Movies

Two Tickets to Broadway (with Sid Silvers, 1951)

Road to Bali (with Frank Butler, William Morrow, 1952)

Here Come the Girls (with Edmund Hartmann, 1953)
Money From Home (with James Allardice, 1953)
Off Limits (with Jack Sher, 1953)
Casanova's Big Night (with Edmund Hartmann, 1954)
The Rose Tattoo (with Tennessee Williams, 1955)
Bachelor in Paradise (with Valentine Davies, 1961)
Move Over, Darling (with Jack Sher, 1963)

TV Series

The George Gobel Show (1954)
Valentine's Day (1964)
Julia (1968)
All in the Family (1971)
The Jimmy Stewart Show (1971)
Chico and the Man (1974)
You Can't Take It With You (1987)

TV Specials

The 42nd Annual Academy Awards (1970)
The 63rd Annual Academy Awards (1991)
The 64th Annual Academy Awards (1992)
Oscar's Greatest Moments: 1971 to 1991 (1992)
The 65th Annual Academy Awards (1993)
The 66th Annual Academy Awards (1994)
The 67th Annual Academy Awards (1995)
The 69th Annual Academy Awards (1997)
The 70th Annual Academy Awards (1998)

NICHOLAS KAZAN

Movies

At Close Range (story, with Elliott Lewitt, 1986)
Matilda (with Robin Swicord, 1996)
The BFG (with Robin Swicord, in development)
Loco for Lotto (with Robin Swicord, in development)

HARRY & RENEE LONGSTREET

TV Movies

The Gathering, Part II (1979)
Baby Sister (1980)
The Promise of Love (1981)
The Sky's No Limit (1983)
Night Walk (1989)
Alien Nation: Body and Soul (1995)
Gunsmoke: One Man's Justice (1995)
A Vow to Kill (with Sean Silas, 1994)
Alien Nation: The Udara Legacy (1996)

TV Series

Fame (1982)
Voyagers! (1982)
Trauma Center (1983)
Hot Pursuit (1984)
Shadow Chasers (1985)
Rags to Riches (1987)

TV Specials

ABC Afterschool Special: Frog Girl: The Jennifer Graham Story (1989)

MATT MANFREDI & PHIL HAY

Movies

crazy/beautiful (2001)
The Tuxedo (story, 2002)

CAROLYN MILLER

TV Series

Here's Boomer (with Daryl Warner, 1980)

TV Specials

NBC Special Treat: I Don't Know Who I Am
(with Daryl Warner, 1979)

ABC Afterschool Special: Sometimes I Don't Love My Mother
(with Daryl Warner, 1982)

CBS Mystery Theater: Mystery At Fire Island
(with Daryl Warner, 1982)

Interactive Projects

Abode of the Spirits (with Lynn Casser, in development)

HAROLD RAMIS

Movies

Animal House (with Douglas Kenney & Chris Miller, 1978)
Meatballs (with Janis Allen, Len Blum & Dan Goldberg, 1979)
Caddyshack (with Brian Doyle-Murray & Douglas Kenney, 1980)
Stripes (with Len Blum & Dan Goldberg, 1981)
Ghostbusters (with Dan Aykroyd, 1984)
Back to School (with Peter Torokvei and Steven Kampmann
& Will Porter and Rodney Dangerfield, 1986)

Club Paradise (with Brian Doyle-Murray, 1986)
Armed and Dangerous (with Peter Torokvei, 1986)
Caddyshack II (with Peter Torokvei, 1988)
Ghostbusters II (with Dan Aykroyd, 1989)
Groundhog Day (with Danny Rubin, 1993)
Analyze This (with Peter Tolan and Kenneth Lonergan, 1999)
Bedazzled (with Peter Tolan, 2000)
Analyze That (with Peter Steinfeld and Peter Tolan, 2002)

TV Series

SCTV (Second City TV) (1976)

ROBERT RAMSEY & MATTHEW STONE

Movies

Destiny Turns on the Radio (1995)
Life (1999)
Big Trouble (2002)
Intolerable Cruelty (in production)

TV Series

Johnny Bago (1993)

ANDREW REICH & TED COHEN

TV Series

Friends (1994)
Minor Adjustments (1995)
Brand Spanking New! Doug (1996)
Mr. Rhodes (1996)

AARON RUBEN

Movies

The Comic (with Carl Reiner, 1969)

TV Series

The George Burns and Gracie Allen Show (1950)
Caesar's Hour (1954)
The Phil Silvers Show (1955)

ED SOLOMON

Movies

Bill & Ted's Excellent Adventure (with Chris Matheson, 1989)
Bill & Ted's Bogus Journey (with Chris Matheson, 1991)
Automatons (with Chris Matheson, in production)

DAVID SONNENSCHEIN

Movies

The Knife and the Rose (with Stuart Geltner, in development)
Tantric Twist (with Stuart Geltner, in development)

TV Series

Shaman Trek (with Stuart Geltner, in development)
Sound Wizards (with Stuart Geltner, in development)
Wizards of Medicine (with Stuart Geltner, in development)

JIM TAYLOR

<u>Movies</u>

Citizen Ruth (with Alexander Payne, 1996)
Election (with Alexander Payne, 1999)
Jurassic Park III (with Alexander Payne, 2001)
About Schmidt (with Alexander Payne, 2002)

PETER TOLAN

<u>Movies</u>

Analyze This (with Harold Ramis, Ken Lonergan, 1999)
Bedazzled (with Harold Ramis, 2000)
America's Sweethearts (with Billy Crystal, 2001)
Stealing Harvard (story, with Martin Hynes, 2002)
Analyze That (with Harold Ramis and Peter Steinfeld, 2002)

<u>TV Series</u>

Murphy Brown (1988)
Home Improvement (1991)
The Larry Sanders Show (1992)
Style and Substance (1998)
The Job (2001)

BIBLIOGRAPHY

Books

Adams, James L. *Conceptual Blockbusting: A Guide to Better Ideas*. Reading, Massachusetts: Addison-Wesley Publishing Company, 1986.

Allen, Woody. *Four Films by Woody Allen*. New York: Random House, 1982.

Aristotle Poetics. Translated by Gerald F. Else. Ann Arbor: University of Michigan Press, 1978.

Burroway, Janet. *Writing Fiction: A Guide to Narrative Craft*. 5th ed. New York: Addison Wesley Longman, 2000.

Crowe, Cameron. *Conversations with Wilder*. New York: Alfred A. Knopf, 1999.

Csikszentmihalyi, Mihaly. *Creativity: Flow and the Psychology of Discovery and Invention*. New York: HarperCollins Publishers, 1997.

Egri, Lajos. *The Art of Dramatic Writing: Its Basis in the Creative Interpretation of Human Motives*. New York: Simon and Schuster, 1960.

Field, Syd. *Screenplay: The Foundations of Screenwriting*. New York: Dell Publishing Company, 1984.

-------------. *The Screenwriter's Workbook*. New York: Dell Publishing Company, 1984.

Fitzgerald, F. Scott. *The Great Gatsby*. Harmondsworth, Middlesex, England: Penguin Books, 1968.

-----------------------. *The Crack-Up*. Edited by Edmund Wilson. New York: New Directions Publishing, 1956.

Froug, William. *The New Screenwriter Looks at the New Screenwriter*. Los Angeles: Silman-James Press, 1992.

Goldman, William. *Adventures in the Screen Trade: A Personal View of Hollywood and Screenwriting.* New York: Warner Books, 1983.

-----------------------. *Which Lie Did I Tell? More Adventures in the Screen Trade.* New York: Pantheon Books, 2000.

John-Steiner, Vera. *Creative Collaboration.* New York: Oxford University Press, 2000.

Johnson, Claudia Hunter. *Crafting Short Screenplays That Connect.* Woburn, Massachusetts: Focal Press, 2000.

Lamott, Anne. *Traveling Mercies: Some Thoughts on Faith.* New York: Pantheon Books, 1994.

Lax, Eric. *Woody Allen: A Biography.* New York: Alfred A. Knopf, 1991.

My First Movie: Twenty Celebrated Directors Talk About Their First Film. Interviewed by Stephen Lowenstein. New York: Pantheon Books, 2000.

Palumbo, Dennis. *Writing from the Inside Out: Transforming Your Psychological Blocks to Release the Writer Within.* New York: John Wiley & Sons, 2000.

Seger, Linda. *The Art of Adaptation: Turning Fact and Fiction Into Film.* New York: Henry Holt, 1992.

Soderbergh, Steven. *sex, lies, and videotape.* New York: HarperCollins Publishers, 1990.

Wehner, Christopher. *Screenwriting on the Internet: Researching, Writing, and Selling Your Script on the Web.* Studio City: Michael Wiese Productions, 2001.

Wharton, Brooke A. *The Writer Got Screwed (but didn't have to): A Guide to the Legal and Business Practices of Writing for the Entertainment Industry.* New York: HarperCollins Publishers, 1997.

Williams, Tennessee. *Where I Live: Selected Essays.* Edited by Christine R. Day and Bob Woods. New York: New Directions Books, 1978.

Articles

Alexander, Scott, Larry Karaszewski, and Milos Forman. "Scott Alexander, Larry Karaszewski & Milos Forman." By Lisa Chambers. *Written By* (April 1997): 42-47 and 77-79.

Cuarón, Alfonso & Carlos Cuarón. Interview by IFC Films. In *Y Tu Mamá También* Production Notes, 10-11.

Doskoch, Peter. "Living Happily Ever Laughter: Learn to Harness the Power of Humor." *The Buffalo News* (November 24, 1996): 10.

Ganz, Lowell & Babaloo Mandel. Interview by Neal Feinberg. In "Dynamic Duos: Writing Partners Share the Ups and Downs." *Creative Screenwriting*, vol. 3, no. 1, 45-47.

Giles, Jeff. "The Farrellys' Wild Ride." *Newsweek* (July 3, 2000): 54-59.

Katz, Susan Bullington. "A Conversation with Lowell Ganz & Babaloo Mandel." *Written By* (May 1999): 24-29.

Payne, Alexander & Jim Taylor. "Adapting and Directing *Election:* A Talk with Alexander Payne & Jim Taylor." By Annie Nocenti. *Scenario Magazine*, vol. 5, no. 2, 104-109 and 189-190.

--. "Writing and Directing *Citizen Ruth:* A Talk with Alexander Payne & Jim Taylor." By Tod Lippy. *Scenario Magazine*, vol. 2, no. 4, 99-103 and 228-231.

Rice, John & Joe Batteer. "Friendship vs. Duty: The Making of *Windtalkers.*" *scr(i)pt*, vol. 7, no. 6, 38-41 and 63.

Scarbrough, Marsha. "It Takes Two: The Write Relationship." *Written By* (April 1998): 20-26.

Van Zandt, Billy & Jane Milmore. Interview by Neal Feinberg. In "Dynamic Duos: Writing Partners Share the Ups and Downs." *Creative Screenwriting*, vol. 3, no. 1, 50.

Wachowski, Larry and Andy Wachowski. "Writing and Directing *Bound:* A Talk with Larry and Andy Wachowski." By Tod Lippy. *Scenario Magazine*, vol. 2, no. 3, 92-95 and 187-190.

293

Walsh, Frances and Peter Jackson. "Writing and Directing *Heavenly Creatures:* A Talk with Frances Walsh and Peter Jackson." By Tod Lippy. Scenario Magazine, vol. 1, no. 4, 217-224.

Wilder, Gene. "Writing and Acting in *Young Frankenstein:* A Talk with Gene Wilder." By Annie Nocenti. *Scenario Magazine*, vol. 4, no. 1, 95-98 and 184-188.

Scripts

Alexander, Scott & Larry Karaszewski. *The People vs. Larry Flynt.* New York: Newmarket Press, 1996.

Allen, Jay Presson. *The Prime of Miss Jean Brodie* (based on the novel by Muriel Spark).

Allen, Woody. *The Purple Rose of Cairo.*

Allen, Woody & Marshall Brickman. *Annie Hall.* In *Four Films by Woody Allen.* New York: Random House, 1982.

---. *Manhattan.* In *Four Films by Woody Allen.* New York: Random House, 1982.

Anderson, Brad & Stephen Gevedon. *Session 9.*

Avary, Roger & Quentin Tarantino. *Pulp Fiction.*

Batchler, Lee & Janet Scott Batchler. *Batman Forever* (original draft).

Boam, Jeffrey. *Indiana Jones and the Last Crusade* (story by George Lucas & Menno Meyjes).

Brooks, James L. *Broadcast News.*

Coen, Ethan & Joel Coen. *Barton Fink.*

Curtin, Valerie & Barry Levinson. *Best Friends.*

Frank, Scott. *Get Shorty* (based on the novel by Elmore Leonard).

Gale, Bob & Robert Zemeckis. *Back to the Future* (fourth draft, March 11, 1980).

Johnson, Claudia & Matt Stevens. *Obscenity* (rewrite, July 2001).

--. *Psycho Bitch* (rewrite, July 2001).

Manfredi, Matt & Phil Hay. *crazy/beautiful* (March 21, 2000).

Payne, Alexander & Jim Taylor. *Election* (based on the novel by Tom Perrotta). *Scenario Magazine*, vol. 5, no. 2, 64-103.

Ramsey, Robert & Matthew Stone. *Life* (January 5, 1998).

Reich, Andrew & Ted Cohen. *Friends: The One with the Stripper* (first draft, September 27, 2001).

Shelton, Ron. *Bull Durham* (May 1, 1987).

Stallone, Sylvester. *Rocky* (January 7, 1976).

Internet Sources

Alexander, Scott, "Interview with Scott Alexander," *Hollywoodlitsales*. <http://hollywoodlitsales.com/archives/alexander.shtml>.

Colleary, Michael & Mike Werb, "E-mail Interview with Michael Colleary & Mike Werb," Writers Guild of America. Edited by Robert J. Elisberg. <http://www.wga.org/craft/interviews/collearywerb.html>.

"Delia Ephron: Keeping the Family Tradition Alive," *Book*. January/February 2001 <http://www.bookmagazine.com/issue14/inthemargins.shtml>.

Elliott, Ted, "Me & My Ampersand," *Wordplayer* 12 October 1999 <http://www.wordplayer.com/columns/wp18.Me.and.My.Ampersand.html>

Farrelly, Peter, "An Interview with Peter Farrelly," *Bold Type*. Interviewed by Anson Lang. 5 June 2001 <http://www.randomhouse.com/boldtype/0698/farrelly/interview.html>.

Gapinski, Natasha, "Gotta Have a Gimmick?" *Absolute Write* <http://www.absolutewrite.com/novels/gimmick.html>.

Mazur, Stephen H. & Paul Guay, "E-mail Interview with Stephen H. Mazur & Paul Guay," Writers Guild of America. Edited by Robert J. Elisberg. <http://www.wga.org/craft/interviews/mazurguay.html>.

Reno, Jeff & Ron Osborn, "E-mail Interview with Jeff Reno & Ron Osborn," Writers Guild of America. Edited by Robert J. Elisberg. <http://www.wga.org/craft/interviews/renoosborn.html>.

Rose, M. J., "The Net Effect of Moviemaking" *Wired* 7 December 1999 <http://www.wired.com/news/digiwood/0,1412,32773,00.html>.

Rossio, Terry, "Writer's Block," *Wordplayer* October 1997 <http://www.wordplayer.com/ letters/lt30.Writers.Block.html>.

"Screen Credits Manual." Writers Guild of America. July 1999 <http://www.wga.org/creditsManual/screen1.html>.

Turan, Kenneth, "Alexander Payne: An Eye for American Idiosyncrasy," *Los Angeles Times* 22 May 2002 <http://www.latimes.com/entertainment/ movies/la-052202turan.story>.

Photo by: Robert Kazandjian

CLAUDIA JOHNSON & MATT STEVENS

Claudia Johnson & Matt Stevens began writing together when they were colleagues on the faculty at the Florida State University Film School. Two of their screenplays — a courtroom drama, *Obscenity*, and a broad comedy, *Psycho Bitch* — were finalists for the 2002 Sundance Screenwriters Lab.

Matt has also written and produced biographies for E! Entertainment Television and writes film reviews for E! Online. His screenplay, *A Really Rotten Christmas*, was purchased by Phase One Productions. He has worked as a script analyst for several companies, including CAA.

Matt's short films have won awards at national and international festivals, and his mockumentary, *The Making of "Killer Kite,"* received the Student Emmy for Best Comedy from the Academy of Television Arts & Sciences. He was a second-unit director for the feature, *Curdled*, executive-produced by Quentin Tarantino.

297

Claudia's plays and screenplays have won numerous awards, including the Florida Screenwriters Award, the American National Theater and Academy West Award, and the Warner Bros. Scriptwriting Award. She is the author of *Crafting Short Screenplays That Connect*, adopted by film schools around the nation, and the critically acclaimed memoir, *Stifled Laughter: One Woman's Story About Fighting Censorship*, nominated for the Pulitzer Prize.

A nationally recognized advocate for free speech, she was the first recipient of the P.E.N./*Newman's Own* First Amendment Award, presented by Paul Newman. She was also a literary advisor for the ExxonMobil Masterpiece Theater's *American Collection*.

Claudia Johnson & Matt Stevens

are available for workshops, lectures, and
consultations about collaborative screenwriting.
Rates and other services are available upon request.

For more information, visit:

www.scriptpartners.com

323-377-9785

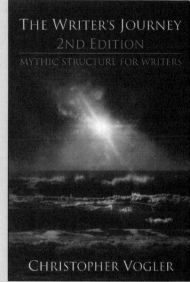

SETTING UP YOUR SHOTS
Great Camera Moves Every Filmmaker Should Know

Jeremy Vineyard

SETTING UP YOUR SHOTS
Great Camera Moves Every Filmmaker Should Know
By Jeremy Vineyard   Illustrated by Jose Cruz

Written in straightforward, non-technical language and laid out in a nonlinear format with self-contained chapters for quick, on-the-set reference, *Setting Up Your Shots* is like a Swiss army knife for filmmakers! Using examples from over 140 popular films, this book provides detailed descriptions of more than 100 camera setups, angles, and techniques — in an easy-to-use horizontal "wide-screen" format.

Setting Up Your Shots is an excellent primer for beginning filmmakers and students of film theory, as well as a handy guide for working filmmakers. If you are a director, a storyboard artist, or an animator, use this book. It is the culmination of hundreds of hours of research.

Contains 150 references to the great shots from your favorite films, including *2001: A Space Odyssey*, *Blue Velvet*, *The Matrix*, *The Usual Suspects*, and *Vertigo*.

"Perfect for any film enthusiast looking for the secrets behind creating film. Because of its simplicity of design and straightforward storyboards, *Setting Up Your Shots* is destined to be mandatory reading at film schools throughout the world."
— Ross Otterman, *Directed By Magazine*

Jeremy Vineyard is a director and screenwriter who moved to Los Angeles in 1997 to pursue a feature filmmaking career. He has several spec scripts in development.

$19.95, 132 pages
Order # 8RLS
ISBN: 0-941188-73-6

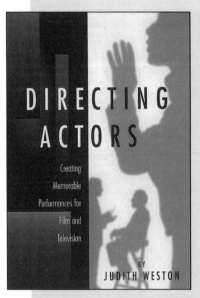

DIRECTING ACTORS
Creating Memorable Performances for Film & Television

Judith Weston

Over 20,000 Sold!

Directing film or television is a high-stakes occupation. It captures your full attention at every moment, calling on you to commit every resource and stretch yourself to the limit. It's the white-water rafting of entertainment jobs. But for many directors, the excitement they feel about a new project tightens into anxiety when it comes to working with actors.

This book provides a method for establishing creative, collaborative relationships with actors, getting the most out of rehearsals, troubleshooting poor performances, giving briefer directions, and much more. It addresses what actors want from a director, what directors do wrong, and constructively analyzes the director-actor relationship.

"Judith Weston is an extraordinarily gifted teacher."
- David Chase, Emmy Award-Winning Writer,
  Director, and Producer
  The Sopranos, Northern Exposure, I'll Fly Away

"I believe that working with Judith's ideas and principles has been the most useful time I've spent preparing for my work. I think that if Judith's book were mandatory reading for all directors, the quality of the director-actor process would be transformed, and better drama would result."
- John Patterson, Director
  The Practice, Law and Order, Profiler

Judith Weston was a professional actor for twenty years and has taught Acting for Directors for over a decade.

$26.95, 314 pages
Order # 4RLS
ISBN: 0-941188-24-8

FILM DIRECTING: SHOT BY SHOT
Visualizing from Concept to Screen

Steven D. Katz

Over 150,000 Sold! International best-seller!

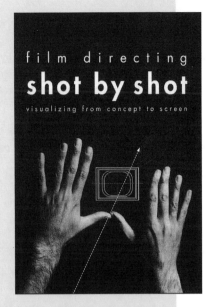

Film Directing: Shot by Shot — with its famous blue cover — is the best-known book on directing and a favorite of professional directors as an on-set quick reference guide.

This international bestseller is a complete catalog of visual techniques and their stylistic implications, enabling working filmmakers to expand their knowledge.

Contains in-depth information on shot composition, staging sequences, visualization tools, framing and composition techniques, camera movement, blocking tracking shots, script analysis, and much more.

Includes over 750 storyboards and illustrations, with never-before-published storyboards from Steven Spielberg's *Empire of the Sun*, Orson Welles' *Citizen Kane*, and Alfred Hitchcock's *The Birds*.

"(To become a director) you have to teach yourself what makes movies good and what makes them bad. John Singleton has been my mentor... he's the one who told me what movies to watch and to read *Shot by Shot*."
— Ice Cube, *New York Times*

"A generous number of photos and superb illustrations accompany each concept, many of the graphics being from Katz' own pen... *Film Directing: Shot by Shot* is a feast for the eyes."
— *Videomaker Magazine*

Steven D. Katz is also the author of *Film Directing: Cinematic Motion*.

$27.95, 366 pages
Order # 7RLS | ISBN: 0-941188-10-8

THE SCRIPT-SELLING GAME
A Hollywood Insider's Look at Getting Your Script Sold and Produced

Kathie Fong Yoneda

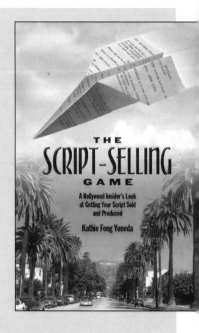

There are really only two types of people in Hollywood: those who sit around wearing black clothes in smoky coffee shops, complaining they can't get their scripts past the studio gates... and then there are the players. The ones with the hot scripts. The ones crackling with energy. The ones with knowledge.

Players understand that their success in Hollywood is not based on luck or nepotism; it's the result of understanding how Hollywood really works.

The Script-Selling Game brings together over 25 years of experience from an entertainment professional who shows you how to prepare your script, pitch it, meet the moguls, talk the talk, and make the deal. It's a must for both novice and veteran screenwriters.

"Super-concise, systematic, real-world advice on the practical aspects of screenwriting and mastering Hollywood from a professional. This book will save you time, embarrassment, and frustration and will give you an extra edge in taking on the studio system."
> — Christopher Vogler, Author, *The Writer's Journey: Mythic Structure for Writers*, Seminar Leader, former Story Consultant with Fox 2000

"I've been extremely fortunate to have Kathie's insightful advice and constructive criticism on my screenplays. She has been a valued mentor to me. Now, through this wonderful book, she can be your mentor, as well."
> — Pamela Wallace, Academy Award Co-Winner, Best Writing, Screenplay Written Directly for the Screen, *Witness*

Kathie Fong Yoneda is an industry veteran, currently under contract to Paramount TV in their Longform Division, and an independent script consultant whose clientele includes several award-winning writers. Kathie also conducts workshops based on *The Script-Selling Game* in the U.S. and Europe.

$14.95, 196 pages | Order # 100RLS | ISBN: 0-941188-44-2

WRITING THE
Killer
SELLING
YOUR STORY
WITHOUT A
SCRIPT
Treatment
MICHAEL HALPERIN

WRITING THE KILLER TREATMENT
Selling Your Story without a Script

Michael Halperin

The most commonly heard phrase in Hollywood is not "Let's do lunch." In reality, the expression you'll most often hear in production, studio, and agency offices is: "Okay, send me a treatment."

A treatment, which may range from one to several dozen pages, is the snapshot of your feature film or TV script. A treatment reveals your story's structure, introduces your characters and hooks, and is often your first and only opportunity to pitch your project.

This is the only book that takes you through the complete process of creating treatments that sell. It includes: developing believable characters and story structure; understanding the distinctions between treatments for screenplays, adaptations, sitcoms, Movies of the Week, episodic television, and soaps; useful exercises that will help you develop your craft as a writer; insightful interviews with Oscar and Emmy winners; tips and query letters for finding an agent and/or a producer; and *What Every Writer Needs to Know*, from the Writers Guild of America, west.

"Michael Halperin's well-crafted book offers a meticulous – and simple – plan for writing your treatment, from its inception to the final polish."
— Sable Jak, *Scr(i)pt Magazine*

Michael Halperin worked as an Executive Story Consultant for 20th Century Fox Television and on staff with Universal Television. He has written and/or produced numerous television episodes. He is the author of *Writing the Second Act: Building Conflict and Tension in Your Film Script*.

$14.95, 171 pages
Order # 97RLS
ISBN: 0-941188-40-X

.ORDER FORM

MICHAEL WIESE PRODUCTIONS
11288 VENTURA BLVD., # 621
STUDIO CITY, CA 91604
E-MAIL: MWPSALES@MWP.COM
WEB SITE: WWW.MWP.COM

WRITE OR FAX FOR A FREE CATALOG

PLEASE SEND ME THE FOLLOWING BOOKS:

TITLE	ORDER NUMBER (#RLS _____)	AMOUNT
	SHIPPING	
	CALIFORNIA TAX (8.25%)	
	TOTAL ENCLOSED	

PLEASE MAKE CHECK OR MONEY ORDER PAYABLE TO:

MICHAEL WIESE PRODUCTIONS

(CHECK ONE) ____ MASTERCARD ____VISA ____AMEX

CREDIT CARD NUMBER _____

EXPIRATION DATE _____

CARDHOLDER'S NAME _____

CARDHOLDER'S SIGNATURE _____

SHIP TO:

NAME _____

ADDRESS _____

CITY _____ STATE _____ ZIP _____

COUNTRY _____ TELEPHONE _____